AUSTIN FARRER : THE ESSENTIAL SERMONS

Austin Farrer

THE ESSENTIAL SERMONS

Selected and Edited by
LESLIE HOULDEN

First published in Great Britain 1991

Society for Promoting Christian Knowledge
36 Causton Street
London SW1P 4ST

British Library Cataloguing in Publication Data

Farrer, Austin *1904–1968*
Austin Farrer : the essential sermons.
1. England, Sermons
I. Title.   II. Houlden, J. L. (James Leslie) *1929–*
252

ISBN 978–0–281–04464–1

3 5 7 9 10 8 6 4

Typeset by J&L Composition Ltd, Filey, North Yorkshire
First printed in Great Britain by
Mackays of Chatham plc
Reprinted in Great Britain by Ashford Colour Press

Produced on paper from sustainable forests

Contents

Acknowledgements

We are grateful to the trustees of the Farrer estate for permission to reproduce the sermons in this book, and to Hodder & Stoughton for those sermons first published in *A Celebration of Faith*.

Chs 2, 3, 4, 5, 6, 8, 9, 12, 13, 17, 31, 42, 45, 46, 47, 48, 51 and 52 are from *Said or Sung* (Faith Press 1960).

Chs 1, 14, 19, 20, 22, 23, 26, 27, 28, 30, 32, 33, 35, 36, 37, 38, 39, 40, 41, 43, 44, 49 and 50 are from *A Celebraton of Faith* (1970), edited by Leslie Houlden.

Chs 7, 15, 16, 18, 21, 29 are from *The End of Man* (SPCK 1973) and chs 10, 11, 24, 25 and 34 are from *The Brink of Mystery* (SPCK 1976), both edited by Charles Conti.

Introduction

Austin Farrer was a giant of a preacher. In his long heyday, from the end of the war in 1945 to his early death in 1968, he enjoyed an ever-growing reputation all his own. The many places and occasions of his preaching testify to that; all the more striking because he was not a man to be away from home and study altogether willingly.

Yet there is something both surprising and mysterious about this popularity. For one thing, though his sermons often began with an amusing story or striking image, they would flow on into deep waters where not every hearer could easily follow and their course could be sinuous. Also, they had a literary quality which did not exactly disqualify them as oratory but was certainly becoming unusual in the pulpit of his day (now it has virtually vanished). And while his theme was usually some central aspect of Christian belief or commitment, it often had a Catholic hue which might seem sectional in its appeal, especially as it was a very special Catholic hue – firmly non-Roman, even anti-Roman, unmistakably Anglican and Oxford Anglican at that; yet there was no better spokesman for universal, deep-rooted, mature Christian orthodoxy. He invites comparison with J. H. Newman or, more remotely, George Herbert. Farrer was a preacher of his time and place. Yet those who heard him, even if not wholly 'with him', often knew they were hearing a voice of uncommon spiritual and intellectual energy.

Some of his utterances now seem dated. Perhaps they are too elevated to suit a mood of Christian realism. In part he suffers from the inevitable temporary disadvantage of being too near to us in time to be read as a classic of a bygone age, too distant from us to seem wholly our contemporary. For example, there is little in his sermons to attract the Christian fired with zeal for liberationism and social justice, and Farrer's use of the term 'practical' in relation to Christian life is likely now to strike readers as meaning 'theoretical'! Yet so well does he lay foundations and so winningly, that average Christian wits may be capable of moving into their own applied theology. He is also likely to be taken as sexist in language: sensibilities were different in the 1950s and 1960s, and in any case most of his sermons were preached to congregations of students in all-male colleges. It has not seemed sensible to update him by altering all his 'men' into 'persons' and his 'he's into '(s)he's. I do not think there was much that was deeply sexist in his theology, which centred on the salvation of the members of our race created in God's image.

INTRODUCTION

Four volumes of his sermons have been published, all now out of print. The first, *Said or Sung*, was his own selection made in the late 1950s. *A Celebration of Faith* (1970) was the fruit of a first trawl of the pile of unpublished sermons, mostly from the sixties, left at his death. *The End of Man* (1973) and *The Brink of Mystery* (1976) were edited by Charles Conti from the same rich store. The present collection of fifty-two sermons, chiefly from *Said or Sung* and *A Celebration of Faith*, has been made with an eye to meditative reading through the year. I have avoided sermons which relate very closely to the life of an Oxford college and assume an affinity with its structure and customs. I have also tended to avoid those which make use of characters and events once topical but now faded. Those presented here are as close to timeless utterances as I could find, though not, I trust, at the price of liveliness.

One sermon per week, but they do not follow the Church's year, except in a few instances. These, so far as shifting Easter allows, have been placed appropriately in the sequence of a year starting on the first of January. Relatively few of Farrer's surviving sermons were closely related to the Christian seasons: most were preached in colleges in term-time when hardly any of the peaks of the year occur. Most of his sermons treated of the central pattern of the Christian gospel, of the believer's response to it in prayer and sacrament, and of our ultimate hope; and in that hope Farrer was more robust and forthright than many Christians have come to be even in the brief period since his death. His points of entry to the message and his emphases varied of course, but readers will find themselves reinforced constantly in a framework of conviction which the great Christian tradition has seen as essential. Rarely will they find it given to them so ripely, satisfactorily or attractively. Farrer combined four-square teaching with apologetic sensitivity: usually the imaginary objector is the Oxford philosopher of his day, and perhaps we have moved elsewhere since then. However, even where such a preacher as this is denied full welcome, he cannot be lightly dismissed, and, for the sake of his genius and his memory, he should be heard with loving care.

Leslie Houlden
November 1990

1
The Painter's Colours

It seems as though we were in for a year of electioneering. It is a discouraging prospect, isn't it? Electioneering is so awful. Everything has to be discussed at a level of grotesque simplification; rational debate becomes impossible. It is often little better in public exchanges between Christians and their critics. I read in the press how a scientific professor exclaims that scientists know more about God's creation than Bishops and Church leaders do. To which an Archbishop retorts, the man is talking nonsense; God's creation involves sacrifice and scientists know nothing about sacrifice. I dare say both speakers are misreported, but taking the exchange as it stands, what can a philosopher do but weep? The professor's remark is, to start with, hopelessly ambiguous. Distinguish the senses, and there's nothing left to discuss; for in one sense his dictum is self-evidently true, in another as evidently false. Who knows about *God's creation*? If by God's creation you mean the physical system God has instituted, then the scientist has a sort of knowledge about it to which no one else, and least of all a bishop, pretends. But if by God's creation you mean 'what the Creator's will intends and achieves', then that is not a subject on which a scientist has a syllable to say. In one sense, the supplier of artists' materials knows what paintings are, for they are certainly unquestionably paints and canvas. In another sense, he knows nothing about it. The painter knows, for he understands the game which is played with these substances.

Well, but if we are to apply the analogy to creation, God both supplies the materials and paints the picture: he is the expert, then, in both fields. Yes, of course, and that goes without saying: God is the universal expert. The most any human experts can do is to think some of God's thoughts after him. The scientist obtains insight into the structure of the materials, by direct examination; but when it comes to understanding, or appreciating the picture God paints, then where are we? If we were utterly incapable of aesthetic appreciation, we could never know anything about a painted picture; if we have some inklings, then perhaps we are in a position to comprehend, if the painter himself will explain himself to us.

Now admittedly human artists are often ludicrously bad at explaining themselves. Their genius is in their finger-tips. They create by a sort of inspiration or possession, as though a power not themselves employed them; they know not what they do. But no such limitation of knowledge applies to God. He knows what it is that he does, and in this he differs

1

most startlingly from us men and all along the line. Jesus said that his executioners knew not what they did, an ignorance which gave them a hope of divine forgiveness. And we are all in the same position, all the time. The only acts which we fully understand and master are trivial acts. If I am playing a game of noughts and crosses against a child, I know exactly what I am doing in placing my mark, for there is no great mystery about the principles of that game. But if I intervene in a discussion on the Governing Body of my College, then heaven knows what I am up to, and my colleagues' guesses at my game are very likely as good as my own.

But God's work is completely perspicuous to him; he does what he means, and means what he does: and so, if he pleases to explain his mind to us, he can.

Scientific professors are perfectly within their rights, if they resent theologians giving themselves airs. Theologians have no claim whatever to be pleased with themselves, for, unlike the scientist, the theologian makes no discoveries: he merely interprets and relays the self-disclosure of God. A scientist may be a creative genius: not so a theologian.

So God paints the picture, and God explains the effect at which he aims; he opens our eyes to it. Such is our parable; like all parables, it illuminates, and like all parables, it is liable to mislead. For if we say 'the world is the masterpiece of the divine painter' we make a grotesquely false suggestion. The painter creates *a* picture; it is as a unit that it has its pictorial being and value. It exists as an arrangement for being looked at. But God does not create *a* world. Admittedly the world offers an arrangement to be looked at, always supposing that any mind is capable of getting it all into focus. Perhaps the seven archangels can manage it; or perhaps only the four cherubim can pull it off. But however that may be, the world's function is not to be a painted show, for men, or for angels, or for cherubim, or for the all-seeing God himself to contemplate. The world's function is to exist and to act with inexhaustible energy, imitating in endless variety the riches of God's own absolute vitality. And this the world does not do as a whole, but only in its constituent parts. To say that the world exists, is like saying that a swarm of bees exists. The swarm only exists, because each of the bees exists, and because they all cling together. We are all aware of the dangerous fallacies which arise through the personification or hypostatization of collectives. There is no Uncle Sam, no Britannia or John Bull and when Adolf Hitler claimed to impersonate the German Soul, there was no need to pay him any extra attention on that ground. But the most staggering of all hypostatized collectives is the world. If I say that there's no such thing as the world, don't think I've joined the Christian Scientists. There's no such *thing* as the world, but all the things in the world exist; and, existing, they make up the world. For God has not only made all the things in the world, he has made them to make up a world; and that's his masterpiece.

2

Now when we claim that God, the sole supreme artist, has revealed to us the drift and the intention of his work, we are talking about God as the creator of each single creature, and not about God as the cosmic designer. As to cosmic design, we may fairly concede to the astronomers and physicists that they know all that is so far known about it; theology has not a syllable to add. Creation, as a revealed truth, is concerned with the existence of single creatures. Now we cannot taste or appreciate creaturely existence except in ourselves, and in others like us. In our friends – why, yes, if we love them as ourselves. In our enemies, oh, far less clearly; for dislike shutters our eyes. In brute beasts, perhaps, dogs, cats, and horses; but ants, bees, slugs and snails – what do you think? I would say, No.

So then, in this range of thinking, human existence is our sample of existence. Taught to appreciate our own being as created, we attribute createdness to a million other things; for we see that they are no more sufficient to exist of themselves than we are.

There is no scandal or absurdity, then, in admitting that the Christian doctrine of creation is centred upon the two-legged creature, man. Our faith teaches us to taste the quality and the drift of our own dependence upon God; perceiving that we exist by his good pleasure, we cannot but know that everything else does, also.

We can perhaps see now that it is not altogether surprising if unbelievers fail to feel the force of arguments in proof of a creator. The arguments can be stated, but they cannot compel belief, as a proof in mathematics can compel belief. Speaking broadly, we can say that men will not admit a creator unless they are willing and able to live out their own createdness in a day-to-day dependence upon God.

I have been saying all along that creation is a doctrine which the Creator himself reveals: the painter discloses to us the nature of his work. You may fairly ask me, how and where does God make such a revelation? Do you really mean to tell us that because an old Jewish writer threw together a pile of age-old myths in the book called Genesis, we are assured of the very mind and speech of God? No, I mean no such thing. The centre and the seal of revelation is Jesus Christ alone. The significance of Genesis is, that it contains the picture of an idea which Christ proved by living it out. For it is not simply that Jesus saw the handiwork of God in lilies, and his providence in the fall of a sparrow. It is that he wagered his life on creative power. Who can raise the dead? No one: in the literal sense, not God himself. The dead are not raised: immortalized men are not galvanized corpses. What is called the resurrection of the dead is a remaking of their life, in a stuff and in a fashion which are known to God alone. If we are made, we can be remade: he who created can create anew. Jesus Christ experimented with creation when he threw himself and all the world's hopes into nothingness, by the death on the cross.

We shall not deeply and honestly believe that the Painter paints the picture until we are willing to be liquid colours under his brush; and how little do we even pray for that, let alone live it! But that is what heaven will be; a life in which the very countenance of God is constantly and visibly portrayed in the changing colours of his creatures' lives. Creation, like everything else, will be perfectly manifest for the first time in heaven. For there, the blessed by their whole existence set forth the manifold mastery of God: and by their lives as well as with their lips ascribe as is most justly due to God the Father, Son and Holy Ghost, one deity in three persons, all might, dominion, majesty and praise, through ages everlasting.

preached in Christ Church Cathedral, Oxford

2
Assurance

I once had a partner in a garden which we worked for our joint benefit. My partner had received an agricultural, I a merely cultural, education. This placed me at a disadvantage. My partner knew when to plant and where to sow, I knew neither; and my attempts to acquire his wisdom were constantly defeated. My partner always justified his horticultural actions by appeal to proverbial maxims, some of which rhymed, while others did not. But unhappily for me, it appeared that maxims grew in pairs, like cotyledons: for every maxim there was another, which was the flat contrary of it, equally rhythmical, equally hoary. Thus all horticultural actions whatsoever could be proverbially justified. When I realized this baffling fact, I was at first merely angry and abusive, and pilloried my partner as a horticultural humbug. But then there was the indisputable observation that what he planted grew, and what he tended flourished. And so I came to see the truth: his wisdom did not lie in the maxims he cited, but in the art of steering a course between the marks which, as it were, the maxims set up.

Life tends to be like this. 'Faint heart never won fair lady', so rush it. But on the other hand, 'Always look before you leap', so take your time. Neither of these maxims will make us wise; one fills the divorce courts, the other multiplies disappointed bachelors. Nor shall we be wise by knowing both; but only if we know when to follow one, and when to follow the other. But it is very difficult. For in the case of the fair lady, unless we have gone a good way in exchanging a faint heart for a bold, we shall not have got any idea what the leap is like, about which prudence bids us deliberate. And if we have really started in on the fair lady, something stronger than reason has already captured us, and cool deliberation is scarcely possible. It is even worse than this; we cannot go any way with the fair lady without a sense of devotion, or at least of loyalty, which makes the whole idea of regarding her as a dubious leap intolerable. And yet, on the other hand, a life-long commitment is no laughing matter.

Such situations have their agonizing aspect, and yet we know there is a way through: a slow exploratory wisdom, neither of the heart only, nor of the head, takes the tiller, and a self deeper than the self we know finds its harbour and claims its true content; and so, by the mercy of God, those who act with heed and good faith are brought to the haven where they would be.

It is much the same with our religion. If we have not been powerfully moved by that divine voice which claims the heart, we shall not even think of asking whether this is, or is not, the real thing. Yet surely we ought to ask; for if it is frivolity to take a wife or husband without the deepest consideration we are capable of, what shall we say of carelessness in giving ourselves body and soul, for life and for death, to the service of Christ? Do we not owe it to Christ himself, since he says, I am the truth? As he offered himself to Thomas to be handled, does he not offer himself to us to be examined? For how is truth known for true but by examination?

On the other hand, how can I question a truth like this truth? For have I not begun to see Christ as the Lord, and does not this acknowledgment preclude questioning? If he is my Lord, my salvation, my wisdom, my strength, my God, is not entire loyalty and, what is more, dependence, my only choice? How can I pretend to doubt the firmness of the rope on which I swing over the pit of destruction? Or, alternatively, how can I pretend to put my weight on a rope I really doubt?

The situation is not without its agony, and it is certainly very unlike what unbelievers suppose, when they coolly talk to us about our rational duty of suspending judgement until we are intellectually satisfied. You might as well recommend to a husband the rational duty of suspending judgement about his wife's fidelity until he has tested it by a sufficient number of ingenious traps and artificial manoeuvres.

Well, but I can still remember being young and saying to myself that a strong impression of the force of Christianity and a movement of the will to love God was no proof that I had found salvation. Consideration may be agonizing, but if we are moved to consider, nothing will stop us; and of all the bad advice that can be given to an inquiring mind the worst is to try not to think. And this I say because, to the discredit of this University and of the faith they profess, there are people going about here and advising their friends never to think or study along any line which raises religious doubt. I do not know what to say strong enough about the cowardice, the unwholesomeness, the stupidity and the implicit lack of faith which such advice exhibits.

The right advice is positive, not negative: not to run away from disquieting considerations but to feed your soul on God. If you believe, your faith must be that God is able to persuade you of his own truth by the revelation he has made; and so you need be afraid of no questionings, as long as you allow a fair field and no favour. What you ought not to do is to weight the scale against faith. How odd it is that Christians sometimes listen to clever atheists but never think of consulting competent theologians, apparently supposing that they have to do battle against giants with their own fists, and oppose archery to gunfire! There are other ways of weighting the scales against faith – for example, by allowing critical inquiry to become an obsession, filling the mind and leaving no room for God or for prayer.

But apart from elementary mistakes like these, we must put up with doubt and questioning so long as we are in this world, remembering that Jesus said 'Why?' on the very cross: 'My God, my God, *why* hast thou forsaken me?' The truth is that our mind is not a perfect unity in this present life; we shall doubt with part of ourselves, on and off, while we are here, but God will more and more assure us against our doubt. For when we are pulled together into one genuine person, then we have assurance of God; or, to put it the other way about, we come to know that nothing but confrontation with God is able to pull us together into a unity of person, mind and will. Faith is the act of the whole man, doubt of a part.

How do I know that I have found him? Not, certainly, because I cease to be able to doubt him; my doubts, in the sense of my active questionings, may even increase. But I know that I have found him, because not even doubt can shake him; he shows himself the stronger and maintains his hold. I know that I have found him, because he does not let me go; except in appearance, and for the while, and by my own fault. But in the drama of our inward battle there is nothing barred – we cannot ever say, 'I can't have found the true God, because if this were he, he would never let me get such a wound; if I were a believer I could never feel this, or think that, or undergo the other.' There are no signs of this sort from which anything useful can be learnt. There is only one sign – the victory of Christ over the worst that can happen to us; a victory he assures us in the end, if we apply to him, and if we wait for him.

'Assurance' is said to be a sign of salvation, and so it is if it is rightly understood: understood, that is, not as an attitude on my part, as in the sentence: 'He approached the Michaelmas examinations with sublime assurance'; no, but rather as an act on God's part, his assuring of me, as in the sentence: 'He had constantly to give his foolish friend the assurance of his unalterable regard.'

He assures me, God assures me, partly through my mind, as when I reconsider the manger and the cross, the words and the works, the sepulchre and the throne of Jesus, and see that they are divine. But he assures me also in my life, through his dealings with me; for he gives me grace. Yes, he gives me grace; and though I spill the water of life upon the ground before his very eyes, not even putting the cup to my lips, he forgives me, and gives me more. As those who cannot love through the meanness and distrustfulness of their minds cease to be able to believe in the love which others bear them, so the despite we do to God's grace destroys our knowledge of it. How do I know that I have found him? Not, heaven knows, because I cannot sin: the nearness of his grace, and the dearness of his love, offer me opportunities for sinning such as I had not when he was further removed; for now I can throw his mercy in his very face. But there is a grace beyond grace, a grace mastering the contempt of grace, the grace of repentance, to which he recalls me; and thus indeed I know, not that I have found him, but that I have been found by him.

The sacraments assure us that he has found us, for in them he makes himself known; those who go in good faith and with self-forgetfulness to his altar will have a steady foundation, lasting and deepening from week to week and from year to year. But, above all, the sacrament of confession and absolution administers the medicine of divine assurance to doubting minds. If I hold God so feebly, is it not, I ask, because he is so shadowy, and so distant? I go to confession, and it is blindingly clear, as soon as I am dealing direct with Christ in his priest, that his love is very present, but that the perversity of my sin is very great. If I sin so much, I ask, is it not that he lets me be conditioned so to sin? I go and confess, and know without a shadow of doubt that my sin was simply my choice, and that as for him, in him is light, and no darkness at all. If I have been so often defeated, I ask, can I any longer hope to fight? I go to confession and in that moment I know that he who raised Jesus Christ from the dead quickens our mortal wills and clears our consciences from the works of death to serve our living God.

Even to us, then, God gives an assuring grace; but there is nothing very special about us, after all, that we should trust his assurances to us, and not trust his assurances to others, who, having better used the divine gifts, have received more. If God had done nothing for me, or in me, I should lack any clue by which to understand what he has done in the saints. But since he has given me this personal clue, let me take it in my hand and follow the thread of gold where it runs on through the lives of others. Their experience will be far more worth my study than my own.

I knew a man once – but this is not the time for reminiscence, and you perhaps have not been so happy as to know living saints. But is not this a university, and have not you been taught to read? Why do St Augustine's *Confessions* gather dust on the shelf and the pages of the Curé D'Ars' *Life* remain uncut? Why is not the Lady Julian in every one's hands, and why are we not ashamed to be ignorant of St Francis de Sales? The person of the Church is one; the saints are the fingers through which we will touch the wounds of Christ, and the eyes with which we will meet his eyes, and the ears with which we will hear his utterance. Their apprehensions, like their virtues, are more than human, they are divine; and uniting ourselves with them, receiving the overflow of their holiness, we will begin to know that it is by God we go to God, and that he whose indwelling unites the Father with the Son joins the body and bride of Jesus to the Father and the Son: to whom, in the bond of that same blessed Spirit, one God in threefold unity, be ascribed as is most justly due all might, dominion, majesty and power, henceforth and for ever.

preached in Pusey House Chapel, Oxford

3

Nice and Worldly

There is a Christian mission being preached in the University, and the prayer of us all must be that those whom it captures may be established in a living faith. But it is not my mission, and I am not presuming here to take the word of their gospel out of the missioners' mouths. What I have in mind is a sort of side issue: I am thinking of the reaction of common sense to hot-gospelling in all its forms. The mission preacher paints the world white and black, he bids us detach ourselves from the kingdom of darkness and adhere to the kingdom of light; and while we are under the spell of his words we see that light shining, as it were, from behind the missioner's head. We can see the heavenly clearness, the single-minded generosity of the life to which he calls us; can see how blessed it would be if we could live for God alone. Compared with the clearness of such a life, our present confused muddle of aims, our self-indulgence, our meanness and our vanity seem dark indeed.

Well, we have heard our sermon. We go out; and there we meet a cheerful friend who says, 'Come and have a drink'. The invitation sounds a bit incongruous with our noble mood; we say, perhaps in a rather feeble way, that we don't feel like a drink. Our friend asks us with genuine concern whether we are ill; and we ought perhaps to reply that no, that isn't the point; the point is that (as the Dickens character says) 'all taps is vanities'. But we have not the courage to take that line and stick to it, so we have a drink after all. The old atmosphere presently reasserts itself; how pleasant, how cheerful, how decent and kind the friend is with whom we are drinking; what a full and amusing life he leads, and how much his company heightens our own pleasure in existing. How good his jokes are; all the better for being a bit wicked; for although he isn't earnest-minded enough to be an atheist, our friend plainly belongs to that unconverted world which the preacher has just been painting black as black. 'Oh goodness!' we say. 'How absurd! Old Robin Johnson a citizen in the kingdom of darkness! The whole thing's nonsense! Have another drink.'

Fair enough; but drinking is no substitute for thinking, and the mission preacher has really got something. Yes, but so has Robin, and how can you make room for them both? God has a use for the saints, that's a clear truth, even if it's a disturbing one; there was that Belgian priest, for example, who ran the leper island alone in the South Seas. No, there is no getting round the saints. But hasn't God a use for Robin Johnson too? The Lord careth not for the strength of a horse, neither delighteth he, says the Psalmist, in any man's legs; his delight is in them

9

that fear him. But when a man's legs, or his wits rather, can cut such pretty capers, can it really be that there is no value in it? And after all, it is not only a matter of cutting capers, there is everything that goes to make up fullness of life. What is a university for? We are not here, for the most part, studying the fear of the Lord, we are studying the riches of the mind. Are we wasting our time? If we believed the mission preacher, should not we have to turn our thoughts another way entirely?

So far I have only been sketching the problem, and reminding you of something which all of you, more or less, have often felt. We must acknowledge the call to be saints, and yet we must find a place for our dear, delightful, unconverted friends. Well, but how? Shall we plant the godly and the ungodly on a level, side by side, and say that God wants them both just as they are, because it takes all sorts to make a world? Surely that is plain nonsense. It is not the desire of God's heart that any of his children should disregard him, however cheerfully and politely they do it. God is our true and only final good; to possess him is to have everything, and to fail of possessing him is total loss. Godliness and ungodliness cannot stand side by side as equally approved of God. The Lord's delight is in them that fear him.

So what are we to say? I will begin my answer from an absolute platitude. Man's destiny consists of two parts: first we live and then we die. That is a platitude, but the next step isn't a platitude. In the eyes of God our dying is not simply negative, it is an immensely important and salutary thing; by living we become ourselves, by dying we become God's, if, that is, we know how to die; if we so die, that everything we have become in our living is handed back to the God who gave us life, for him to refashion and use according to his pleasure.

We live, we die: God's concern with the one is no less than his concern with the other. Our religion is summed up in two pictures: God the creator breathing into man's nostrils the breath of life; God the redeemer dying for man on the cross, and breathing out his life into the keeping of his Father. Creation and crucifixion are the two poles of our faith, and each of them is God.

What is it, then? God desires that we should grow, live, expand, enrich our minds and our imaginations, become splendid creatures. He also desires that we should die, should be crucified on the cross of Christ Jesus, should surrender all we have and are to him; and he desires that we should die that death spiritually before we have to die it physically; that we say to Christ, 'Take me, crucify me on your cross, for I cannot do the crucifying for myself. Make my sacrifice part of your sacrifice, nail me to it and do not let me slip.' God wants that, for his delight is in them that fear him; and truly to fear God, to reverence him as his holiness demands, is to make a complete sacrifice of ourselves to him. There is no fear of God that stops short of that.

What then is the relation between living and dying? In a perfect Christian life, if we can talk of such a thing, the dying and the living would go on side by side from the start; life would be full, constantly enriched, and also constantly surrendered to God. But even in a life which has been Christian from the beginning, where there has been true surrender, true sacrifice from childhood onwards, there often comes a point of sudden change when the providence of God seems to say to a man, 'You have enriched yourself, developed and spread yourself enough. Hitherto your business has been to live and grow; henceforward your business shall be to serve my will, to use all that you have gathered, rather than to go on gathering more.' And when we look on men who have answered such a call, the saints who have given themselves to God and mankind without reserve, everything else looks cheap by comparison. As to the growth, the development and flowering of Christ's own humanity, we have almost nothing recorded except those few precious words of St Luke, 'He advanced in wisdom and stature, and in favour with God and man.' What Christ teaches us in all his recorded ministry is not living but dying, not how to be ourselves, but how to surrender ourselves to God, and for God's sake to mankind.

Well now, what after all are we to say about our dear, delightful, unconverted friends? We must say that so far as their lives are wholesome or truly human, they are splendid manifestations of the power to live; but that they have not yet learned to die, they have not made even the first step along that more difficult path which Jesus Christ opened up for us. What has the providence of God in store for them? Perhaps they are going to hear the voice of Christ in this world, this year, next year. Perhaps our stupidity and the grudging pharisaism of our religion is going to repel them. Perhaps the worldliness and dilutedness of our faith is going to sicken them. Perhaps they will not find the cross of Jesus in this life. What then? It may not be by their fault; or if it is, perhaps the fault that has made them miss the truth has been no greater, very likely less, than the fault which makes me, who have the truth, respond so feebly to the truth I have. I am not their judge, I am not my own judge; there is only one judge, and may he have mercy on us all.

Suppose, then, that they are accepted in the sight of that judge; do they simply get off their dying? By no means: 'Flesh and blood', that is, the mere natural life, says St Paul, 'cannot inherit the kingdom of God.' To get to God they, like us, have not merely to undergo death, they have to achieve death, have to make a positive use of death, to throw off their self-bound being so that God may receive a willing material for his own love to remake. I see it in a picture: here we all are, believers and unbelievers, and there away before us is God, the goal of us all, whether we know it or not; and between us and him is the river of Christ's death, the river in which self-will must drown, if we are ever to rejoice in a better and more blessed will, the will of God. Some of us have waded a little way into the waters of that death, some of us have not so much as wet our feet, but we have all to go through, whether in this world or in the next.

Do I talk of water? The apostle talks of fire, and so did Christ. Many, says St Paul, will be saved, though they bring a world of rubbish with them, but none of them will be let off the ordeal of fire. I will quote St Paul's words: 'Let every man take heed how he builds. If a man's building be of gold, silver, precious stones, wood, hay, stubble, every man's work shall be shown up; for the day will show it up, because it is revealed in fire, and the fire shall try every man's work, of what sort it is. If a man's work is burnt up he shall suffer loss, but himself shall be saved, yet as one pulled through the fire.' We see that there is no getting to God without passing through this fire, for, says Christ, 'every man shall be salted with fire'. The fire is salt, cleansing, healing, salutary, it is the fire of Christ's own sacrifice purifying us from self, making us fit for God, and in God for our true happiness. May God give me more of that holy fire here, so that I may not wait for another life before I begin to find and love and serve my only true good, my merciful creator. May God give me grace not to run from this fire, nor to throw away the cross; but may he give me grace besides to recognize his handiwork in all men; to acknowledge that converted or unconverted, he made them, and filled them with all sorts of excellences. I must pray indeed for men's conversion, but I must pray meanwhile for their happiness, and for their growth in mere humanity.

So now let God be praised for all his work, whether of redemption or creation; that to him, the only blessed God, Father, Son and Holy Ghost, may be ascribed as is most justly due all might, dominion, majesty and power, henceforth and for ever.

preached in Trinity College Chapel, Oxford

4

The Gentleman-Apostle

They used to tell schoolboys – perhaps they still do; you should know, your experience of school being a trifle more recent than mine – anyhow, they used to tell us that St Paul was a fine example of a Christian gentleman, because just look what perfect manners his letters display. Well, since then I have looked at St Paul's letters a great deal, and I am not so sure about the perfect manners. Fortunately his letters contain something more interesting than lessons in politeness; but so far as the manners go, they seem to me a bit on the elaborate side. They are the manners of a Jewish exile doing his best; they have not that perfect ease which only an assured position and an English public school can give.

He is of course really doing his best, but it is a bit too obvious. If I had been a Christian elder at Rome I am not sure that St Paul's tactful beginning to his Roman letter would have set me at my ease. But as I am not a primitive Roman elder but only a decadent English theologian, I am rather fortunate than otherwise to have the Apostle writing as he does. Just because he has to try so hard to be tactful, I can see what he is thinking, I can feel the trouble he takes to get the other man's point of view. He may not be such a good model of manners as the man who says the right thing by instinct, but he is a more useful example of the working of God's grace; for I can see pride losing the battle to gentleness, as the Apostle writes.

He begins by telling the Romans that he is the emissary of Christ's kingdom, and that these are the terms of his commission: to reduce all nations to submission before the invisible throne of the Lord and his Anointed. Among the rest of the nations, he says, there are you Romans; so I greet you in the name of my King.

As though feeling that this is somewhat overbearing, he makes a new start. 'Not that I have to reduce you to submission', he says. 'You believe already, and I join with the whole Christian world in thanking God for your faith, and in praying for its increase. So I long to see you; not to convert you, you do not need it, but in case I may be able to confer on you some spiritual gift to strengthen you.' Once again St Paul feels that this is a bit much, and comes in with the corrective. 'I mean', he says, 'to have my share of encouragement among you, through your and my common Christian faith.'

Here St Paul is so tactful that he falls over his words and is almost untranslatable: 'to be co-comforted in you through the mutual faith of you and me'. This is really no way to talk, and I don't think it is a model of easy manners. It is the sort of thing which accompanies the shuffling of feet and the dropping of teaspoons. Not that it matters much now; the teaspoons, if any, have been picked up long ago; and tactful or clumsy, what St Paul says is both sincere and exact. It is useless for a Christian apostle or a Christian bishop or a Christian priest to pretend he has nothing to give, no spiritual gift to share with his friends; or what is the good of him? He dare not deny his commission. Has not Christ promised to bless the preaching of his word, and the ministry of his sacraments? Confess to me and you shall be absolved, listen to me with faith and you shall hear God speak; I bring you the sacrament in my hands, it is the Body of Christ.

But on the other side, St Paul knows the experience of sharing spiritual gifts, and how much more he receives from the faith of others than he is ever aware of giving them. For what we give to others is what Christ gives to them over our shoulders. He gives it to them, not to us, and we do not even handle it. And what Christ gives to us through our fellow Christians, he gives likewise over their shoulders and into our hands. We receive that, we handle that, we have some appreciation of what that treasure is. So St Paul knows that when he comes to Rome he will come in the full power of the Holy Ghost; for has not Christ made him his Apostle? But he also knows that what he himself will experience is more like this: 'to have my share of encouragement in your company, by the mutual working of your faith and mine'.

'The mutual working of your faith and mine'. Believing in God is in fact a common undertaking. It is the greatest of human enterprises; and, like other important enterprises, it is only possible of achievement by common endeavour. Faith is not the possession of the single mind alone, it is the possession of the Church. It is personally real, of course, but it lives by communication and interchange. Sometimes one or another of you will say to me, 'I try to remember the presence of God when I pray myself, but it is much easier when we worship together'. That is not a discovery which would have greatly surprised St Paul; for what is it but 'a share of encouragement in company through the mutual working of common faith'?

Well, but are not we being fooled? Are we not simply yielding to the suggestions of mass emotion? We might be, of course; but in fact we are not. We have seriously and with consideration accepted Christ. But if so, it is absurd for us to say that we will cultivate our faith under no conditions but the most adverse, the most killing and solitary. Allow me a profane parallel. It would be foolish, of course, to yield to the mere charms of female company; but one who has seriously decided to love will hardly refuse all company with the object of his affection, merely to make sure he is not fooled.

What I am sayng is, I believe, important to every one; specially

14

important, perhaps, to you. For it is easy to make a fatal mistake about achieving religious maturity. We cannot go on depending on the faith of others, as Christian children do. We have got to have, as we say, a faith of our own. Or as that might seem to rate our powers of spiritual discovery a little too high, let us say we have got to make the faith that we have, our own faith. But that does not mean that we have got to have it by ourselves; and if we attempt it, we are presently frozen out.

We have to go on our own feet indeed, but we climb together as alpinists do, bound in one chain by the mutual working of common faith. And if any of us fails to co-operate, he does not merely spoil his own life, he betrays the common endeavour and weakens all other believers.

There are many ways of sharing faith. St Paul, having heard of the faith of the Roman Christians, as he says, wants to have a share in it; so he proposes the sensible method of walking down to the quayside at Corinth, and looking for a boat to Rome. We, similarly, have heard of the faith of St Paul; and though no ship will take us into his company, the fact of reading his letters will do almost as well. We can travel in time as well as in space; and I am aware that I might profitably spend much more time than I do reading the words and the lives of the saints. I never return from such visits into the past without thankfulness and, as St Paul says, a share of encouragement.

But most obviously there is our common life here and now. And if you find that faith lives by common worship, if that is your experience, then you may agree that our pious founder was not only pious but wise to give us common prayers not only every week, but every day. And why, day by day, do we throw away our opportunities?

Whose faith is the Christian faith? I have said that it must be ours, but cannot be ours alone; it is the faith of the Church. But there is a deeper wisdom still. The Christian faith is the faith of Christ; not only the faith which believes in Christ, but the faith which Christ believes. St Paul cannot abate the claims of his apostleship, because he cannot deny the Christ who made him an Apostle; and Christ – he cannot deny his mission, because he too believes, believes in his own saving work; to deny it would be apostasy from the Father, and to die for his mission is the act of his faith. It is Christ's dying and rising faith which overflows, which runs as it were in the veins of all Christian men. Our communion is with Christ; and it is because Christ, by faith, lives in our fellow Christians, that our faith lives by communion with theirs, and theirs with ours.

preached in Trinity College Chapel, Oxford

15

5

The Potter's Clay

I read a report in my newspaper to-day about some new work on cosmology; that is, I take it, on the general nature and development of the physical world. I find sentences there which cause me great astonishment. Several of you, I daresay, could help me to see what some of it means. Or perhaps you would be ill-advised to take me on; some pupils are hopeless, and the last time I competed in mathematics I came thirteenth (paired) among fifteen. I fear I should not grasp the sense of your formulae. Anyhow it is clear to me that cosmology is subtle and complex, that I hardly know the first thing about it, and that the author of the early chapters of Genesis knew less about it than I do. We may form the impression that he had an inquiring mind and a strong curiosity about the origins of things; but alas, he had no data to go on, nor had he been taught the method of looking for them. He had to build his story out of parables and dreams, and the confused traditions of the tribe. As a result he added nothing to our knowledge of scientific cosmology; he simply described in vivid figures what he saw by faith of God's shaping power: the power which shapes things, and above all, men, here and now, and not once long ago in a fabulous morning of the world.

God moulded man, he says, of clay, of moistened dust; and since he said it, we have never been able to get those hands of God out of our minds, those deft omnipotent shaping figures, pulling and pressing and marking the clay, so that the image of the modeller's thought rises a living thing under their compulsion. But what are these hands of God? And how are they related to that infinite complexity of cosmic force about which you are going to teach me one day, if my mathematics are not too bad altogether?

It might do well if I look first at my own hands. That will be easier for a start; and here they are on the desk before me. How many parts, I wonder, do they each contain? And when I choose to flex my fingers or turn a page of my paper, how many different physical motions, how many items of process, one acting upon another, does it involve? I wonder, but I do not know; I am as ignorant of physiology as the author of Genesis was of cosmology. I do not know, but neither do I need to know, not being a medical man. Without any skill to analyse or anatomize my hands, I can use my hands; more than that, I can live in my hands and (I might almost say) be my hands, when I am absorbed in a work of manual skill. My purpose runs in my fingers and fulfils itself. And whatever researches you may make into my bodily structure, my work remains unaltered, unassisted and unhindered by your learning.

16

I turn back now to those hands of God which shape Adam (that is, they shape mankind) according to the biblical fable. What is the author saying when he writes of these hands? It does not concern him, clearly, by what infinite complexity of forces, by what pattern of mass and motion, those hands are composed. Perhaps those hands of God are nothing less than the whole world. It does not concern the biblical writer to say; but this is what concerns him: Does he or does he not truly discern by faith a life controlling and directing those hands, and that life, divine? Does God's work obey God as my work obeys me? – far more so, indeed, if God is almighty. What can I make at the best? Very little. I have been taught to use my tongue and my pen; I can spread ink over the paper, I can sprinkle sounds on the air. It is not much; yet even from these slight tokens you have the direct perception of a mind at work. Now set before yourself the people you most love or admire, and see if you can acknowledge God's handiwork in that charm of wit, that constancy of kindness, that breadth of understanding, that inexhaustible imagination, that reliable force of courage, or whatever most delights you in a man.

After these things the word of the Lord came to Jeremiah, 'Go down to the potter's house, and there I will cause thee to hear my words.' The prophet went, and there the man wrought his work upon the wheel; and when the vessel that he made from the clay went wrong in the hand of the potter, he made it a different vessel instead, as he thought good to make it. Then the word of the Lord came to the prophet: 'House of Israel, cannot I do with you as this potter? As the clay in the potter's hand, so are ye in my hand,' saith the Lord. No escaping then from those hands; those hands did not make us once, like magic toys, and turn us free to run; the house of Israel is still clay in the hands of God, neither is there any end to his shaping of them. All their existence is the shaping of God. But here a new thing comes in, which was not in the story of Adam's creation. 'The vessel went wrong in the hand of the potter'. How? In the hand of the Jewish potter whom Jeremiah watched it well might, but the potter who makes the house of Israel is almighty. Will he fumble with the clay? He will not fumble with it; he will meet faults in it, though. There is a lump here, and there it crumbles; here something too stubborn and resistant, there nothing firm enough to make a shape. For the clay in which God works is our free will, and though he gave it us, it is free.

Notice how the prophet or, rather, God's word that comes to him, relates our free will to the work of God. God is always beforehand and holds the mastery, for is not he God? Nothing comes of the clay, of our life, that is, but what God makes of it. The clay makes no shapes for itself, except crazy shapes by distortion of the shape intended; a crack here, a lump there, a ruin and a confusion. The true life of the clay is to spin into symmetry under the maker's hand; yet nothing results, either, by the mere force of the hand, unless the clay is fit and responds. The

17

skill of the divine potter is an infinite patience of improvisation. No sooner has one work gone awry than his fingers are pressing it into the form of another. There is never a moment for the clay, when the potter is not doing something with it. God is never standing back and watching us; his fingers are on us all the time. The world is his, from every side he touches and presses us. If we love his will we take the shape of it. If we are lazy and selfish, his fingers oppose us and make war on us, and crumble us back into obedience. We repent, and without a moment's delay the ever-active fingers are moulding us back into the divine image.

This means that the present obtains an urgency it would not else exhibit; we cannot with a tranquil detachment inquire, What would God do with me if I were pleased to serve him? We have always to ask, what is God doing with me now? What is his love doing with me now? Can I endure to frustrate him a week, a day, an hour, longer? Can I grieve him any more, by leaving him only the work of warning and judgement to work upon me? What is required of me that I may live in his grace, and move in his will, and receive the imprint of his likeness?

God made man in his own image, his own similitude (says Genesis) and breathed into his lips a breath of his own spirit. So man became a living soul. In these phrases the whole work of God upon man is summed up as it were by anticipation, the whole work through all the tract of history. For where is that image of God in the human being, where is that living soul alive with the very spirit of God? The work was not yet complete, certainly, when Jeremiah went down to the pottery and saw the house of Israel still on the potter's wheel. But is the work never completed? Is the clay shaped and spoiled and shaped again for ever? Do we wait for an imaginary perfection in a Utopia hereafter?

The work of the potter is completed, and the divine likeness is revealed, when the clay is perfectly prepared to take it. And how is the clay prepared? The potter found the clay he needed in a sepulchre outside Jerusalem. There a human body was left as clay, emptied of the life-giving spirit by which it had been a living soul. This clay was prepared for the potter's use by sacrificial obedience; by flogging, crucifying, death. He who breathed into Adam's clay a breath of his divine Spirit breathed into this clay all the fullness of that Spirit, and he became a living soul. No, says St Paul, the old Adam was that; Christ, the new Adam, is not merely a soul living in himself, he is life-giving Spirit. His life overflows, it imparts itself to those whom he unites with himself.

There is no end indeed to God's making of man. But God has not set the goal of the process in an imaginary future, where we cannot see it. He has set up the goal; it is revealed, it exists, the work has been finished in Christ. What never ends is our receiving the grace of Christ, our growing up into the image of Christ, until we see the face of Christ.

preached in Trinity College Chapel, Oxford

6

The Burning-Glass

In the name of the Father, and of the Son, and of the Holy Ghost. That is how we are taught to begin our discourse, placing what we say under the protection of God, that we may speak on his behalf, not on our own. And if it is the general rule for preachers to clothe themselves with the holy name and lose themselves in the truth they preach, more particularly it applies when we preach on the grace of God. For no one of himself can preach the grace of God, he can only stand aside and let it shine; the dart of light comes out of the body of light, and the sharp point of the dart which touches and pierces us is called the grace of God.

Let us begin with the New Testament. Grace, on the lips of St Paul or St John, is often an equivalent almost for God himself. 'By grace were ye saved.' Well, but by what are we saved? By nothing but the act of God. Grace then is God, or the saving act of God. St John says that God is love; it is almost an accident that he nowhere affirms him to be grace. Grace is the love of God in its most lovely aspect. If we say that God is love, we establish the substance of him, we say that he is the pure act of inexhaustible self-giving. If we call God by the name of mercy, we show the face of his love turned upon misery and need. But if we call him grace, we manifest the generosity of his love. Grace is gratuitous, nothing merits or calls for it. Suppose I were to preach to you about giving things to God, and you were to reply, 'But who can give anything to bounty itself?' Bounty itself – a fair New Testament translation of your remark might be, 'How can I repay the grace of God?'

When the Church calls God love, or grace, or mercy, she is not subscribing to the vapid doctrine that all we mean by God is the presence of these qualities, wherever they happen to appear in the world. No, God is God, even though there were no world to reflect his goodness. We start from that. God is God, an infinite intensity of personal life. But when we ask what is the life of God, we say, 'An everlasting act of love.' And this love shines variously in different relations. Between the Persons of the Godhead it is good-pleasure and social delight. Towards the miserable it is mercy, and towards the undeserving, grace.

God's generosity is not, like ours, a principle on which he acts from time to time. He neither slumbers nor sleeps; he never wakes up into action, he acts always; his bountifulness is what he always bountifully does. Of the variety of that bounty I will not speak – creation, preservation, so many blessings of this life – but I will speak of the heart of bounty, Jesus dying on the cross for us men and for our salvation.

Indeed when St Paul (to take him for our example) speaks of grace, it is of this that he speaks. Jesus dying is the place, and substance, and act of grace; and the colour of grace in it is its being free and unmerited. 'While we were yet sinners,' says this Apostle, 'Christ died for us ungodly.'

Now it is a general principle that the flavour of everything is brought out by contrast, sour by sweet and light by darkness. We are told to taste and see that the Lord is gracious, and our palate feels it most by contrast with some opposite. And so grace most shines in St Paul's pages when it is opposed to merit or desert. 'God being rich in mercy, for the great love that he bore us took us dead in our transgressions, and bought us to life with Christ. By grace are ye saved. He raised us up with him and set us in heavenly thrones with Christ Jesus, to display in future ages the abounding riches of his grace, and his loving-kindness to us in Jesus Christ. For by grace are ye saved through faith; it comes not of you, the gift is God's. It comes not of achievement, lest any should boast; for we are his handiwork, created in Christ Jesus for the achievement of a good, which God has prepared for us to walk in.'

By Jesus's dying and rising, that is by God's grace, not by our work, merit, achievement or desert. Such is St Paul's contrast, as though he were saying: The fire is kindled by no business of ours, no preparing or striking of matches on our part, but by sunlight falling through the burning-glass of faith. Now such a contrast focuses attention on that precise point where the sunlight does the work of the match, and lights the tinder. Such a contrast leaves it for others to measure the shaft of light reaching from the sun to us, and concentrates all attention upon the very end of the shaft, tapered to a point by the lens, and piercing the dry leaves with a needle of fire. So, in thinking of grace, the Church has come to turn from the fount of light which is God in God, and the shaft of light which is Jesus in his incarnation, to look at the very needle of light which pierces the heart. But though we may choose to attend to the burning-point, what draws to that point, and makes that point, is nothing but Jesus Christ, God and man, burning his way through the wall of the heart.

I think we have taken this parable far enough; for what we have to do is not to give external descriptions of God's grace, but to stand out of his way and let grace do its work. And grace will not do its work by our thinking about burning-glasses, but by our watching and hearing and eating and drinking Jesus Christ. Perhaps with all my burning-glasses and stuff, I am merely putting off the moment when I tell you what it is for a Christian, and so I suppose for me, to have the grace of God. The moment has come; and what am I to say? To speak as though we had anything seems presumptuous; yet we cannot be so ungrateful to God's mercy, as to deny that he has given us grace. It is useless to preach unless we can claim some taste of the things we describe; just enough taste of them to interpret what we hear from the saints, or see in them.

Once again, therefore, what is the grace of Christ? It is that Christ penetrates us, and that this penetration has real effects. It is our prejudice to think that all persons are separate units, and that we communicate only by signalling to one another across physical spaces by physical signs, whether gestures or words. Such is our prejudice. It is called common sense, but it simply is not true. In the world of the spirit our prayers invade and enliven one another; and what are our prayers? They are our souls in action. The saints support and carry us; their life is the life of the Church. But the saints themselves, and we, are supported and enlivened by Jesus Christ. For he, being God, is also man; he crosses from the divine side to ours, to share with us as we share with one another; to be the heart in that community of spiritual creatures which serves the Father Almighty.

So grace is Jesus Christ entering us, Jesus Christ under the skin, the sacrifice of Jesus and the resurrection of Jesus spreading and fulfilling themselves in us. As the well-known prayer expresses it, 'Soul of Christ hallow me, Body of Christ save me, Blood of Christ enflame me, Passion of Christ strengthen me.' And does the grace of Christ so abound, that he gives himself to those who thus pray? Yes, we have seen it in the saints, in those whose wills are crucified, who in praying such a prayer desire nothing so much as that it should come to pass. But the crucifixion of the will – how slow a thing it is, and for most of us in this life, before we have achieved it our powers begin to fail and our habits to form, we become old and difficult and foolish, we die, and we have not been saints. May God, while there is time, give us the crucifixion of the will; for here also the resources of his grace are still unexhausted. We come to throw ourselves on grace, but it is by grace that we throw ourselves on grace. Before we touch the cross, Christ has shouldered it; before we shape a prayer, Christ has prayed it. Let the prayer of Christ, let the sacrifice of Christ, placed in my baptism under the root of my heart, break upwards and displace the sunny rubbish of self-will, to become my prayer and my resolution.

The saints who have crucified their wills are the visible incarnations of grace. Grace triumphs in them during this mortal life; they love the love and will the will of God. And though we are not so, God gives us grace, even to us. We are incorporate in Jesus with all the saints, we eat and drink him in the sacrament. And are there no fruits? Certainly there are fruits. There is the fruit of continual repentance. Again and again our most uncrucified will is reunited with the cross; we are forgiven and accepted as living parts of Christ. Moreover by grace we receive many good desires, and the expulsion of many that are evil. We pray for those whom we dislike, and care for them; we pray to do the duties we detest, and delight in them. Such are the fruits of grace; and to such fruits ordinary Christians can testify.

21

I need hardly say that the effects of grace are put down by unbelievers to suggestion, individual or corporate. Nothing comes in from outside they say; it is all something into which we think ourselves. In a sense, Christians do not disagree; nothing comes in from outside; it is just us, thinking ourselves into our best nature. It is just us; but what are we? That is the point, what are we? According to the unbelieving philosophy, we are complex single beings; but according to faith, we are complex double beings. At a level deeper than that which any science studies, Christ feeds with himself the springs of our action. Nothing comes in from outside; when we act from the resources of divine grace, all the action and all the thought is in us; but it is Christ in us, feeding the deep root of the will; Christ, giving himself to be our self.

For we must use figures and parables; but how they mislead! The parables of grace – and we have Christ's own authority for them – speak of the branch drawing sap from the vine, and the seed building the plant from the materials of soil and rain. But grace is no process of nature, no ray of light kindling into flame, no soil or water feeding a vegetable root; it is the sheer bounty of God. And so when we preach the grace of God, this is what we preach: 'We are ambassadors on Christ's behalf, as though God did beseech you by us; we implore you on Christ's behalf. Be reconciled to God. Him that knew no sin he made sin for us, that we might be righteousness of God in him. Working with him, we beseech you also not to receive the grace of God in vain. For, he says, in a favourable hour I have heard thee, in a day of salvation I have succoured thee. Behold now is that favourable hour, now is that day of salvation'; this is the day to receive what God most longs to bestow, Jesus Christ, everlasting joy and inexhaustible grace; thereby to serve and praise the one Almighty God, unity in three Persons, Father, Son and Holy Ghost, both now and ever.

preached in St Mary the Virgin, Oxford

7

The End of Man

What happens if you put a pair of rabbits on a desert island? Supposing, that is, the island is really desert, quite empty of animal life: no foxes, for instance, no buzzards. Well, the rabbits multiply and they eat the grass. You might think that when the grass won't support any more rabbits, the colony stops increasing merrily and the population stabilizes. Not a bit of it. They all begin to starve on the same day, they all get deficiency diseases, and all but a handful of them die. Indeed they may all die: then there's an end of rabbits.

The globe is our rabbit-island. There are no buzzards or foxes to keep the human rabbits down. It has taken us all these millennia to reach global capacity; we're nearly there. When there is nothing more to eat, we are not so likely all to die of deficiency diseases; we are more likely all to blow one another to bits. And so there'll be an end of man. The writers of science fiction do not find the possibility amusing – for annihilation is annihilation, and about nothing there is nothing to be said. So they save a handful of their human rabbits, to be the Noah's Ark of a universe and start a new round of history. But suppose there is no Noah's Ark: suppose the destruction is complete – how much does it matter, if there's an end of man?

But before we consider that portentous question, let's give the science fiction writers their heads. We will agree then that the handful of humans survive, but in what form? Their genetic character is greatly affected by nuclear fall-out. Never mind, nature copes somehow, and, with a violent mutation, settles into a new biological balance. The human race survives, but the human creature is unrecognizable for what it was; suppose anything you like – we walk on our hands, we see with our ears, we hear with our noses. Our passions and feelings become quite differently balanced; we see the world upside down and ourselves inside out. Meanwhile we excavate the ruins of the Oxford science area, recover the brilliant discoveries of the twentieth century, and go forward so to elaborate our material civilization that life becomes a completely different affair from what it was. We look back on the records of previous centuries and find the activities of former men no nearer to us than those of bees and ants. What has happened? Men have admittedly had descendants: but are these creatures men? Could we come to the end of man, and go on into something else?

So there are two possibilities: we blow one another up without remainder, and there's an end of man. Or we go on to the end of man, and after; for if we become another animal altogether, then there's an end of man; just as there's an end of an undergraduate, when he takes his degree; though not in the same sense as there's an end of one if, failing to take his degree, he takes his life.

Either way, there could be an end of man. But then on either supposition, what about THE END OF MAN: the end, that is, for which he was created? For the end of man is not just that he should come to an end; any more than it is the end for which a violin is made, to be jumped upon by a hooligan: but that it should play sweet music. On either of our sensational alternatives, when man ends, will the end of man have been achieved; will the human music have been played?

It is fortunate that philosophy lecturers do not attend Pusey House sermons, for were such a man here, he would be boiling in his seat. 'Do we not tell our pupils', he mutters, 'ten times a year that comparisons between artefacts and living creatures are utterly fallacious?' An instrument is made to do a job. Very well then: that's its end. Living creatures have no end prescribed to them except that they should live. They themselves create ends by adopting pursuits. There is no such thing as the end of man: the ends of men are what they make them.

Very well; nothing has an end, unless it has a maker: and if we were atheists perhaps there'd be no more we could say; for then we should not think we had a maker. All the same we have. Certainly he does not make us as a man makes a machine; and so our relation to our end will not be like that of a machine. A machine is limited to a fixed end. But in fact we took the example of a violin, of which the ends are not fixed, but in a manner open and infinite. True, a violin will only play violin-music; but cannot we vary and enrich the music for ever? There is no end of the music, no end to the fiddler's art, the violin has an end which is endless.

So with the end of man. To speak of 'the end of man', as a Christian speaks of it, is not to speak of fulfilling that biological existence which we share with slugs and snails, or even with plants and trees. The nerves, the fingers and the throats of men form a complex instrument on which the discourse of reason can be played; action can be thought, and thought can be enacted; and thought is more truly endless even than music, for it has more dimensions. Why, musical composition is itself one of the forms of thought: and how many more there are!

So then, either our supposed new race can think, or it cannot. If it cannot, then it will not be able to pursue THE END OF MAN. But if it can, then whatever happens to its physical constitution, or to its cultural pattern, it can continue to pursue that glorious end.

Thought is unlimited in its nature, though the bodily fiddle on which we play that music is so limited. Thought can go anywhere, and so can the passion and the desire which accompany it. So the end of man is not fixed by the instrument with which he thinks, nor by the heart with which he loves. The universe is ours in which to expatiate, to spread ourselves. Our end is fixed not by our faculties, but by what there is most worthy to be loved and known; and that is God, God in himself, God in all his infinite works and ways. For all knowing is a knowledge of God, and all loving is a loving of him, where there is purity of heart.

So then, if they have hearts to love what is lovely in itself, and minds to contemplate without coveting, our imaginary grandchildren will have undergone no change which frustrates THE END OF MAN, whatever happens to the shape of their bodies or the pattern of their lives.

Ah, but suppose the fiction of our novelists to be false; suppose no human handful survives the global war; suppose the race perishes without remainder: then surely the end of man has been snapped off short and never once attained: God's providence must acknowledge defeat. Yes, if God's heart is set upon a never-ending progeny of human souls. But why should we suppose so? Perhaps he will have had enough. After all, it does not take a nuclear war to make death universal. Death is universal; and none of us attains THE END OF MAN before he dies. Let the race perish from the earth: all those who have been saved in Christ are made alive with him, and proceed to the possession of that infinite good which here they blindly sought. God is the end of man, and God is not seen in this life, but at the best believed, even by the pure in heart.

The most insidious error of our severe philosophical theologians is to set aside the life to come as a thing indifferent, a matter of no concern, which Christians may or may not believe. What? Do we see God in this life? Is it a matter of no concern, a thing indifferent, whether we are ever to attain our only end? If it is indifferent to our earth-bound thoughts, is it indifferent to the heart of God? They think too meanly of his love to us who call this hope in question. Belief in this infinite and invaluable gift, this partaking of God's eternity, is the acid test of genuine faith. Leave this out of account, and you can equivocate for ever on God's very existence: your talk about God can always be talk about the backside of nature, dressed in emotional rhetoric. But a God who reverses nature, a God who undoes death, that those in whom the likeness of his glory has faintly and fitfully shone may be drawn everlastingly into the heart of light, and know him as he is: this is a God indeed, a God Almighty, a God to be trusted, loved, adored.

The end of man is endless Godhead endlessly possessed, but that end flows back in glory on our mortal days, and gives a hope and meaning to whatever Christians do for love of God or love of one another. For we are all heirs of everlastingness, and whatever we do or are furnishes material to the hands which out of perishing stuff create eternal joy.

We cannot, in this life, wholly possess the end we pursue; for man cannot reach his end, until there is an end of man – until we cease from self, and turn outwards on God and on the children of God. And such

25

self-forgetfulness is not attained in a mortal body. Flesh and blood, says Christ's apostle, cannot attain the kingdom of God. See, I show you a mystery – all need not sleep the sleep of death, but all must undergo this change, though it be in the twinkling of an eye, at the last trump. For the trumpet shall sound, and the dead shall be raised incorruptible, and we shall be changed. For this corruptible being must put on incorruption, and this mortal put on immortality. And Christ himself more simply said, 'He that would gain his life must lose it'. So there must be an end of man, that man may possess his everlasting end and, emptied of himself, be filled with God. All must be caught up and transformed in that death and resurrection which Christ fulfilled for us, and to which he unites us through his sacrament, the medicine and the pledge of immortality.

preached in Pusey House, Oxford

8

All Souls' Examination

When I was a young man I used devoutly to believe that fellows of All Souls were selected by a simple test: they were given cherry pie to eat. If they spat the stones they were disqualified for boorishness, and for smoothness if they swallowed them. The serious competition lay between those who, with various degrees of elegance, got the cherries into their throats and the stones into their spoons.

I have lately been disabused of this simple belief. Recently at any rate the candidates have been doing papers, among them an essay; the subject was sin. I cannot help thinking that the All Souls' examiners would have done better to stick to ordeal by cherry pie. For what in the world could they expect a lot of young men more clever than wise, and more wise for the most part than Christian, to make of sin? I did not see the essays, but I cannot suppose they were any good. For sin is not a subject, not, that is, a subject by itself; it is simply the negative aspect of my relation to God; and it makes one feel slightly sick to contemplate a roomfull of young men, too polite doubtless to embarrass their examiners by the profession of any faith they may have, writing on sin for the space of three hours: or rather, if I know them, not on sin but on sin-language; a sort of talk, they would say, which renders self-reproach portentous and engraves the memory of past misdoing with the acid of guilt. The essayists would go on to ask the purely rhetorical question whether such a way of thinking about our moral lapses served any good use, and so pass rapidly on to consider the causes or the cure of so morbid a habit of thought.

Well, but in such an essay not one word would have been said about sin. For my sin is not what I think about myself, it is what I do to God. I have no doubt whatever that a consciousness of sin unrepented and unatoned is highly destructive of the mind that entertains it. It is a poison as pernicious as any All Souls' essayist or *New Statesman* critic likes to say it is. But it is useless to conclude, 'So don't let us have it,' because there it is. To get sin out of the world I must get God out of the world, and I cannot. He is about my path and about my ways; his love is on the road before me, opening up those good works in which he predestines me to walk, and standing in the way of those follies to which I incline. I see that he opposes my wilful passage; I put my foot on the accelerator and drive through his opposition. Sin is what I do to God, wilfully violating his majesty and flouting his good pleasure. He meets me everywhere in so many forms, and specially in his breathing image, the human form divine. Again and again I trample him down. My sin is what I do to God; whether I am conscious of doing it or whether I am not, I do it; there it is, and if I become conscious of God I shall not remain unconscious of my sin.

But he forgives me, that is the great thing. Yes, he forgives me, every day and every hour; and as he is infinitely generous and infinitely great, I may try to comfort myself with the reflection that it can cost him little to forgive the pinpricks of such a midge as I. After all, I may say, I myself do not find it all that difficult to forgive; keeping up quarrels is a bore. I may envy men the spirit to be angry for forty-eight hours, but I cannot imitate them. My indignation burns itself out in five or six. I have no desire after that to chase people for the wrongs they do me, it is too much like work; anything for a quiet life, and when I have decided to drop the whole thing, I say I have forgiven.

Well, that is one temperament, a temperament quite common among the semi-civilized and especially among dons. It is nothing much to boast about, and it offers no sort of analogy to the forgiveness of God. For when God forgives me, whatever he does he does not decide to .let me alone, or to let it go at that. If he decided to let me alone I should drop out of existence; for in him we live and move and have our being. What would happen to me if the breathable atmosphere could decide to let me alone and were to stand back from me on every side, leaving me in a vacuum? But God is not like the atmosphere either, for though air sometimes becomes wind and wind hurricane, yet for the most part air just lies about and lets itself be breathed. Not so God; he is never inert, he is master, he is the sovereign will, he is always at work on me; if he ceased from creating me I should cease to exist; he does not let me be, he continues to sustain me. Nevertheless in so far as I profane and falsify my relation to the well-spring of my life, I begin to shrivel and perish, I am on the way that leads to everlasting death. If God forgives me while I continue to go to the devil, what shall it profit me? I go to the devil just the same. God forgives me, for he has no pleasure in the death of the wicked, but rather that he should turn from his wickedness and live. But whatever his good pleasure may be, I go on dying in my wickedness. God forgives me with the compassion of his eyes, but my back is turned to him. I have been told that he forgives me, but I will not turn and have the forgiveness, not though I feel the eyes on my back. God forgives me, for he takes my head between his hands and turns my face to his to make me smile at him. And though I struggle and hurt those hands – for they are human, though divine, human and scarred with nails – though I hurt them, they do not let go until he has smiled me into smiling; and that is the forgiveness of God.

When a human judge acquits his prisoner, he simply gives sentence; he speaks the words, that is, and a clerk makes marks with ink in a book;

the judge does no more. It is for his officers to show the prisoner out, and it is for the prisoner to walk away on his own feet. Do you imagine that God is like the judge? Or that God ever pronounces mere words which are but sound and breath? Men's acts are inexpressive, they have to explain them; men's words are inefficacious, they have to enact them. God's words and acts are not thus divided; his acts are self-revealing, the language of his heart, his words are self-fulfilling, the instruments of his will; 'Let there be light', he says, and there is light. When God forgives, he does not simply pronounce or simply record a sentence; when God forgives, the well-spring of life turns from bitter to sweet, the acid of sin ceases to corrode, and living waters irrigate the soul. We stop shrivelling, we begin to grow.

'I believe in the forgiveness of sins,' says the Apostles' Creed, making the article hang upon belief in Holy Church Universal and Communion of Saints. One of our oldest authorities for the origins of the Apostles' Creed speaks of 'remission of sins through Holy Church' as that which the candidate for baptism was asked to believe. The creed, after all, is a baptism creed, and baptism is a washing for the remission of sins, administered by Holy Church. It was reasonable enough that the candidate should be required to profess belief in the very rite he came there to undergo. And so we have it without ambiguity in the parallel form of the Church's ancient creed called Nicene; 'I believe in one baptism for the remission of sins,' we recite every Sunday in the Holy Eucharist.

When the Holy Ghost moved the Church to put these articles into her professions of faith, it was never supposed that the intention was anything so vague or platitudinous as to declare that God bears no grudges, or that he would much rather see men repent than see them go to the devil. No, the intention was to proclaim that God had taken certain measures to make his forgiveness effective. He had taken a pair of human hands with which to turn our stiff-necked heads, and bring our eyebeams into the line of his own. And in accomplishing this – so gentle he was, yet so strong – he died and he conquered; that was the price of it, for that was the means to it; that indeed was the act of it. The death of Jesus is the forgiveness of God taking effect, the very act of our remission. The judge on the bench speaks acquittal, the Saviour bleeds forgiveness on the cross.

But, says the theology of the creeds, don't imagine that you can creep into a quiet corner, and make your peace with God. You may indeed begin that way, you can't end that way. You must come out into the open, you must give yourself up, must surrender to visible justice; for the Christ who turns your face to his own is still in the world, and you must meet him there. He has a mystical body, a Catholic Church, a Communion of Saints. And if you will not surrender to his human body,

29

you are not reconciled to his divine person. In the Catholic Church you meet the very symbols, the stuff of his saving passion: bathe in the waters of her font as in the stream that flowed from Christ's side, take the bread as his body, hear the absolution as from his lips; above all, love the Christians as Christ; for what you are to love in them is Christ – Christ fashioned and growing in them, as he begins also to grow in you.

'Thy sins are forgiven thee', said Jesus to the paralytic; for though he pitied his paralysis, he grieved more for his sins. Those who stood by exclaimed that God alone could forgive sin – which was indeed very true, being of the nature of what our philosophical friends call a tautology; for since sins are defined as offences against God, they are certainly not forgiven unless God forgives them. Just as it would be no good my forgiving one of my friends his abominable conduct to his wife; only his wife's forgiveness could forgive it. Only God can forgive sins and – this was what Christ's critics really mean – he does it invisibly in the court of heaven, he does not speak forgiveness on earth through any man's lips. They are wrong, says Jesus; and he heals the paralytic before their eyes as the best evidence he can give for the claim that the Son of Man has divine authority on earth for forgiving sins. Not God only but man, not of course just any man, but the Son of Man, the representative man, the proper man, the divine man, has this authority. His is God's pardoner on earth.

St Matthew, telling the story, adds this conclusion: The people when they saw it wondered, and glorified God for giving such authority to men. 'To men', why the plural? The Heavenly Father has given such authority to the Son of Man; but those who say 'to men' evidently have it in mind that the power can be extended; if one man has it, there is hope others may share it. So the crowd may seem to hint, but are they right? For are there men with whom the unique man, the Son of Man, will share such a privilege as that of forgiving sins?

It seems a wild surmise; and yet unless the Evangelist had thought it to be significant, he would hardly perhaps have troubled to record the random word of an ignorant multitude. Let us turn a few pages of his Gospel, and see whether Jesus transmitted his powers to others, or not. 'Thou art Peter, and upon this *petra*, this rock, I will build my church, and the Gates of Hell shall not master it. And I will give thee the keys of the Kingdom of Heaven; and whatsoever thou shalt bind on earth shall be bound in heaven, and whatsoever thou shalt loose on earth shall be loosed in heaven.' This to Peter; but a couple of pages further on, to all the apostles: 'Whatsoever ye shall bind ... whatsoever ye shall loose ...' They, under Peter's leadership, were to give and withhold, to grant baptism and remission to the penitent, while withholding these privileges from the frivolous; to discipline and, if need be, to expel the unworthy

Christian, to readmit and pardon the contrite. The Son of Man has power on earth to forgive sins, but also through him God has given such an authority to men.

God had given such authority to men, and the multitude glorified God. You will observe, they glorified him, they did not curse him for this; they were not true Protestants, it seems, this multitude; they did not complain that a man, a pardoner, a priest was being brought in to stand between themselves and God. And why did it not occur to them to make a complaint springing so naturally out of human pride? Because of Christ's miracle. Christ had shown, by making the healing of paralysis a sign of sins forgiven, that sin is a deadly disease, a darkness of the heart, a palsy of the hand. Any one who can cure this disease is evidently a benefactor; so God be praised, and may he be pleased to multiply those who can exercise so blessed a ministry. What the multitude saw was no mere assurance that in the court of heaven God forgives sins; they saw the act of a Son of Man empowered by God to bring forgiveness down to earth; to show them the face of God, to make them turn their stubborn necks and take their pardon from his eyes.

The Son of Man read the heart, he knew what was in men. He could absolve them without confession. His ministers, the successors and delegates of the apostles, are not so. Some of them have had some share of Christ's penetration, and have wonderfully known the thoughts of their fellows. Such gifts are rare. Christ's ministers cannot absolve you unless you make them a full particular confession. Prayers for absolution are common in public services, but they are merely conditional. Your confession in the liturgy is only general, and the priest can do no more than declare your forgiveness if you are penitent. But are you? He cannot assure himself that you are, and so he cannot say, 'By Christ's authority committed unto me I absolve thee from all thy offences, in the name of the Father and of the Son and of the Holy Ghost.'

I have sinned. I have offended the majesty of God by contempt of his love and by violation of his will. And I have incurred blood-guiltiness, for I have left poor Lazarus covered with spiritual sores to perish in the street. What am I to say? I have done this evil in thy sight; cleanse me from blood-guiltiness, O Lord, and my tongue shall speak thy praise. Turn my face again and change my way; reunite my will to everlasting love. I know, I believe that you forgive me in heaven, but you have sent your forgiveness on earth to lay hold upon me in the Son of Man. He embraces his enemies and yours on the cross. I will go and find him in the man he has empowered. I will go penitent, but I will come away more penitent; for I shall have met God in the human form, and he will have blessed me. By his blessings I will believe his love, and so my heart will be renewed; and walking from blessing to blessing I, sinful man, will not despair to achieve my pilgrimage and come at length to my Father's house in peace; there to behold the face from which I shall never again be able to turn away my eyes, chained to the God before me by the God within, and in the Son adoring the Father through the indwelling of the Holy Ghost; ascribing to the everlasting Trinity all might, dominion, majesty and power, thenceforward and for ever.

preached in Trinity College Chapel, Oxford

9

Christ is God

I have been asked to arrange for you a course of sermons on something very plain and entirely fundamental, on Jesus Christ himself. And first, why he is said to be truly God.

It is one of the most tiresome things about dons that if you ask them questions they don't supply the answer, but reformulate the inquiry; and in the present case, however I may wish it, I don't see how I am to avoid this sort of tiresomeness. For what you want, I suppose, is a plain answer to the question, why any one should think anything so extraordinary as that a certain Galilean Jew was God Almighty. And my first reaction is to say that before we attempt to hit such a nail as this on the head, we had better get a little clearer what nail we are trying to hit. We want to be shown that a certain man was true God. But first we must see what it would mean to say of a man that he was truly God. It *could* indeed mean all sorts of things, and has meant all sorts of things in various mythologies. Our question is what it meant, say, to St John, when he was speaking neither of Augustus Caesar nor of Hercules, but of Jesus Christ.

If we were to ask one of our philosophical friends what is the question which has 'Jesus is God' for its answer, he would probably say, That is easy. Either it answers the question, which man was God (Jesus was); or it answers the question, what sort of being was Jesus (he was the divine being). But, in point of fact, the disciples of Jesus were not asking either of these questions. They were not like the Tibetan priests looking for a newborn Dalai Lama, and asking in which man among men God had appeared. Nor were they looking at a certain gifted man and saying, This Jesus, is he human or more than human? What they did ask was, This Jesus, what sort of a son is he to God? And they answered, He is a proper Son, and so he is what his Father is. His Father is God, and he can be no less.

That this was how they thought is plain from St John's Gospel. St John begins with a few lines of inspired speculation. In the beginning, he says, there was God with God, expressing him as word expresses mind, his only-begotten Son; and he became a man of flesh and blood. Having read these bold speculative words we turn to the chapters that follow, expecting perhaps to be shown how Jesus is the eternal Word of God in fleshly expression; but we hear no more about it. What St John has collected for us is any speech or action of Christ which reveals his sonship to God. Plainly then, in St John's mind, what proved Jesus to be

God-with-God and eternal Word of God was his being such a Son, that he must be credited with being a proper Son; that is, of the same nature as his Father; 'God from God, light from light, true God from true God,' as the creed has it.

If a pagan wanted to prove that a certain apparently human figure was really God, or, to use pagan language, was really a god, the first thing he would set out to show would be that his hero acted by his own power, and without asking any one's leave. And as we work our way into St John's Gospel we may begin to think we are going to find the same thing demonstrated about Christ. He will not follow his mother's advice at Cana of Galilee, he does his first miracle in his own fashion and at his own time. And in the same way he makes a point of acting independently of his brethren about the time and manner of his going up to Jerusalem. But looking further, we see that he detaches himself from his mother or his brethren only in order to attach himself to his Father in heaven. The trouble about his acting on the motion of his family would not have been that he would have failed to choose for himself; the trouble would be that he would have chosen for himself, chosen to fall in with their ideas; whereas he must choose nothing for himself, he must do his Father's will in all things.

The pagan would wish to show that his divine hero was supremely original, but St John's testimony is that his divine Saviour is utterly derivative. This is the point which the Jews in the Gospel dialogue cannot understand. They accuse Jesus of claiming to be someone, of seeking his own glory, of bearing testimony to himself. His reply is that of himself he is nothing and claims nothing; that is just how he differs from us men. We seek glory for ourselves, and we seek it from one another. Jesus has nothing to do with anything of the sort. What he does do is to speak the words his Father sent him to speak, and perform the acts his Father puts into his hands. He cannot forbear to claim that these are the words, the acts of God, for then he would be failing to do his errand. He must demand submission to the messenger of God in the name of God, even though he happens himself to be the messenger. But 'messenger' is inadequate; a messenger merely reports a set of words entrusted to him, but what is entrusted to Jesus is the very life and love of God, to be lived in the world and made to shine and to save. If I give a written message to the College Messenger he can say, 'All right, sir,' and put it in his pocket. If I give him a verbal message he can say, 'All right, sir,' and put it in his head. It is all right, because when his pocket is crammed with notes and his head with messages, he has still plenty of room for being himself. But if I say to him, 'Don't take a message, just go and be me,' it isn't all right any more. He must reply, 'No, I am afraid I can't do that, sir; I am not you, I am myself, sir.' Sons in this world can no more be their fathers than messengers can be their employers; but the divine Son can say, 'He that hath seen me hath seen the Father.'

The evidence, then, that Jesus was God-from-God and God-with-God, was that a life had come into the world which gave back to God the picture of his own face, and the love of his own heart. And the second evidence was the power of it. By union with this life men received a share in something not human at all, an eternal divine sonship. 'To as many as received him he gave the power to become sons of God, to them that believe on his name; who not of blood, nor of the will of the flesh, nor of the will of man, but of God were begotten.' He could not give us a share of what he had not got; before all adopted sonship like ours, comes the true natural sonship which is his.

We have then to consider in Christ primarily what he claims, what he is, what he does to us. There are also supporting evidences of an exterior kind preceding, accompanying and following his earthly life.

The evidence preceding his advent is the remarkable history of Israel, a nation distinguished from all others and held together by nothing but the faith that God would establish his Kingdom through this people. Now, in a way that is far too various and too complete to be described here, Jesus fulfilled all the strands of prophetic hope; not in a soulless, mechanical way, but in a divine, living and unpredictable way. Such a preparation for Christ, and such a fulfilment in Christ seems a work truly worthy of God.

The evidence accompanying his earthly life is his miracles. Spiritual men have at all times done wonderful things; if Christ had not done any it would have surprised us. His divine nature is not proved by his miracles, but it is confirmed by them. Antiquity was credulous, and the evidence is difficult to sift; but only stubborn prejudice will deny that Jesus was a worker of wonders, and more especially that his mighty acts slipped from him like the running over of a divine power which could not be hidden. He did not exert himself to do miracles, still less to exhibit them.

The evidence succeeding his earthly life is his resurrection. His friends were convinced by it immediately, and turned into a believing church by it. His enemies never claimed that they possessed or could exhibit his body. The resurrection sealed the Father's acceptance of the Son's supreme sacrifice.

Last of all we may put what we will call retrospective evidence. When the disciples came to look back and ask how the divine Saviour had come into the world, the answer was, By a divine and virginal birth. Faith will accept this retrospective evidence as in agreement with what faith already believes, and as something divinely appropriate; but the virginal birth cannot convince unbelief, for how are we to produce the witnesses?

It is almost absurd to count over the heads of evidence at this rate. It is more like a catalogue than a sermon, and it would be quite useless if I were not reminding you of things you know already. I will make just one point now, and it shall be something quite general. It is this: all of this evidence is addressed to faith, and to nothing but faith.

The issue which faces us is to recognize true God when we see him. And what is the organ or faculty for recognizing God? The eyes for colour, the ears for sound, the method of logical thought to test an argument. But with what power shall God be recognized? With no single power, but with our whole life and being. Why, you cannot discover your true friends, or the wife you ought to marry, with less; so how should you discover God with less? It takes all of man to acknowledge man, it takes more to acknowledge God; it takes God, the Holy Ghost speaking in the heart. To believe in Jesus we must co-operate with the Spirit of Jesus, the Spirit wherewith Jesus has colonized our minds.

If you ask, then, 'Shall I not be able to talk away the evidence for Christ's godhead? Shall I not be able to make up plausible theories to account for everything without an incarnation?' I will reply, Yes, you will be able to talk it away; but God, when it pleases him, will show you that you are deceiving yourself by so doing. 'Well then,' you may say, 'but if I admit the evidence, need a miracle-worker be God?' I answer, No. 'Need a man who claims what Jesus claimed, be God?' I answer, No. 'A man appearing as risen from death?' No, and so with the rest. But what is the proper response of the will and intellect and the heart, to the whole evidence of Christ? That is the question which, once answered, has to be answered all over again in every vital decision of life. That is the question of which I pray Almighty God to teach you the answer; or, if you have found it, to remain constant in your decision.

For 'if we accept the witness of men', as we do in a court of law, 'the witness of God is greater; and this is the witness of God, his testimony to his Son. He that believes on the Son of God has the witness in him. He that believes not God has accused him of lying, by disbelieving the witness he has given concerning his Son.'

But we, praying that our lives may answer our words, in union with the Church on earth and the Church in heaven, ascribe to the Father who testifies, and to the Son of whom he testifies, and to the Holy Ghost who is the living testimony of the Father, all might, dominion, majesty and power, henceforth and for ever.

preached in Trinity College Chapel, Oxford

10

Predestination

For whom he did foreknow, he also did predestinate to be conformed
to the image of his Son, that he might be the firstborn among many
brethren. Moreover whom he did predestinate, them he also called.

Rom. 8.29

To enjoy peace of mind, you should take care not to listen to yourself.
For if you listen to yourself, you will observe how you repeat yourself. It
is most shaming, when you tell the same story twice to the same person;
for you are caught out then. But it may be really worse when you aren't
caught out; when you hear yourself palming off the same bad penny of
spurious wisdom on one person after another, and realize that you will
probably go on doing it as long as the supply of victims lasts. Where is
the don, I wonder, who could write down his standard answers to
undergraduates, say on the subject of their careers – could write them
down in a clear hand on a piece of paper, and read them through steadily
and not wish he were dead? Or may it be that an unbelieving don might
feel a tolerable complacency over his performance? After all, worldly
wisdom is worldly wisdom, and it is possible to steer young men in the
direction of mental comfort and financial competence; there are a
number of noble platitudes on these themes which will bear a deal of
repetition. What is so awful is to be a Christian don, and to listen to
one's own muddled compromises between worldly wisdom and divine
vocation.

'My uncle', says the pupil, 'has rather a decent solicitor's business, and
he'd like to take me on. But sometimes I think I'll be a parson.' 'Well,' I
hear myself replying, 'it's certainly a shame if these family firms are let go.
But then, of course, the Church is perishing for lack of priests. The
parson's life, though, is a terrible life and his family starves. You want to
be very sure you are called to it before you plunge in. On the other hand,
it may be God just won't let you off.' But either God does let him off, or
he lets himself off; and then he draws the conclusion, perhaps, that he is
free to please himself; God won't mind. So his life is left without any
sense of a divine destination – a pretty effect of my Christian advice. I
suppose I should have asked him to consider whether he was divinely
called to be a money-lending solicitor. But the words died on my lips; it
seemed such humbug. Or should I have thrown in an unasked-for
sermon, to the effect that the divine destination of our life should
be found, not so much in the way we earn our bread, as in the way

we share it? But then, unasked-for sermons are a social outrage, so I don't take this line, either, with the unfortunate pupil who asks my advice.

Well, I am a more or less incurable case now – I'm over fifty, and the nonsense I have talked I shall go on talking. Let's think about you, for of you there is still hope. Do you see your life as having a divine destination, either in terms of a calling, or of personal claims to be met, or of anything else?

The trouble is, I'm to preach to you about divine predestination. But if you have no divine destination, however hazy, in front of your eyes, you may see no sense in the question whether it is, or isn't, the effect of a divine *pre*destination, appointing you to such a path before ever you were born. If you have no notion of your life's being carried on the current of a divine will, what is the use of discussing whether that current is, or is not, irresistible?

But if you really know nothing of a divine will directing your path, then where is your faith? Where is your faith, if you never look a day ahead, no, not even an hour, to see what God destines for you? Where is your faith? Yet you have faith; though, like the rest of us, you are one part faith and nine parts faithlessness, yet it is that one part of faith with which you identify yourself, when you collect yourself into one piece, and kneel before the God who made you. 'Lord, I believe: help thou mine unbelief' is the prayer of us all. It is certainly mine, and will be so, barring a miracle, to the day of my death, when I hope he who gave me this faith will show his face to me.

But meanwhile we have faith – you have faith – and in what? Doubtless in that Lord whom you invoke for aid against your faithlessness. Your faith is in him; not in his bare existence, however, but in his active power; or rather in his powerful act, by which he gives and increases faith, and leads you in the way of everlasting life. This is the object of your faith, the act of God doubled and redoubled upon you, one in intention, manifold in effect: preservation doubled upon creation, and providence doubled over both; redemption added above all, making you afresh, with grace to defend what redemption has renewed, and inspiration to guide it, seating the providence of God in your very heart. All these are the several currents of one stream, the running river of almighty action, the tide of mercy which carries you into illimitable life. If you have faith, your faith is in this all-supporting act of God on which you float; a flood of which none has sounded the bottom, and none has visited the source.

But now, to believe predestination, what is it but to see the evidence of saving power, to know that Mercy sweeps all barriers away, securing the end at which his action aims? Each step of omnipotence is almighty: he adds stage to stage, he does not leave off till all is perfect. 'Whom he foreknew, he did also predestinate to a conformity with the image of his Son, making him a firstborn among many brethren. Moreover, whom he predestinated them he also called; and whom he called he justified, and whom he justified, glorified' (Rom. 8.29).

To say that we are predestinated to salvation and to say that our salvation is planned is to say the same thing; and no one can complain that the idea of planning is a stranger to the world in which we live. There are, indeed, two sorts of plans – there are Western plans and there are Eastern plans. Eastern plans tend to be ruthless, to handle humanity as mere material; they are something done to men, rather than anything that men achieve. Western plans are elastic, they are mere assignments for free agents to fulfil; as a result, they tend not to be carried out. There is a dilemma here, which it is difficult to resolve. When men plan for their fellow men, either they make the plans fit tight, and then they strangle the men; or else they let the plans hang loose, in which case the men get out of hand. But when God plans for men, it is not like this. His plans for us are close, not loose, they fit us like a glove; for the thought of God goes with our every motion, divine care clothes us like the atmosphere. And yet, his thought for us does not constrain us; what he designs for us is that we should freely act; what he creates is liberty. To enter into God's plan for us is to be most sovereignly ourselves; it is through giving us the power and courage to be ourselves that he fulfils his purposes in us. We can do nothing positive which does not give effect to everlasting love; the more creative we are (if we must use this arrogant word) the more we give expression to his will; for he is the sole creator, and to create through us is his design.

We cannot escape from God, any more than we can escape from the atmosphere; but then we do not want to; for why? we should cease to breathe. We can never draw a line and say: 'God on that side, I on this.' God is on all sides; he has beset us behind and before, and laid his hand upon us; such knowledge is too wonderful: we cannot overtake it. Should we begin to reckon his counsels, his designs for us, they would be more numerous than the grains of the sand; therefore, says the Psalmist, when we awake from sleep, we are present with him; for his designs open out in front of us before we have opened our eyes; they spread through the opportunities of the dawning day, and take shape in the good works he has created for us to walk in them.

'My boy,' says the stage schoolmaster, 'God has created you an Englishman, and he has sent you to Fagchester. The rest is up to you.' To us? No, no, no, and a thousand times no; we will go on in God's great predestination, fulfilling the thought which is the breath of our being, and abiding in Christ, by faith.

I hope it is now plain that to talk about predestination is no more than to talk about the God who is the object of faith, the God (that is) who saves. But there is something else in the world besides salvation – there is the perversity from which we are saved. Free beings have abused their freedom, and multiplied every sort of evil; and it was to remedy this that God acted in his predestining grace, entering us and working through our freedom from within. But not all have admitted the heavenly guest; and here lies the mystery of predestination – not in the salvation of those who are obedient, but in the refusal of those who disobey. We run into irresolvable contradictions, whatever we say about this. How shall we safeguard God's justice, and not attenuate his saving love? A regard for his justice will incline us to say: the lost are lost and the saved are saved, by reason of their willingness or unwillingness to co-operate with God's grace. As he wishes his sun to shine on the evil and on the good, or his rain to fall on the just and the unjust, so he showers grace on all; but some accept it, others do not.

This sounds highly reasonable from the aspect of justice. It does not speak the truth about the riches of grace. For this is the glory and the depth of grace, that God persuades sinners; that there is no will so wicked, he has not converted it. What? Is there a man in this chapel whom God has enlightened, and who will dare to say: 'Salvation was offered to all, but while others declined, I had the merit to accept?' It would be better to die than to make such a boast. No; God, who offers salvation to all, prevails on me to accept it, and to renew, to persevere in, that acceptance. May he give me the gift of persevering to the end!

But then, if there is no will so perverse that God has not converted it, why has not he converted all? I cannot tell; I cannot fathom his counsels, for 'how great is the sum of them'. And they are incessantly at work, calling us to co-operate with them, and to be their instruments. How do I know that God will not prevail at length with all? How do I know what means he may devise here or in other worlds hereafter to warm cold hearts, or reconcile rebellious wills? His warnings not to neglect present opportunity are addressed to me, and I acknowledge the justice of them. But if he threatens me with hell, it is that he may give me heaven, turning my feet from the path of sadness which I have deserved to tread. It is hell to be out of God, but he speaks of hell to draw me into God. He has not forbidden me to pray for the salvation of any man, and he has commanded me to work for the salvation of those he has given me. Rather than scowl at a high justice I cannot comprehend, why do not I yield to a present kindness which I can feel and know? Why do I not do the certain will of God here and now, by co-operating with his purpose to enlighten and to save? Of one thing I am certain: if God at length shows me his face, I shall find no lines of cruelty in the countenance of love, and in the well-spring of light no darkness at all.

Our Anglican Articles, with a contempt for theoretical truth which is almost comic, declare predestination to be a most sweet and comfortable doctrine for the elect, but full of danger and discouragement for the ungodly. 'Just like the Church of England', may be our first reaction. Well, but what's the matter with the Church of England? The authors of the Articles were perfectly right. Predestination is true, but the godly alone can understand it; the ungodly cannot. And why? The ungodly man sets his will against the will of his creator, and, because his creator is almighty, complains that he is himself reduced to impotence. He is blind, because he commits the ultimate error – not theoretical but practical: the error of turning his back on the living truth. The believer can see, for he embraces Truth himself; he unites his will with the creator's will, and so he learns the mystery of love. He finds that there are no hard lines to be drawn between God's love for him and his for God. God loves us into loving him, and the love by which we love him is the Holy Ghost. And yet the more his love is divine, the more it is ours; we are never so much ourselves, as in the act of love which God inspires, never so alive as when we are clay under his fingers, and never so free, as in being predestinated.

Our freedom is a sharing in the freedom of that Son, who is divinely free to be all that his Father begets in him, and wholly himself in being the home and vessel of the Holy Ghost. To whom, therefore, with the Father and the same Spirit, one God in three Persons, be ascribed, as is most justly due, all might, dominion, majesty, and power, henceforth and for ever.

preached in Pusey House Chapel, Oxford

11

The Silent Christ

St John in his Gospel seems determined, whatever may happen, to show the wisdom of God, and the foolishness of man. St Matthew and St Luke have a story about an officer whose boy was healed by Christ; but their story will not do for St John: his tale exactly reverses the point of theirs. Instead of Christ's offering to visit and heal the invalid and the officer's begging him not to bother, but to pronounce the word of power from where he stands, St John shows us the officer begging Christ to make the visit, and Christ convincing him that his word suffices. There is no visible sign: nothing impressive is done. The man goes home, and finds the crisis of the fever past. The neighbours can say if they like, 'Good old Nature! Keep the healer away and the patient recovers.'

That was the second miracle Jesus did at Cana of Galilee: and the first contains a similar point. Mary, who had said to the angel, 'But no man has had me,' says to Jesus at the wedding, 'They haven't any wine.' 'Let me be,' says Jesus, 'it isn't yet my moment.' Mary, like the officer, gives in, and leaves it to her Son. 'Behold the servant of the Lord!' she had said to the angel. 'Just do what he says,' she remarks to the servants. Jesus, it would seem, chose a moment when he could speak to them without anyone noticing; and so hardly anyone there had an idea where so much good stuff had come from. It was very generous of the bridegroom, no doubt; but what on earth made him keep the best till last?

Still St John does not feel that he has sufficiently rubbed in the point: and he follows up the two miracles of Cana with the story of the Pool of Bethesda with its intermittent spring. There is a man there superstitious enough to think that if only he could get in when the water welled up fresh from the bottom, he might be healed. 'But I've no one to put me in', he says to Jesus. 'couldn't you just. . . ?' Once more the mercy of God cuts across on a different line from the man's half-desperate hope – 'Take up your bed and walk!' There is no need to wait for anything, or to carry out any sort of performance. Just have what you want. Leave it to me; the wine will be forthcoming when it's wanted. Go home and look at the boy; you'll find he is better. You want to walk, don't you? Well, walk!

What is the use, what is the meaning of all this harping on a single string? It is not just something about the way miracles happen. Mind you, St John believed the miracles he reported; and it would be very silly and irresponsible of us to doubt that Jesus was the most powerful of spiritual healers, the mightiest of wonder-workers. That does not mean,

42

of course, that we are bound to credit every detail of every such story which was attached to his name. St John is certainly not interested in digging the core of history out of the husks of legend. What he wants to do is to pick the stories which best illustrate the ways of Mercy with mankind.

But why use bodily miracles to teach us truths of the spirit? So far from miracles helping to explain, they are of all things the most in need of explanation. Why use miracles? Why, because we are miracle-lovers; and the first thing for us to get into our heads is that we are asking for miracles all the time. We Christians, like the bridegroom at Cana, are obliged to put on a party for mankind; we are bound to offer all comers divine fellowship and inextinguishable joy. And where's the wine? Aren't the supplies dry? What can we drain from the bottom of the barrel? Perhaps Mary will take heart and say for us, 'They have no wine.'

Our children, or friends, brothers, sisters have got the fever: they are revolted, unbelieving, passionately set on stupid aims; and what can we do? Nothing; 'Saviour come down ere the child die.'

But it comes nearer home; we are paralysed ourselves, tied down by our bad habits, our unforgiving minds; there is, no doubt, the pool of regeneration close at hand, but we can't somehow crawl to it – if only something would happen! If only someone, something, would pick us up and throw us in!

The first thing, then, is to realize that we want miracles, and that we do not know how miracles are to be done; a small point since it is not we who are going to do them. I find in myself this foolishness, that when I call in the aid of a workman over something I can't repair, I have to tell him what I think to be the cause of the trouble, and how it should be mended. The poor man is merely fogged by my suggestions; but at last I let him look at the bother for himself; a broad smile of intelligence spreads over his face, and his clever hands go to work. Why tell divine wisdom what to do? We have only to show our need.

The other point that stands out is the immediacy of the divine mercy. There is no need for any preliminary business for it to take effect. Jesus need not visit the officer's son; the cripple need not wait for the water to stir or for someone to carry him over to it. There is simple and immediate attention to our need as soon as it is known. Now to many of us this is the very touchstone of faith. Can you believe that every moment you have only to turn to Christ to be accepted with him?

Here I propose to make a digression, which I shall hope to tie back into the argument later on. A great deal is said nowadays about the importance to our health and happiness of free relations between the sexes. What does a Christian say about this? I think a Christian distinguishes. On the one side there's physical appetite which has just got to be controlled within the limit of God's law; and on that issue the

Christian won't give an inch. On the other side there is the intimacy of affection, which Christian virtue can very well separate from gross physical satisfaction; and it is this that is psychologically so important, and so full of blessings. For in a relationship of love we are assured of an immediate welcome, if the love deserves the name. We do not have to justify ourselves to be accepted, we do not have to show off to be appreciated, we do not have to prove it wasn't our fault to be felt for. So in affairs of love, short of marriage, a Christian will pursue trust, loyalty, and above all honesty and openness, an intimacy of the mind, not of the body.

That is my digression. The reason why I made it was that I want to ask how Christians can dare to think less of divine than of human love. We are simply and immediately accepted with Christ's mercy. There is the warm corner of our welcome, the hearth where the fire never goes out; we often cannot forgive ourselves, but always, before we sit down by the blaze, or spread out our hands, God has forgiven us: he is our friend, he is on our side, he wants to give us all we need.

He does not, needless to say, want us to be shirkers or grabbers, idlers or egotists, playboys or exhibitionists. But then, once in his company, we do not want to be these things. It has often been thought that a human love-affair, besides relaxing our tensions and warming our affections, would put an edge on our virtue. Perhaps it sometimes does. It very often doesn't. But this is the love of Christ, that he cares for us as we are, and makes us as good as we let him. And so Christ manifests his power without sign or noise. The wine is in the pitchers. The boy is well again. The cripple is on his feet. 'How is it', said his disciple Jude to Jesus at the supper, 'that thou wilt manifest thyself to us, and not to the world?' Jesus answered, 'If a man love me, he will keep my word, and my Father will love him, and we will come unto him and make our abode with him.' Such is the hidden Epiphany, the silent self-manifestation of Christ.

preached in Keble College Chapel, Oxford

12

Atoning Death

Preachers become flatterers; we charm your ears, and make the act of attention involuntary. It is all very well; but we run the risk of disgusting the best part of our audience, people who wish to learn, and feel no objection to fifteen minutes' hard thinking. To-night, anyhow, I shall make no attempt to imitate the Pied Piper of Hamelin. I shall give you a stern theological lecture, and if you will make no effort you will not hear me through. But you will make the effort, surely. We are approaching Holy Week; and before we keep the mysteries of Christ's death we ought to reflect on the salvation we commemorate. How does the Saviour's death profit us? What are we to think of his Atonement? From time to time some of you startle me by referring to the Atonement itself as a revolting heresy, invented by the twelfth century, and exploded by the twentieth. Yet the word is in the Bible. We have to consider, not how much we disagree with Luther or Calvin, but how we are to be saved.

Well, then, I will try to give you a theologian's report on the result of theological study. I will tell you as carefully as I can the essence of what I see the New Testament to contain about Christ's atoning sacrifice.

To begin at the beginning, with Jesus Christ himself. He came to a people who expected a Messiah, but did not at all expect him to die for their sins. You must not think that this was mere superficiality on their part, or that they ignored sin, or supposed that it could be put right without any one dying the death. No: they had the fifty-third chapter of Isaiah in front of their eyes, just as we have it before ours; they read of that servant of the Lord who was wounded for men's transgressions, by whose stripes men are healed; who poured out his soul in death, and was numbered with transgressors; yet bore the sins of many, and for transgressors offered his intercession. See, they said, this figure is the figure of the true Israel; faithful to God, we are persecuted, we perish. It is the heathen and the unfaithful of our own nation who sin, but it is we who, by our patient suffering, are called to vanquish the evil. Our martyrdoms are the acceptable sacrifice by which the world will be redeemed. And when? In that day when our sufferings are complete, and God, returning in mercy, sets us on high, as it is written in the same prophecy: Behold, my servant shall be exalted and lifted up and made very high; to the astonishment of the heathen, and to the confusion of mighty princes. And how will God exalt us in that day? By sending to us the Son of David, King Messiah. He will be strong, and he will make us great. The sufferings are thine, O Israel, in this present time: but the glory is King Messiah's, and thou too shalt share it.

So preached the Rabbis in a hundred synagogues, and Jesus doubtless heard them. But he was not satisfied with their doctrine; he could not agree that they rightly divided between the sufferings and the glory, giving the sufferings to Israel and only the glory to Messiah. For what is Messiah? And when Jesus asked that question, he was asking, What am I? Is not Messiah *the* man, the proper man, as it is quaintly said in Martin Luther's hymn: 'But for us fights the proper man, whom God himself has bidden?' And must he not, by the divinity that is in him, take up the whole destiny of man, the whole redeeming part of the servant of God, the sufferings as well as the glory? *The* man or, in Christ's Jewish phrase, the Son of Man, must suffer, and be rejected, and killed, and so come to that death from which he will arise to glory. So said Jesus, to his disciples' great amazement.

The proper man gets right what a sinful race gets wrong, his is the proper manhood, he fights the proper battle, he dies the proper death, giving into his Father's hands the proper gift, a soul unselfish and undefiled; and he gives it with a proper giving, that is, with all his heart. And so he reaches the proper fulfilment, an everlasting union with the life of God.

Well, here is something containing mysterious depths, and yet presenting a surface meaning which we can understand. Yes, we will agree, this was the proper man. But now we come to the point – 'For you,' says the proper man, going to his death, 'my body is broken for you,' or, in another place, 'the Son of Man is come to give his life a ransom for many.' 'For you,' 'for many' – how are we to understand this 'for'? If the proper man dies a right death, how shall that avail us, who are in much danger of living so trivially that we shall die all wrong, and grudgingly surrender into the hands of God nothing that he can use? What is this little word 'for'? If we understood that, we should understand Christ's atoning sacrifice. He went to his death, he rose, and was taken up, and left that little word 'for' sticking in his disciples' hearts.

The Spirit came down at Pentecost to interpret Christ's words more largely, and especially this 'for'. We read the interpretation all over the New Testament, and above all in St Paul.

To understand St Paul it is essential to start in the right place, and not to put the cart before the horse. The proper starting place is the true use of death. In the animal order, death is just a physical fact, the scrapping of the outworn machine. But man is not an animal simply, and God has assigned to the death of man a spiritual purpose also – the casting off of a lower nature, with all its corruptions, and all the hold sin had on us through it. Death is ideally, then, a death to sin; but we, alas, cannot die this death. Our body lies, but our spirit cannot cast off sin and flesh together, for our heart is given to our fleshly self and not to God. But of Christ it can be said, 'The death he died he died to sin once and for all:

46

the life he now lives, he lives to God.' For the sin which had beset him, but to which he had not yielded, was left, uselessly besieging the empty fortress of his body, while his spirit departed in purity to God; and when he rose again, it was in a body which was not open to the assaults of sin.

Now if Christ's death had just been something that a man consented to and underwent, it would have been a pattern for our imitation, and no more. But because it was an act of God, it had in it an infinite power, to the radiation of which no limit can be set. Christ's dying into life has the power to carry us all through the same motions; and so, what we have to do is not simply to imitate, but to adhere: to take hold, by faith, of this strong swimmer in the gulf of death, who not only supports us, but makes us swim with him. For we do not hold him with our hands; we consent that he should hold us by his spirit. And his spirit is an invisible bond which has this strange power, that it links our hands to his hands, our feet to his feet, our heart to his heart, in such wise that, without visible contact, our hands move as his hands move, and our feet follow the motions of his feet; and yet we are not dragged through the movements we make, we make them freely; for our heart is linked to his heart; it all comes from there.

So Christ dies our death, and achieves our life for us; and we die our death, and enter into life, through him. And this happens because, on his side, God is in him; and on our side we take hold, adhere or believe.

So far we have said nothing of atoning sacrifice. But what this is we shall immediately begin to see, if we recall that the sin which is conquered, and the crooked death which is put straight, is not Christ's death or Christ's sin, but ours. This is not fairyland; evil cannot be annihilated by the waving of a magic wand; it has to be met, suffered and redeemed. Well, it was man's evil, but it was the Son of God who met, suffered and redeemed it. How plain it is, then, that he has stood in for us, that he has paid our price! And this was driven home by the very manner of his death. For he died on a gallows, when, as the thief who suffered with him said, he had done nothing amiss. For our sakes, says St Paul, God made him the very image of sin, the very figure of a curse, that we might become all divine innocence in him.

It was one action, one sacrifice, by which Christ saved us; the Bible, and especially St Paul, holds that unity fast; but dwells now on one aspect of it, now on another. If we consider how utterly undeserved it was, we call it grace; if we consider the cost, we call it atonement; if we consider the effect, we call it new life, redemption, sanctification.

St Paul piles figure upon figure in the attempt to describe what cannot be described, and especially the sacrificial cost. Since sacrifice in the literal sense was familiar to the ancient world and especially an institution with the Jews, he uses technical terms of sacrifice. Under the old law we were allowed to kill sheep in expiation of our offences, but now there is a better, indeed the only true sacrifice, Christ. Such things the Apostle says; but there is one thing that he does not say. He never says that Christ propitiated the wrath of God, or propitiated God at all. Well, but, you will tell us, he does say that Christ is a propitiation. The English versions say so; but you can take it from me that the English versions are wrong. Expiation, not propitiation, is the proper sense; we propitiate a person, but we expiate a crime. God himself, says St Paul, so far from being wrathful against us, or from needing to be propitiated, loved us enough to set forth Christ as an expiation of our sins through his blood. 'Expiate' means simply 'purge away', 'take the guilt out of'. God provided in Christ's death the spiritual cure for our sin; that is what St Paul is saying.

If St Paul did not say that Christ propitiated God's wrath for us, still less did he teach that God poured his wrath on Christ, or cut him off from grace, as a substitute-sinner on the Cross. Nothing of this sort is to be found in the Bible. When Christ is said to have been made a curse or made sin for us, any one competent in the usages of Jewish speech ought to know what is meant: simply that the Father allowed Christ to be crucified, and so to act before men and angels the part of a sinner and of an accursed man. And that, surely, is quite enough.

I have sinned: but Christ it was who died. The way back from sin to freedom is through suffering and death; through his, not mine. I must accept every day his infinite generosity and acknowledge my impotence to atone. I must adhere to him, that is all. He asks nothing but sincerity of my adherence; all the rest is his. And so every day I may dare to celebrate that bloodless sacrifice, in which the Christian is bodily united with the death and resurrection of the Lord, our salvation ever new, our inseparable life; to whom with the Father and the Holy Ghost be ascribed all majesty and power, now and ever.

preached in Trinity College Chapel, Oxford

13

Early in the Morning

'Very early in the morning on the first day of the week ...' As I try to find my way into this subject, I see ahead the formidable risk of my never getting into it at all; so strong is the temptation to sit down by the wayside and pick daisies, or perhaps I should say, not so much pick daisies as puff dandelion-clocks. 'Early on the first day of the week.' Here is a temptation to moralize on time; and if we once start we shall never stop, for time contains all the morals there are. What is time, anyway? There is no such thing. Is it a series of blank spaces on a chart, weeks, days, minutes, hours; blanks which we can book up beforehand, but can only fill in when we reach them and live through them? What a lot of room there is in the blank pages, as we look ahead through our diary; and when we look back over the old entries, how little room we find there was for the things we hoped to have done and never managed to do. I meet my pupils at the beginning of Michaelmas term. 'Have you been round the world this summer?' 'No, just poked about a bit in Devonshire.' 'Then you've read a nice lot of books?' (this we say with a special tutorial smile). 'No, there never seemed to be time, somehow.' 'Well,' says the tutor coming clean, 'I have done about a third of what I meant to do, myself.' But hope springs eternal – the long vacation was sixteen weeks, the term is eight, and I wonder if there is a single one of us who is not seriously convinced that he will get more done in the term than he did in the vacation.

Time, looked at like this, seems to be nothing but a bad joke, and yet in the end it is no laughing matter. Sixteen weeks and eight are twenty-four, and fifty-two of them are a year, and you have not got more than fifty of those in which you can hope to do much good; while as for me – we will draw a veil over that.

Well; but Christ rose from the dead on the first day of the week, and God, whose life is alone steady and not made to run away from him like sand, will give us a share of his everlastingness; that is our blessed hope. Yet we go to eternity through time; it is a crumbling bridge, but we have got to walk across it, not go down with it; and so it is not surprising that religion takes a great account of time, and always has done so.

When Christ died and rose on the first day of the week, he made a revolution of all things, and among others, of our attitude to time. Before Christ we used to keep the seventh day, but Christ rose on the first, and now we keep that.

Well but, you may say, this is a merely comic revolution; there is no

49

real difference between the seventh of the week and the first. It is purely arbitrary. If some dictatorial government were to decree that henceforth Monday should be the first of the week, then Sunday would be not the first but the last; or, for that matter, we might stop counting in sevens altogether. Quite true; it is only how we view it; but then the importance of time lies in how we view it. The Jew saw himself giving the seventh day to God, we see ourselves giving the first; and there is all the difference in the world between the two.

The Jewish system seems very sensible. Do not indulge yourself, do the slogging first; fulfil your practical duties, get your work out of the way and clear a block of time for God. If you took this attitude, not so much perhaps to your religion, but to your amusement, it would be an excellent thing. Earn your leisure by your work. Which of you does? The good Jew, whom Christ caricatures for us in his parable, comes into the temple and tells God that he has earned his Sabbath. In a world of slackers he has not slacked; he has kept his fasts, paid up his tithes and held the devil at bay; he brings his eyes bright, and his hands clean, into the temple of God.

Jesus Christ changed all this, did we but realize it. Very early in the morning on the first day of the week, before any one had done a stroke of work or acquired a jot of merit, he rose from the sepulchre, bringing new life to his disciples. What then began had nothing to do with last week's work or last week's sins; they all seemed centuries away. The old world for Christ's disciples had ended in calamity, had gone down into a gulf of darkness; the earth had crumbled under their feet, they had nothing to stand upon. But here was something as new as the creation of the world where no world was: new life straight from the hands of the only living God. The women at the sepulchre took one look, they turned and ran from the place.

But they came to their senses when they had seen Christ himself; and thereafter early on the first day of the week – originally on the eve but in after years on the morning – they assembled to begin the week with Christ's resurrection, to eat him in bread, to drink him in wine as he had commanded them, and so, departing, to live Christ for another week.

What are we to do with our religion? By God's own act, and by our baptism, we are the body of Christ. You and I and the rest, we are the body of Christ in this place, his hands, his feet, his lips, his heart. But what are we to do about the yawning gulf which opens between this Christhood of ours and our actual performance; our laziness, selfishness, uncleanness, triviality and the painful absurdity of our prayers? This gulf which yawns between what Christ has made us and what we make of ourselves – if we take it seriously it is a tragedy, and turns the religion of joy into the sadness of a sour conscience. If we take it lightly it is a farce, and we may laugh; but if we laugh we shall presently cease to believe.

What shall we do? What else but the very thing Christ's disciples did from the first – early in the morning on the first day of the week reassemble the whole body of Christ here, not a member lacking, when the sun has risen; and have the resurrection over again. In that moment, dead to the past and trusting him for the future, bathed in his blood and strong by his victory, united by his person, loved and forgiven by his Father, in that moment at least we are what he has made us; the gap is closed. And indeed he will be with us through the week; all our work, all our prayer, all our companionship will be fertilized from that root.

This is the basic Christian pattern. Everything else is secondary or optional. The primitive Christians simply kept the week with a weekly Easter, their Sunday Eucharist. It was centuries before they had a calendar of yearly feasts, centuries before any service but the Eucharist became a regular part of Christian life; not till late in the Middle Ages that laymen began commonly to edify themselves at home by reading the Bible.

What do you think St Peter or St Paul would have said if you had told them that you feared always to communicate, lest it should go stale on you? They would not have known what on earth you were talking about. It would have been all you could do to bring them to conceive the possibility of such emotional frivolity, such reckless individualism in a Christian man. What, is the body of Christ to lack a member because you are not feeling soulful? Don't you know that Christ wants you here, that he has died to give you what you here receive, that this is the weekly resurrection of the body of Christ?

'But I can't communicate without faith.' Why no, but every Christian has faith; otherwise he would not be a Christian. If you have the faith to be called a Christian, you have the faith to communicate. To communicate is only to treat your Christianity as real. For what is your Christianity, if it is not your being a member in Christ's body? That you are an almost dead member we may grant, but if you believe that this is what you are, then you must surely believe that what Christ wishes to give you is a share in his resurrection. And there is nothing unusual about you; all members of Christ are dying members as soon as they become detached from the body and from the Head; we have no life in ourselves.

We cannot communicate unprepared, but why not prepare? The one vital thing is to get as much clearness of mind as at the time you can, about God's holy will for you. I say, as much as you can get at the time; no one asks of you the impossible. Know what you must repent and what resolve, open your heart to God and to your neighbours for his sake, and come; and if you are in a difficulty find a priest; what are we for?

Well then, let those of us who are qualified present our Redeemer every Sunday morning with the materials of his body, and give him the opportunity he so much desires to make himself present and visible in this place. And those of you who are not qualified because undecided, unbaptized, unconfirmed, I pray God to give you the light you need, and join you in that sacred union which is as wide as earth and as high as heaven, the company of saints, the extension and overflowing upon us of that immortal love whereby, in the Holy Ghost, the Father and the Son are ever one, and enjoy all glory and all bliss in all eternity.

preached in Trinity College Chapel, Oxford

14

Faith and Crutches

When the lesson for the day contains a really awful text, it seems mere cowardice not to preach about it. And what can be more shocking than this? *Thomas, because thou hast seen me, thou hast believed. Blessed are those, who have not seen, and yet have believed.* There are such aggravations of outrage here, one doesn't know where to begin, or where to end. But perhaps we can reduce the scandal to two sentences. First, our whole view of the world is to depend upon a physical miracle; Jesus, who died, has bodily returned. And second – as if that wan't bad enough – the physical evidence, which would alone suffice to prove the physical miracle, is not to be asked for. Thomas, that sturdy-minded empiricist, has all our sympathies. If he can see, feel and explore, he is ready to be convinced; not otherwise. He has all our sympathies, but not the Evangelist's approval nor Christ's, either: blessed are those who have not seen, and yet have believed.

Did I say I would reduce the scandal to two sentences? I was over-hopeful: I must add a third. For, having apparently frowned upon Thomas for requiring signs in proof of faith, the Evangelist goes straight on to say that Christ worked many other signs beside the few wonders he has recorded in his gospel; but he has written those he has written, that his readers might believe, and have life in Christ's name through their faith. What are we to make of this? Miracles are to be the motives of our belief; and yet those who required the miracles to be shown, were at fault. It sounds as if St John was half ashamed of miracle, and yet cannot do without it. And even Christ himself, the Christ who speaks through his page – but no, he cannot be ashamed of miracle, unless he is ashamed of himself; for he is a walking miracle, the miracle of miracles, a man alive from the dead. And how can he be ashamed of the faithfulness of God which raised him, or ashamed of the compassion, which sent him back with speech on his lips and kindness in his eyes, to make himself known alive among his friends?

Perhaps, after all, we have not understood St John and our first false move was to moralize his story. We wanted to give good marks, and bad marks: Thomas was to have a bad mark for asking physical evidence, those content with hearsay were to have good marks. Or again, we wanted to talk the language of ought, and ought not: Thomas *ought not* to have required the evidence of his senses, hearing evidence *ought* to suffice. Look back once more at St John's text: you will find no foundation in it for such black-and-white judgements there. St John is

53

black-and-white enough when the occasion calls for it. Israelites ought not to think they can advance God's cause by murdering the innocent. Men who begin to see a chink of spiritual light ought not to shut their eyes against it. St John is black-and-white enough on points like these. But he does not suggest that Thomas *ought not* to have required sense-evidence. When Thomas said to his fellow-disciples, 'Unless I see and touch, I shall not believe,' what do you think it was? Was it a refusal, or a boast, or a confession? A refusal – I won't believe; or a boast – I'm too clever to believe; or a confession – I shan't be able to believe? He was a friend and disciple of Christ's, who had risked his life with him; how could he refuse to believe that God had raised him from the dead? or how boast of sceptical detachment, who had committed himself to a cause, body and soul? No, surely it was more like a confession: That's the sort of man I am; I shan't be able to believe, unless I believe my own hands, and eyes. If, when he said this, Thomas was telling the truth, he could hardly have done better; do you think he would have done better if he had lied? If he had pretended to believe, when he didn't? When we come to Christ in our prayer, shall we tell him a pack of lies? Shall we pretend all sorts of noble sentiments we do not have: pretend to believe in him as firmly as we believe our own existence, pretend to care for his holy will as warmly and constantly as we care for our own comforts and ambitions? Of course not; for whom could we hope to deceive? Not him: we could only deceive ourselves. No, we will confess ourselves as we are, and know that he will treat us on our level, and according to our need, as he did Thomas: reach hither thy finger, and feel my hands; reach hither thy hand, and put it in my side; go not in lack of faith, but believe.

Jesus gave himself, that was all, and he gave himself to each according to his need, to each in his proper function; to Thomas into his arms to be handled and felt; to Peter and the rest to be seen, listened to, and conversed with; to the Church afterwards through the apostles' witness, and in the sacraments; in the lives of saints, and in the deaths of martyrs. He blesses those who are willing to let him make himself known in the way that he chooses; he blesses them, but he does not curse Thomas for his sense-bound mind and his physical demands. He does not curse him, no; what does he say? Reach hither your finger, and see my hands; take your hand, and put it in my side; and cure your unbelief.

But to return to St John's ambiguous attitude towards physical miracle. Except you see signs and wonders, you will not believe, says Christ to the frightened father, whose son was at the point of death. And again, at the raising of Lazarus; Christ is the resurrection and the life of men, whether he calls Lazarus from the tomb or not. What use does it serve, to bring back one dead man among so many millions; and then only that he may die again? Are not God's good purposes for us better fulfilled, when things follow their natural course; since we must die, is it not better to die once in faith, than to receive a violent resuscitation? Lazarus's return seems to be a concession of hardness of heart.

Christ's miracles were long ago, and perhaps you, like Thomas, do not easily believe them. If so – since you cannot travel back in time – you might like to consider some miracles more accessible to examination. Among many good ideas our Protestant reformers had, there were naturally some less good: and one of the most calamitous was the dogma that miracles ended with the New Testament. No doubt there was endless folly and credulity in the mediaeval Church, which needed to be pruned. But to deny all miracles of saints was to go in the face of evidence, and ultimately to destroy the grounds of belief. You might get hold of the life of the Blessed Curé d'Ars, who was not a mediaeval man, but was alive when my grandfather was born; and you will find it difficult to resist the evidence of his miracles, or indeed the supernatural character of his whole life. Yet his attitude to miracle was as ambiguous as Christ's attitude, or as St John's. There was one cripple in particular who pestered him for a cure. The saint preached at him time after time, to reconcile him to his condition. Since the doctors could not cure him, why would not he shoulder the common burden of his condition, and by his Christian patience offer a daily sacrifice, by which he could help his neighbours to bear their troubles and to love the will of God? The saint who told him this had a right to speak: he was himself a great sufferer, though he did not say so. It was all no good; the cripple could not accept his calling. 'Very well,' said the Saint, with tears in his eyes. 'Put your crutches in the corner, and walk out.' And he did.

That miracle is a concession to our condition who will deny? God will go no further in miracle, than we extort from him. But then the whole work that God did in Christ and still does for our salvation is a concession to our condition, extorted by our need for his compassion. Every line, every page, of the Gospel records the concession of divine wisdom to human folly.

'For look how high the heaven is in comparison of the earth: so great is his mercy also toward them that fear him. Yea, like as a father pitieth his own children: even so is the Lord merciful to them that fear him. For he knoweth whereof we are made: he remembereth that we are but dust.'

But for our sin, and our infirmity, he need neither have died, nor risen from the dead; that he did, we have every reason to rejoice, and to thank the mercy that has no end.

preached in Keble College Chapel, Oxford

15
The Death of Death

We are all mortal; and so it is no use a clergyman's treating it as a matter of surprise, that occasions for him to read the burial service are not infrequent. If a man had a parish of 24,000, he might expect to bury one a day. I do not want you to work out the arithmetical basis of that calculation, for if you are so occupied you will not be listening to what I want to tell you. If the priest works the sum, his arithmetic can remove from his mind any surprise he might feel at the frequency of such ceremonies; but nothing (it may be) will cure him of the surprise with which he finds himself, time after time, assuring the mourners on the authority of St Paul that we shall not all sleep the sleep of death, but we shall all be transformed, in a moment, in the twinkling of an eye, at the last trump; so that we, who have hitherto led a flesh-and-blood existence, will be changed into the substance of glory.

I do not know how useful it is to relay St Paul's speculation to the Christian mourners of today, but I do think it is worthwhile our reflecting on it, just because it involves us – creatures of flesh and blood – in a head-on collision with Omnipotence. No doubt we think, or half think, we have to undergo such a collision in a disembodied state, when there will be no more evasion, and we meet Truth himself face to face.

But when we think of this, our imaginations are not moved: for we have a hazy feeling that anything might happen to a disembodied spirit: we know not what we shall be and for all we know meeting with deity may be all in the day's work then. But the mental shock is real, if we conceive of ourselves such as we now are undergoing that divine encounter. What would happen? St Paul says, we should be changed; and we do not need to go outside those few words, to touch the height of amazement. We should be changed: changed – and how? St Paul speaks of the seed corn changed into the plant of wheat, and others, more appropriately perhaps, have talked of the chrysalis becoming a moth or the larva a dragonfly. I once lay in a punt on the Cherwell, spellbound for an hour, watching the dragonfly miracle; and indeed it was amazing enough. Yet it certainly did not happen in the twinkle of an eye, but through an agony of birth: slow, yes, agonizingly slow. Nor was it a miracle, after all, for it was all in the way of nature: the expansion of what had been folded, the liberation of what had been compressed. For in the works of nature God works naturally; that there should be dragonflies at all, not to mention men, is a breath-taking wonder, if we think of those mere rudiments of being from which such creatures are evolved – not surely without a power divine. Yet the Creator's will has waited ages for such things to work themselves out by the action of inborn energies, under the infinitely subtle and unforced persuasion of invisible providence.

But *then*, says St Paul, in the twinkling of an eye, we shall be changed: God will no longer wait for the ripening of nature nor restrict his action within nature's bounds; for this is where nature ends. We shall be changed, in the twinkling of an eye, for all this bodily being of ours will utterly melt at the touch of our maker and offer not a moment's resistance to his purest thought, his most absolute will; suddenly our being will become the simple print of his intention for us.

You and I may pray, as our Saviour taught us, *Thy will be done*, and wish we may be wax in the hands of Almighty Love; and Mercy will accept our true desire, while knowing how slow is the ripening of our virtue and how many obstacles the coarseness of our flesh and blood opposes to our maker's purpose. But it will be otherwise when we are changed, in the twinkling of an eye; then God will have his way with us, and to experience this will be to know God indeed. For the invisible Creator is known to his creatures in his creating of them: and when he freely and without obstacle fashions us, he will be perfectly known, felt as it were in the pressure of his fingers and read in the expression of his creative thoughts. Shall not we be ourselves the embodied thoughts of God, when we are changed?

But what are we doing? We've let St Paul's speculation run away with us. Is nature to melt in the rays of insupportable light that God may be all in all? Not, perhaps, without first passing through a natural death: perhaps in spite of St Paul, we all shall sleep, before we are any of us changed. Certainly, whatever St Paul may have thought, he slept the sleep of death, he and all the generation he addressed; they did not hear in this world the blast of the archangel, the trump of God.

Still, we needn't be too hard on the Apostle. How was he to know the very form and timing of events yet to come? He was bound to think that some day, and in some way, the whole being of the saints must become glass to God's thoughts and wax to his will. So much for looking forward – and then, as for looking backward, he had seen it happen. Had he not seen the Lord, the risen Lord? At one point nature and history had melted in the immediate ray of power. A body was laid in the tomb, a living, speaking glory issued from it.

To think with meaning of Christ's resurrection we must look behind the world; for from within the world such an event is supremely unnatural. We must dare to look into God, and see how no created thing is at all, but by his will. And *then* what may seem unnatural is the way in which God gives created nature rights against himself and shapes his will on her slow, groping motives. How natural, that Almighty Purpose should simply prevail; how natural that nature's rights should be withdrawn; how natural, how inevitable, that God at length should gather the harvest of his patience, and that, in the ray of immortal light, we should be changed: that something created should be as he would have it.

But when? Looking forward, St Paul hoped to know but did not know. Looking backward, he knew. Once there had been nothing God should wait for; when a life was lived, and a death died, in simple self-offering to God, that God's love for all the world might be achieved. When we shall melt in the will of God to be re-fashioned, it will be the pain of fire, says St Paul, so attached are we to the darling self we love, so fearful of the God who kills to make alive. Not so the resurrection of Christ. The killing had all been done already: there was nothing he had not offered up, nothing that had not been dissolved in his natural being, when his conscious mind was reduced to a snatch of verse just floating over the rising oblivion, *Eli, Eli, lama sabachthani*. The killing had all been done; how then should the making alive be withheld? Would not the Son's perfect sacrifice have forced the Father's hand, if that had needed any forcing? Ah, no; what can be more covetous of opportunity than God's immortal love, his life-giving grace? He flows in like the tide to fill every cranny that opens: repent, and in a moment he has filled your heart. Christ's sacrifice was completed in his burial, and in a twinkling of an eye he was changed.

And now, do you see, I have scarcely overtaken what was supposed to be my starting-point: what has Christ done for us by his resurrection? What for us? But nothing one can say on this subject is much better than silence; what shall we say? He has given us the substance of glory. Being changed in God, he is the heart of heaven and he draws us into association with himself: the action of the man-in-God, the God-in-man, is an action he shares with us and entrusts to us. We have yet to be changed, to melt in the will of God – and even so, we already possess by association, and by attachment to Christ, that victorious and transfigured life after which we aspire. Our end is unchangeably far – our fusion in God, our new-creation. And yet in Christ it is near, it is possessed: if any man be in Christ, he is – not shall be, but is – a new creation.

Ah – but like ignorant children, making toys of their mother's jewels, or like postal sorters passing packets and not thinking what they contain, we handle our only treasure, the pearl of great price, and scarcely regard it. But that is not the matter of any single sermon, that is every sermon. Think what you have – be what you are – take your paradise.

The Christ of resurrection did inspire and may inspire terror, for he is what we shall be on the other side of the fire, and we fear the fire. Yet we read that the fear of the disciples turned to familiarity and kindness, for whatever the risen Christ be in himself he came to meet them and returned into the place and into the forms of flesh and blood; he talked, he listened, he gave himself to be touched, he shared their food. For the man-in-God, the man utterly molten and fashioned in God's will, is not separated, not fenced off from us. How would that serve the loving will of which he is made the sensitive instrument? We fear the fire – yet all the fire will do will be to make us happy in living out the love of God; and Jesus, who needed no fire beyond the suffering of his passion, was moved by love to return among his disciples as the dear man they had known; and our painter, whatever you may think of his art, was no fool in the thoughts he conceived, when he showed our Saviour on his rounds in human guise, patiently knocking at the doors of our hearts.*

preached in Keble College Chapel, Oxford

* A reference to 'The Light of the World', by Holman Hunt, in the Lady Chapel of Keble.

16

Pearls of Great Price

The kingdom of heaven is like unto a man that is a merchant seeking goodly pearls; and having found one pearl of great price, he went and sold all that he had, and bought it.

Matt. 13.45–6

This is not really a sermon, but a tutorial discussion broken loose. We all know that tutors must not preach at their pupils. But they must be allowed their compensations. The sermon suppressed in the study may be permitted to break out in full spate across the Chapel floor.

But for a start we will go back to the study. My pupil has been explaining to me his views on a very well-worn philosophical text. The old philosopher is trying to make out a case for the superior pleasantness of a virtuous life. Cads, the philosopher has to admit, often seem to have a glorious time; but, he says, only seem to. Their pleasures are more apparent than real. The commentators (whom my pupil is also acquainted with, in a distant sort of way) join in a howl of derision. Nonsense, they say, pleasures lie in seeming: they are as real as they feel. If cads feel pleased over their caddish delights, then they *are* pleased. It is nonsense to call any felt pleasure false.

But my pupil for once (and how rarely this happens!) disagrees with the commentators and champions the ancient sage. 'What these people say', he remarks, 'may be all very well in theory, but I'm sure Plato is on to something. What he's talking about – well, it's what happens when you get a bit drunk. First of all you think you are having a marvellous time. But after a bit, you see you weren't, really; it was all a fraud.' 'Well,' I say, 'but what was a fraud? You felt jolly, didn't you, while it lasted? That wasn't a fraud. And the drink went down nicely: that wasn't a fraud, either.' 'No, that wasn't the fraud,' says my pupil, 'but there was a fraud, all the same. The fraud was, I thought I was absolutely at the top of my form, and making marvellous jokes. But looking at it afterwards, I see that I wasn't exercising the mastery of wit I thought I was, I was being pretty feeble. So my being pleased with myself was a take-in. And I'll tell you another take-in,' he continues. 'I thought I was getting to know one or two of the other characters at the party wonderfully well and better than ever before. But after the event, I can see I wasn't really. We weren't getting to know anything: we were just getting warmed-up together.' 'I dare say you're right,' I say, 'and of course it isn't my line to recommend insobriety as the path to mutual acquaintance. All the same, you wouldn't say, would you, that getting warmed-up never leads to any genuine discoveries? Take falling in love. What's so fantastic about it is, that all the commonplace trash in the poets is perfectly true. When you're in that state of mind, you see everything with amazing vividness: the violets look twice as blue and the song of the thrushes is ten times as sweet. And what you see in the girl – well, she's just a girl, admittedly, but God made her, and there's an awful lot in her to see, as there is in all his works; and if for once you can see some of what's there to see, surely that's nothing to complain of; that's not a fraud, is it?'

My pupil views me with compassion: dear, dear, the romanticism of these middle-aged men! 'No, but there is a fraud,' he says. 'You think the girl's IT, and of course she isn't.' No; and so, for all there may be in her, she is to be dropped, is she, as an impostor, who had falsely pretended to be IT? Like a merchant man, seeking goodly pearls, who found one pearl of great price and went and sold all that he had, and bought it. For this was it, the truly perfect pearl. What is IT; that which is no fraud, so that we can never wake up sober and say, I thought that was it, but of course it wasn't really.

Now, perhaps, we can appreciate the meaning of St Peter's declaration, recorded for us in the second lesson. What do men say that Jesus is? Some say this, others say that. But what do his disciples say? St Peter speaks for them: 'Thou art the Christ.' You can seek a learned answer to what the fable meant, by searching the Old Testament, and later Jewish books. But for a practical answer, 'You are IT' might do. St Peter has found what will never be a fraud. To work with Messiah is to do what you are for, and to help achieve what the world is for. And the pearl of great price, once found, is always in our pockets, or rather, in our hearts – we have only to put our hands into our bosoms, to find it there. For there are always Christ's commands to be obeyed; there is always Christ in heaven, so that we can any time lift up our minds, remember him, and share his living thoughts; there is always Christ to be sought next morning in his sacrament. We need never be put off with frauds: we can always be having, and doing, what we are for. This is IT.

After the drinking-party, there is the morning of cold reflection, which remorselessly peels the false colours off the previous night's glories; and there are many such inevitable hours in life, the sobering ends to cheerful periods for instance when a man gets a bad, or no, degree, and reassesses the value of his career as an undergraduate bridge-player. Our last hour on earth might seem to provide the most searching of all soberings-up. Only then, with the aid of medical skill and medical mendacity, we may hope to skip the consciousness of it, and sink into eternity on cushions of morphia. But no, this is too good to be true, justice cannot be cheated so, there is a day of reckoning.

Seated high, the Judge will reign:
All that's hidden will be plain
And no unrighted wrongs remain.

In former times what struck men about the Day of Judgement was that it would forbid men to get away with their crimes, but what may strike us about it, is that it will make us acknowledge our follies. Then we shall see face to face that supreme Good, which day by day and year by year we have neglected for toys and trifles. And the more we read in his eyes the light of mercy, the more grounds we shall have to condemn our own perversity, for having turned our backs day by day, and hour by hour, on so kind a Creator.

St Peter himself has a black crime to confess in that presence – he denied his master; yet nothing can alter the fact that he devoted his life to the service of Christ, braved persecution and incurred martyrdom. But we, who live a more mixed and ordinary life, and have made no visible heroic sacrifice – how will it be for us? It is not that the Christ of God cannot be sought and found and served in an ordinary life. It is that we shall have to consider in what proportion of our life we have remembered the pearl which God has placed in our bosoms. That will be our Day of Judgement.

What advocate can I command
What plea, alas, shall take in hand
When the righteous hardly stand?

The Christian poet who describes the Last Day appeals to his judge:

O King of fear and majesty,
Saving whom thou savest, free,
Fount of pity, pity me.

Thou soughtest me with toil and pain,
Thou hungest on the tree to gain
My pardon; surely not in vain.

'Thou soughtest me' – the kingdom of heaven is like unto a man that is a merchant seeking goodly pearls, who, when he had found one pearl of great price ... Why, what have we been saying? Have we not, in our unconscious egotism, been reading Christ's parable the wrong way round? We have been comparing the kingdom of heaven to the pearl of price, and ourselves, or the heroes among us, to the merchant man. And yet that is not what Christ says. The kingdom of heaven, he says, is like a merchant man – and when Christ says 'the kingdom of heaven', as often as not he means 'the Royal Majesty of God' or, more simply, 'the Divine King'. God the King, then, is like a merchant man. But if so, what is the pearl? Look at the other parables with which the evangelist aligns this, and you will see. God is a peasant, who wants a crop, and he does not mind how much of the seed miscarries, as long as there is a harvest. God is a fisherman, who wants a catch: he does not mind how much rubbish comes in the net, as long as there are fish worth picking out. He is a shepherd, who will leave his flock to fend for itself, while he drags after the one lost sheep. He is a merchant man, who has set his heart on one pearl of great price, and thinks everything well lost, to gain it. So what is the pearl of price?

Remember, Lord, thy arduous way
In quest of me, and hear me pray:
Lose not the found, on judgement day.

Thou soughtest me with toil and pain,
Thou hungest on the tree to gain
My pardon; surely not in vain.

You are the pearl of price. A loyal and obedient heart is what the King of Heaven thinks the world well lost to win, and since he puts such a price on our souls, he has the best right to bid us not to undervalue them. He who will buy Peter with his precious blood is he who says to Peter: 'What shall it profit a man to gain the whole world, and lose his soul? Or what shall he trade in exchange for his soul?'

The parable of the pearl, then, describes the King of Heaven's quest for us, not our quest for him. And yet it is not perverse to take it the other way round as well. For we cannot go wrong, to imitate God. And if he sets an infinite value on the image of his face where it is shaped in us in mortal clay, we cannot go wrong, to value it in its heavenly original, or to love that Son, in whom the Father's heart supremely delights.

But though there is a two-way traffic, the King of Heaven seeking us, we seeking him, no one can doubt which of these searches is the more effective for our salvation. He has set his heart on us, and this is the best hope any of us can entertain: that our setting of our hearts on him is sufficient to make the bond between us a reality, so that he may draw us to himself, and in that other world pull us through the fire that purges us, and burn our rubbish away.

There result from what we have been saying two very simple truths. God is priceless to us, for what he is makes him so. We are priceless to God, for his kindness makes us so. Why then should I remember God, and serve God, day and night? Because he is all that is worth having to me; and because I am infinitely desired by his love. It needed no Christ to teach us that God is our sole and everlasting Good could we but attain him; what Christ showed us was that God desires us with all the love of his infinite heart.

preached in Trinity College Chapel, Oxford

17

St Mark

In the heavenly state I daresay the satisfaction of earthly curiosity will not seem important. But looking at it from the earthly side, I can feel a lively interest in the hope of some day seeing St Mark and discovering who he is. For I know him, and I do not know him; rather as you might know a telephone voice you never met, a voice who often talked with you but who never talked about himself; the competent secretary of some important person with whom your business often lay. What colour are his eyes? You do not know. Where does he live? You do not know. Is he single, married, a father, childless; what his his hobbies and tastes? No information on any of these points; and yet he has a characteristic way of handling his employer's affairs, which makes him a familiar person to you. You may say you know the way he thinks. It is in some such fashion that the careful students of his gospel may reckon to know St Mark.

We know him, but how little we know about him! He may be the John Mark concerning whom the Acts of the Apostles inform us. But then again he may be some other Mark. He may have written at Rome a few years after St Peter and St Paul died, at a time when Jerusalem was under siege, and Nero had just been murdered, when the world was in confusion and no one knew what would happen next. That would be in AD 68, some forty years after the crucifixion, and as likely a year, perhaps, as any for St Mark to compose the first of all gospels. But no one can prove beyond a doubt that he did not write three years earlier or fifteen years later and, it may be, not at Rome at all.

Happily for us, the certainty of the Christian faith does not depend on the answering of these questions one way or another; and I think it is worth insisting a little on the point. For people are often and mistakenly inclined to reason as follows: Christ is set before us as a historical figure; the documents about his history are the Gospels; the authorship date, character and sources of the Gospels are open to dispute; and so nothing about the historical Christ can be indisputable, or better than a matter of pious belief. Such reasoning is entirely false, for the simple cause that our primary witness to a historical Christ is not any of the Evangelists, but St Paul. And with St Paul the case is quite different: he is himself a historical character of flesh and blood; his great letters are genuine beyond doubt, and can even be accurately dated.

It may help us to appreciate the force of the evidence if we apply the time-scale of the twentieth century to the first century of our era. Here you are in the late '50s, are you not? You are, let us suppose, the congregation at Corinth. The man who taught you your Christian faith, St Paul, is a man of the age of your present College Chaplain though in other respects dissimilar. He is sometimes here, sometimes away touring the Mediterranean, but not for reasons of health. Last term, so to speak, he sent you a letter taking you severely to task for giving his deputy, a man called Stephanas, a terrible time. Some of you were maintaining preposterous opinions; among others, that there is no resurrection; in refutation of which, the Apostle's letter reminds you about the bare facts of the gospel he has always preached. They concern Jesus of Nazareth, a man born with the century, about five years older than St Paul himself, and many years younger (of course) than many hale and hearty persons still living, than our own senior fellows, for example. This Jesus died in the early '30s – as it would be in our century, at the dead middle between the two wars. He was buried, he rose again and conversed with many people, St Paul being the last. His familiar companions are still mostly alive, and well known to St Paul. Paul does not see eye to eye with them about the law of Moses, but about the facts of Christ's wonderful life, death and resurrection there is no disagreement among the Apostles.

It is through St Paul, then, that our faith is rooted in history; and a firm root it is. And so it is not necessary, even if it were honourable, to press the evidence about the authorship, date or sources of the Gospels further than it will go. Here are men, the Evangelists, built like St Paul and like ourselves upon the common faith, the apostolic witness, writing anyhow early in the history of our religion, when there were memories of Christ still to be gathered, and when the Spirit of the same Christ was still most active in the special work of revelation. The Christ of hearsay was interpreted for them by the Christ in the heart. And so under the double control of memory and inspiration, the Gospels were composed. To cold historians they have not the same evidential value as St Paul's words; but to those of us who have already believed the Apostles and become Christians, the Gospels carry conviction; for the Christ we believe in speaks to us as a real person from the gospel pages. To borrow St John's language, the shepherd calls, and the sheep know his voice.

And yet, as I began by saying, alongside the voice of Christ there is the voice of his interpreter, of each evangelist; among whom, to speak for myself, I dearly and specially love St Mark. This is St Mark's day. What then, in the few minutes I still have, can I tell you about the mind of this glorious saint? We must stick to the broadest lines, the principal stages which he brings out in the development of his story.

In the first part of his gospel healings predominate. And if we did not know what was still to come, we might say, What sort of a religion is this? It is a medicine, apparently, for securing health and sanity. But if so, it enters into competition with every other medicine. If science can do more for men than faith and miracle, science is the better medicine, the better psychiatry, and supernatural grace may retire from the field.

But we have no sooner formulated our objection than the scene changes. He who had healed the paralysed foot and restored the withered hand, he who had opened the eyes of the blind begins to say, 'If your hand is your undoing, cut it off and cast it from you. Off with the offending foot, out with the covetous eye; make sure of everlasting life, however the pursuit of it may maim and limit you in this present world.' He who had raised the dead before, now calls for martyrs: 'Take up your cross,' he says, 'and go with me to die.'

Ah, we say, this may be terrible, but this is religion; Christ, like Churchill, is calling for heroes. It is not, after all, 'What can we get out of God?' That was only a beginning, a religion for children. Now it is, 'What can we do for God?' This is the religion of men. Let us turn the page, and read the story of their finest hour. We turn it, and what do we read?

'Amen, I say to thee, before the cock crows twice thou shalt thrice deny me ... He came and found them sleeping ... They all forsook him and fled ... Peter began to curse and to swear, I know not the man ... And' (the very last words of St Mark's authentic text) 'they went out quickly and ran from the tomb, gripped by an ecstasy of terror, and said nothing to any one; for they were afraid.'

Shall we reduce St Mark's Gospel to three lines?

God gives you everything.
Give everything to God.
You can't.

True, there is a fourth line; Christ will make you able, for he has risen from the dead. But this is almost overshadowed in St Mark's Gospel by the emphasis on self-distrust. St Mark seems even more afraid that his readers will trust themselves than that they will distrust Christ's risen power.

Well, perhaps the Mark of the gospel was the John Mark of Acts, after all. And perhaps all this emphasis on desertion, running away, the failure of good intentions has something to do with that most painful text in the Book of Acts: 'Barnabas wished to take John called Mark with them; but Paul thought it not well to take with them him who had turned back from them in Pamphylia, and not gone with them to the work.' If the Evangelist is that Mark who had once turned back, and of whom St Paul had thought the worse for his turning back, then he had evidently learned from his turning back what God wished him to learn from it: that it is not in us to follow Christ, it is Christ's gift.

Happy is the man who learns from his own failures. He certainly won't learn from any one else's. Here I am on a safe ground, for you are all failures, are you not? when it comes to serving God. So there is no fear of my missing my target in any of you, and especially, perhaps, just at the end of a vacation. Vacations tend to be spiritual disappointments. It is humiliating how, when you get back into your families, childish faults of temper reassert themselves which you hoped you had outgrown; humiliating how, as soon as you lose the encouraging company of your Christian friends here, your religion languishes. You have not prayed nor worked nor controlled yourself as you hoped to do. God has given you much; you have not given anything worth mentioning to God. Well, St Mark (if he is indeed the same man) went back from the work in Pamphylia, and in Gethsemane none of the disciples behaved with credit. It is by these desolating experiences that God teaches us to trust him, not ourselves. The more emptied out you are, the more hope there is of your learning to be a Christian. Now is the very moment – there will never be a better – for you to put your trust in the God who makes something from nothing, who raises the dead.

preached in Trinity College Chapel, Oxford

18

A New Creation

Hail the day that sees him rise
Glorious to his native skies

So sings Charles Wesley – or perhaps not Charles Wesley, but Thomas
Cotterill, credited with having altered the words in the year of our Lord
1820. But never mind which of them it was, since neither of them is
going to answer my rhetorical question. My dear Charles – or ought I to
say, my dear Thomas – what do you mean? You seem to be saying the
same sort of thing as:

See the canny Scot return
To his native Bannockburn

Only that the glorious person of whom you speak had his birthplace
somewhere among the celestial galaxies, not in the less habitable half of
this island. Well, since – my dear Thomas, or should I say, Charles – you
are not in a position to answer me, I must try to play your hand for you
out of dummy. And I feel pretty confident that you would reply that I
am interpreting you too literally. For, you would say, when Christ
returned into his native and celestial glory, it was the divine life of the
Son of God that so returned, since as for the human life of Jesus, the
birthplace from which it entered on its course was at Bethlehem, not in
the skies at all. And to call the skies, or any other place, the birthplace of
the Son of God must be taken to be a figure of spech, for the 'mysterious
begetting' of the Son of God does not have a time, still less a place: it is a
timeless dimension of social love within the beginning of the Godhead.

Besides (our orthodox and learned hymnographer continues) our
scriptural warrant for what we say is in St John's Gospel, in the prayers
of Christ: 'And now, O Father, glorify me beside thee with the glory I
had beside thee ere ever the world was.' Evidently the skies are not the
native place of the divine Son, for he was with his Father when there
were as yet no skies for him to inhabit. So much, I think, the very
orthodox hymn-writer must be bound to say. But at the next step in the
discussion I lose all confidence in my power to ventriloquize an answer
on his behalf. This is when he is called on to face the obvious question:
'Then what makes you say "native skies?" You say it's a figure of speech;
well, lying has been called a figure of speech. Why use a figure of speech
which is 100 per cent misleading?' I do not know what our hymn-writer

would say to this. We must do the best we can for ourselves. What shall we say? I should say that the force of the figure is that of a simple comparison. We are virtually confined to this planet; and even the Americans and Russians to the solar system. Outside lies the unimaginable spread of astral space, which constantly radiates upon us, and out of which, perhaps, aeons ago, our little system was somehow blown together. Well now, put the whole universe of galaxies in the place of our little world, and say the following formula: 'As our little world is cradled in outer space, so is the universe cradled in God's immensity.' Or, to put it otherwise, 'the universe is the sky of our little world: God's immensity is, as it were, the sky of the universe.' Such is the figure of speech, for what it is worth; but I am not sure that Dame Julian of Norwich was not better inspired, when she saw the universe as a very small thing, like a nut, lying in the palm of God's hand.

But Dame Julian is not our present business; let us return to Wesley's hymn. 'Hail the day that sees him rise/Glorious to his native skies.' He says 'rise' you will notice, not 'return', and that is not, I think, simply for the sake of the rhyme. For the marvel is not that the celestial Son of God returns where he belongs, but that the earthborn Jesus rises into the native heaven of that divine life which had become man in him. The manhood he has taken, he does not relinquish: 'Though returning to the Throne/Still he calls mankind his own.' He is not the man of flesh and blood which each of us now is, but he is the man glorified, which each of us may hope by his grace to become. And what we shall be in glory, we do not know, except that we shall be most fully ourselves, through being full of God.

So, then, the dear man who lived and died for us is gone beyond the limits and the confines of this world into the immensity of God. But that does not mean that he is merged and lost in the placeless life of Godhead, like a drop of water in the ocean. It means that there is a new creation, a new world beyond this world, a world not of flesh and blood, nor a world of interlocking physical energies, but a world of which the substance, not yet known to us, is the new-minting of God's hand, a world of Christhood, of glorified human nature, of Jesus, and of all those united with Jesus, and, through him, united with the life of God.

It is the obvious meaning of the Ascension faith that Jesus is in some sense taken out of the world – not so that he might be made distant from us, but so that he might be freed from the limitations of physical being and new-minted in the image of the Glory of God. And so there are two worlds: our universe, the place of God's natural creatures; Christ's heaven, the place of God's glorified creatures. In either world God is everywhere present by his power and his grace; but more fully in that other world where the hearts of the redeemed offer no obstacles to his invisible action, and most fully in the glorious man, Jesus Christ, whom he has made personally one with his divine life. The mind of God speaks from his lips to the citizens of that country; they see the love of God in the kindness of his eyes.

There are two worlds, then; and if we do not call that other world 'heaven', then what are we to call it? Those theologians who say that 'heaven' is an image which means nothing to our age had better be careful what they say. To localize infinite God in heaven, or anywhere else, is a gross metaphysical error; in this or in any other age. But if there is not a society of persons in bliss, new-created and centred on a glorified Jesus, then our Christ is nothing but a dead Jew and to talk of Christianity is sentimental folly. But we know a living Christ, and we know he is not unaccompanied; and what shall we call that company, but heaven?

There are two worlds, the old and the new creations of God; but if they are two, then how are they related to one another? Surely the answer of our faith is plain. Our world does not contain Christ's, but Christ's world embraces ours. Since Christ's world is not physical, it is no part of our universe: for our universe is nothing but an interaction of energies, a tissue of dynamic space, and what is not physical has no place in it. No lines of radiation which any telescope can follow will reach it, no curvature of light will show the pull of its influence. But our world is in Christ's heaven: for that is a world where spirit touches spirit. Those heavenly minds can know whatever minds are opened to them by God's will and permission; so we are present to Christ; and so he inflows upon us.

There is no way from here into heaven, while this life lasts; but all heaven adopts us. And so faith strikes boldly at the heart of heaven, and starts with the Christ who makes us his. To lift up our hearts, and put them with the Lord, is the beginning of our eucharistic action; and so it is of all Christian prayer. We have just to remember that we are in his world, known, yes and loved through and through, by the man in whom is the Godhead; and then to form our prayers as the extension of his thoughts.

'It is expedient for you', said Jesus in St John, 'that I depart from you.' Expedient! expedient that he should so place himself that he might furnish a living line of love from every believer's heart to the heart of God. Expedient – but will it seem expedient, when on the day of judgement we are made to see what treasures of grace have been poured before us, and how our neglect of them condemns us? But it will be expedient, since he also died for us. We will take refuge with the precious blood.

preached in Keble College Chapel, Oxford

19

The Legacy

When Jesus died on the cross, says St John, there came away three things from his body: breath, blood, and water. He bowed his head, and breathed out his life. They ran the spear through his side, and there flowed out water and blood. The fact can be physiologically interpreted, but that's not what interests St John, as we see when we turn to his first epistle. What, he then asks, is the present and living evidence of the gospel? The evidence is threefold, he says: the breath, the water and the blood. The threefold legacy of the dying Christ is alive in the Church to which he bequeathed it. It is set out in his sacramental gifts: his water is their baptism, his breath the spirit of their confirmation; his blood the wine of their chalice. Well, a Christian may say so; but how should the esoteric ceremonies of the Christian congregation be what St John says they are – God's evidence to the world, a testimony which nothing but wilful blindness could resist? Why, because the sacramental realities fill the life of the Christian. The water stays with them – they are pure; the breath breathes through them – they are inspired; the blood is in their veins and they are ready to be martyrs. *There* is the witness of the breath, the water and the blood. St John's doctrine is merely summarized in the Jesuit prayer for everyday:

> Breath of Christ hallow me
> Body of Christ keep me
> Blood of Christ inflame me
> Water from Christ, wash me

A church in which these aspirations were sincere, and these petitions granted, would be the Church of St John, instinct with the threefold witness of the breath, the water, and the blood. St John's Ephesians did not hold meetings to see how they could galvanize themselves into a mission; they were a mission and the gospel ran like wildfire, as we are historically assured, up the Anatolian coast.

Of the triple witness, two strands are plain enough. If Christian lives were pure, they were pure; if the blood of the martyrs ran, it ran. So much for the water and the blood. But St John tells us, the breath is also an evidence, a palpable fact – the Christians are inspired, you can't gainsay it. And what sort of a fact is it? What *is* life in the Spirit?

Well, have you encountered it? If you have, we needn't waste time on definitions. John Locke, we remember, offers us the definition of a certain substance as being a metal, yellow, heavy, ductile, malleable, fusible and fixed, and soluble in *aqua regia*. Many thanks for the definition, John; and now please hand me a bit of the stuff, and I shall know what you are talking about. Oh, it's *gold*, is it? And if you have had the true metal in your hands – have known a Christian alive in the Spirit, or ever made the acquaintance of such a being through his writings, look at him, don't look to me. For my part I'll fix my eyes on one or two specimens and report what I observe; and you can check from your own observations.

My spiritual man – may I call him Angelicus? – is characterized less by enthusiasm or visible zeal, than by self-forgetfulness. He has strong and persistent desires, or concerns, indeed, but they are not about himself. Neither are they specially about me; and that is vexing. I wanted Angelicus to be my friend, and so he was, in a way: he gave himself completely to me when the two of us were together; but when there were others present his heart was just as much with them. I wrote him the most amazing letters, and he answered them pleasantly. Pleasantly but shortly; I'm sure he wrote much longer and more frequent letters to the most tedious people, if they happened to be in any sort of worry or to need bolstering up. Call that friendship? It was maddening: he even seemed to like the wretched creatures. Why, he might just as well have been God himself: Angelicus, the man with the God's eye view – only that suggests an Olympian survey, from a great height; say a God's eye view if God's eye were right down on the floor, and just behind everyone's head, and inside everyone's mind at once, if you can imagine such a thing. Oh, but it is, isn't it? Yes, of course, you're perfectly right: the eyes of the Lord do run through the whole earth.

The God's eye view is seeing everything for what it is, and loving it for what it's worth. And that, I suppose, is what you'd call spiritual-mindedness. But when one's said that, one still hasn't got Angelicus. It isn't just that he is spiritual-minded: he's more than that – he's inspired; his spiritual-mindedness, if you see what I mean, goes with a whizz. How shall I put it? You and I, when we pray, climb up a few inches out of our selfish and worldly little bodies and take a look round in God's larger air, and it's wonderful, and exhilarating, though a bit difficult to breathe. We think a few noble thoughts, and make a few decent resolutions; but we can't struggle free. We acknowledge some extra duties, which we perform with pain, and place a few restraints on ourselves, which we observe with reluctance. There we are, stuck half in our bodies and half out; hadn't we better plunge right back into flesh and be hearty animals? This half in, half out, is an awful business. What I would, that I do not: wretched man that I am, who shall deliver me from this body of death? But Angelicus – he's out and away: what God loves is lovely to him; he's up and after it.

The true Christian is inspired. Don't waste your time wondering whether his inspiration falls in the province of psychology or of divinity. The psychological processes through which a free concern for God's will rises in the heart need have nothing special about them; it's the same old heart-strings thrumming away, even when they are playing a divine music. Life in the Spirit manifests itself in very various forms of psychological spontaneity, but psychological spontaneity, as such, is not life in the Spirit: only such spontaneity as gives rein to heavenly-mindedness. This is a very old piece of Christian wisdom. Test the spirits, says St John, whether they be of God. And the touchstone of their genuineness lies not in how they seem to come, it lies in what they say.

When St Paul cries out for wretchedness and asks who shall deliver him from his corpse of a body, he goes straight on to give God thanks for Christ the Lord, through whom he obtains that deliverance: for it is Christ who actually brings him into the vivifying stream of the divine life. The life and act of God is indeed, everywhere, but as poor Job complained, it is another matter to follow the veins and find the pulses of it. The life of God is everywhere, for the Creator everywhere descends into his creation and goes along with every one of his creatures by knowledge, by concern, and by action. To live in the Spirit is to go with God; but how shall I go with him, unless Christ sets me on the way?

In the Supper discourses in St John's Gospel, Christ promises the Paraclete as a second self, as an overflow of Christ. But, as that Gospel makes clear, Christ himself lived first in the very overflow of God. Angelicus is no more than an expression of Christ: Jesus is the very man who lives outside himself, who lives in the Spirit.

The primitive Christians, who read their Bibles very simply in Greek, found verses in the Old Testament which leapt at them from the page in letters of flame. For instance they found this in the Book of Numbers. What is to be done, asks Moses of the Lord, to shepherd Israel when he has passed away, lest they scatter like a leaderless flock? And the oracle of God replies: take Jesus,* the man in whom is the Spirit, and put your hands on his head ... Jesus, the man in whom is the Spirit; Jesus, the vessel of the Holy Ghost; Jesus who goes outside his animal being, to make the heart and eyes of God his own. When Jesus left his village setting, and made the family of God his family, 'we must go and get him,' said his kindred, 'for he's jumped out of his skin,' – and how right they were, except that there had been no jump. Jesus had never been inside his skin as ordinary human animals are, pent in this body of death. He had lived in a larger air: he had been in the Spirit of God.

* Joshua (Hebrew) = Jesus (Greek).

It was by being outside himself – by being ecstatic in the literal sense of that word that Jesus brought the life of the Blessed Trinity into our world; for it is in ecstasy and in mutual indwelling that the marvellous life of the Godhead consists, God our Father goes out of himself to be all in his Son – this is the first ecstasy: and the Son goes out of himself to live by that very indwelling of the Father in him – that is the second ecstasy. There is a third ecstasy when there is a creation, and God comes out of himself to be all and everywhere and all things in his creatures. It is the fourth ecstasy, when the creatures of God go out of themselves to be in the God who indwells them. But this ecstasy the creatures of God scarcely achieve, until the Son of God takes on the form of a creature, and lives therein the ecstatic life; and when he died on the cross, he gave it to us for a legacy. Then he made his will, as he hung a-dying: he gave Mary to John, and John to Mary; he left us the breath, the water and the blood. We come here to claim the legacy of Christ. Ah, how much more he longs to give, than we to claim. May this very love release us from the body of this death.

preached in Pusey House Chapel, Oxford

20

Thinking the Trinity

When we were in America – and it feels odd, I must say, being in America. They treat the academic visitor as a talking book; the text is something you published twenty years ago, but footnotes, they hope, are going to spurt *viva voce* from your living person, wherever they stick a pin into you. Under this sort of treatment, you can see that it is difficult not to grow a trifle pompous. And so there we were in a corner of New York, holding an open forum (or was it a colloquium?) and laying down the law about the action of the divine providence in the balancing of goods and evils. Some discussion ensued; until a Jewish scholar, whose presence had been hitherto unnoticed, pricked our little bubble for us. Not that he broke in – he waited for a full pause in the conversation; and when he spoke, it was with much gentleness. He had one of those thoughtful Jewish faces that seem to be moulded by a sense of their people's suffering, but at the same time by a patient faith in the God of Israel. He found it surprising, he said, to hear Christian theologians speculate so confidently on the place of pain and disaster in the counsels of God – a mystery which, not unnaturally, had occupied the Jewish mind a good deal. He said that he would express his own sense of the matter in a Jewish form, by quoting a rabbi of older days.

The rabbi's pupils came one morning and sat before him. They asked him the providential reason of some natural evil that had befallen – let us say that it was a neighbour's premature death. 'My children,' said the rabbi, 'there are questions into which a man may enter, and there is no way back out of them. Again, there are questions a man may enter upon, and there is a way back. And it is the first part of wisdom, when any question is proposed, to decide of which sort it is. Now I tell you that the question, why God permits this or that natural evil, is among the questions allowing of no way back, nor of any answer. And why? I will tell you this also. The Holy One (Blessed be He!) filled all immensity before the world was, and there was no place where he was not; and so neither was there any place where a world could be; for he was all, and in all. What did he do? He drew back the skirts of his glory, to make a little space where he was not; and there he created the world. And so, where the world is, there he is not. And that is why we look in vain for his hand in the chances of nature. Nevertheless (Blessed be He!) he has visited us with his lovingkindness.'

So said our Jewish philosopher; and when he had spoken, we had little appetite for resuming our previous discussion. We wanted to ponder the words of his ancient sage. There seemed to be a deep sense in them, but not a sense that lay on the surface. Obviously it takes you nowhere, to speak of God's being present or absent, in any plain way, at one place or another. In one way, he is everywhere absent, for no place bodily contains him. In another way, he is everywhere present; since whatever exists manifests his present will that it should exist; and as the Psalmist says, 'If I go down into hell, thou art there also.' For hell would not be, if God's will for its existence were withdrawn from it.

What, then, had the rabbi meant, when he spoke of God's vacating a space to allow for a world? We asked our Jewish friend, and he said the meaning was this: God gave the world room to be itself. He would not so inhabit it as to make it the passive reflection of his own ideas; or like the machine which does no more than embody the design of its constructor, and perform the wishes of its manipulator. God made the world, but he did not just make it; he made it make itself; for only so could it be itself. He released a half chaos of brimless forces as alien from his own being as anything could well be; and they blinded away, not in the paths of a godlike wisdom, but according to the very limited principles of action implanted in each. Nevertheless (said the rabbi), the Holy One has visited us with his lovingkindness; by an invisible art, and by a secret attraction, he has brought out of a blind interplay of forces many organized intricacies and much sentient life.

What, then, is the moral of the fable? The world is not like God, though it reveals his power and his glory. Nature is infinitely wasteful, but God wastes nothing. She is unfeeling; he is compassionate. She is blind; he is wise. For at the beginning and bottom of nature, there is a withdrawal, we may almost say a self-banishment, of God. Nature is not divine; we cannot be nature-worshippers, except by projecting upon nature a gilded image of our dreams. God made the world in unlikeness to himself; we look there in vain for the lineaments of his face. He made man in his own similitude, and it is in the face of man that we must look for the countenance of God.

Or rather, not in the face of man, but in the faces of men, turned towards one another; the light of understanding that passes between their eyes, in a sense that sounds through the interchange of their speech, in mutual liking kindled from heart to heart. Man's mind, not his bodily frame, is the similitude of God; and mentality always was a social, not a solitary, thing. We learnt to talk, because they talked to us; and to like, because they smiled at us. Because we could first talk, we can now think; that is, we can talk silently to the images of the absent, or we can pretend to be our own twin, and talk to ourself.

I can talk to myself, but it is hard work. How easily (alas for my pupils!) does my speech flow when I talk to them; with what sorrow and reluctance did I drive myself when I was preparing this sermon, although it was for people who have given me as much reason to like them as any people alive, and although the subject is of all others most fascinating. Yet it was a labour to compose, simply because you were not there, but only the visionary ghost of you. I had to pretend you; it was the best I could do.

God does not have to pretend; that is where he differs from us. He speaks with himself; but the self with whom he speaks, and who takes the responsive part, is a dear and real person, the Son of his love. And what they exchange between them is no fragmentary expression of a passing thought, it is the whole mind and heart and substance of their godhead.

That is all Christians know about the life of God. We can weigh it, and turn it over, and phrase it a hundred ways; we can consider it in relation to a hundred things; can guard it against a hundred misconceptions. But it all comes down to this; this is all we know. And even then, as you will be quick to tell me, we cannot know it; it baffles understanding. We cannot think of different persons, unless they are identified with several lumps of flesh; still less can we conceive a thought so powerful, that it really constitutes the Other in the mind, instead of merely pretending him. And so we cannot think the Blessed Trinity. But then, it is not required of us to think the Trinity. We can do better; we can live the Trinity by grace of the Trinity.

As I have implied already, the life of the Trinity is represented in us after two different fashions: in society with one another, and in discourse with one's self. Each fashion of representation has its special merit. Our society with our friends mirrors the reality of the Trinity: it is real society and the persons involved in it are real persons. A man's discourse with himself better represents the oneness of the Trinity: the divine Persons are as close to one another as a man's own thought is to a man; yes, and closer than that. Sometimes Holy Scripture speaks of a divine Father and a divine Son; and that is to speak of a society between kindred beings. Sometimes, on the other hand, Scripture speaks of God and his Word; and that is to use the figure of a single mind and its uttered expression. And I think you will find there are no other ways Scripture does take beyond these two, in writing of that supreme mystery.

It follows that we live the Trinity, in some sense, just by being men; and it is no blasphemy to say that this dear Trinity of ours, in all the companionship it engenders, or indeed, of which it consists, is the offspring of the divine Spirit. More particularly in the special work of a college, where the younger learn from the elder, and the elder find happiness in the vitality of younger wits, you have an enactment of the Blessed Trinity; a Trinity in which there is a Father and a Son, and yet no disparity, but an equal delight of each in each. But then again, it is specially characteristic of a college, that our studies, with all accompanying sidelines of mental stimulation, drive us to exercise in a more than trivial way that high privilege of a rational being, to enter into converse with himself, and to beget upon his own thought a new achievement of understanding.

Any man, then, who has the character to be either a thinker or a friend lives the Trinity in some fashion, whether he is a Christian or not. Has not God made us all in his own similitude? We can achieve nothing truly human which is not also in a manner divine. And we may wonder without end at the simple fact, that anything so godlike as common friendship, or as ordinary rational discourse, should be actualized in physical bodies. These things are the masterpieces of the Creator, and in these he delights.

And yet the Blessed Trinity has a higher delight in us, and we a more heavenly partaking in the life of the Trinity, by our being Christians. We may see how this is, if we recall that what the divine Persons love in one another is not something that just happens to be; it is the perfect truth of eternal godhead. The Father loves the Son for perfectly expressing this; the Son adores the Father as the fount and archetype of all that his own being expresses. So Christians, in so far as they are Christians, like in their friends not what merely happens to be in them, good or bad; they prize in one another with a special regard what is sincerely good; that is to say, what expresses the goodness and the beauty of God. They see the will of God in one another's lives; they love the Creator himself in his handiwork.

Or again, to speak of that other looking-glass of the Trinity, the discourse a man has with himself. That *alter ego* in the mind with whom we converse need not be the mere complacent shadow of our own desires, the bosom flatterer who is our own worst enemy; nor even the mere logical judge, the inner critic who forbids our getting away with dishonest argument. The Christian may go further; he may draw into converse with him an imagined other self who speaks for the very will of God. He may square his account with eternal truth and sovereign majesty, so far as he can find them in his heart, or see them bear upon his present life. Then suddenly he is not talking with himself at all, or with any system of his own imagining. The other person of his inward colloquy takes on the very name and character of the Creator. The principle of an eternal law warms with the kindness of a Father's care, encouraging us to speak with him as sons. So a Person of the divine Trinity, the Father of Heaven, shows through one of the parties to our inner dialogue. But no sooner has this happened, than the other participant is similarly transformed. When we respond in filial duty to so heavenly a Father, our very self reveals the action, and expresses the person of his heavenly Son. Who does not know that when we genuinely pray, it is Christ who prays in us? And as for the bond of mutual liking which unites the two persons of our colloquy, it is no other than the inspiration of the Holy Spirit; for where the Father and the Son are, there is he.

What I have spoken of is no exalted mystical ecstasy; it is just praying, or even, without the form of prayer, any attending to the presence and will of our Creator. *Tota Trinitas illabitur menti,* the whole Trinity moves into the mind, says the great St Augustine, writing of this very thing. But we have better authority. 'We will come, and make our abode with him,' says the Christ of St John's Gospel. 'We' – that is, the Father and the Son, by the indwelling of the Holy Spirit. And with whom will they take up their abode? With the man who 'will keep my words', says Christ; who guards and honours by his obedience this treasure in the soul, this viceroy of heaven in the heart, the revealed thought and will of the godhead; a word able to come alive and to address us from the lips of God, drawing us into that happy converse, which brings the Trinity to earth, and raises earthly life to heaven: where to the Triune Sovereignty alone is, was and shall be ascribed, as is most justly due, all might, dominion, majesty and power, in all eternity.

preached in Trinity College Chapel, Oxford

21
Consecrated Bread

The scientific history of words tends to be disappointing. How many distributors of school prizes have gone to town on the noble assertion that education is a drawing-out, not a putting-in! Historically speaking they are wrong. Education is just a raising or a bringing-up. Take another case – our family name. We were solemnly told by our uncles that a farrer was a farrier or *ferrarius*: to wit, a blacksmith, a fine, muscular fellow. Alas, nothing of the sort: the Farrers were nothing more interesting than fair-hairs, Danish lads infesting Northumbrian shores; not blacksmiths in fact, but whiteheads. Or there's the word 'university': a glorious idea, *universitas studiorum*, the whole gamut of faculties, all the things there are to know! That's not a university, we say of some one-eyed place: it gives degrees in nothing but business economics. As usual, history lets us down: it wasn't *universitas studiorum*, the whole gamut of studies, which gave us the word, it was nothing more interesting than *universitas studentium*, the whole body of students in a given place, say Paris or Padua. Never mind, you may say, to hell with etymology; the false derivation gives us a true and beautiful idea. The whole round of the universe of knowledge, or at least, of enquiry, that's the university: everything from Egyptology to nuclear physics, from pitch-and-toss to manslaughter. Our Senior Tutors, woe to their souls, channel us into lines which suit the teaching staff, and they treat us as tutorial fodder, not as hungry minds. But that's simply an abuse; once we are in the university, we have the right to satisfy our intellectual cravings. So what shall it be? What shall we take? In all this university, this universe of enquiries, what shall I take? John is taking Law. I shall take French and German. Goodness! I hope I'll get through the prelim.

And there's another thing. Suppose I do take what I like, and manage the job, what about all the other subjects of knowledge which by my specialization I neglect? Well, it can't be helped; one can't attend to everything in a limited time. The great thing is, to get some foothold on the continent of exact and disciplined thought; one can always branch out from there in any required direction. Surely a man who's read Plato and Aristotle can master the directions for working a sewing machine. So, reinforced by these comforting considerations, you look at the universe of enquiry, and you decide what you will take.

As you like to look at it, the choice seems either portentous, or trivial. If you take your studies seriously, you set a lifelong direction to your mental interest by the choice of the subject you take; but then again, you have, perhaps, no very solid grounds for taking one before another: you are moved by a detestation of Anglo-Saxon, or a desire to be different from your elder brother. Your choice is not like the choice of God, when he decided what he would take. He also looked out upon and surveyed a *universitas*, a universe of wise and perfect thoughts, his own; but these thoughts of his, unlike the strengthless insubstantial thoughts of men, had embodied themselves in solid shapes and living creations, they had become a world. The Creator's thoughts are actual creations; because he thinks us, we exist. And in this universe of his substantial thought, God chose what he would take, and bind himself to, for ever; one line, one lot, one portion of creaturely existence. For at all costs he was determined that he would gain a foothold on the continent, our continent of human life.

If he was to do so, how narrow was the choice! God was to be man, then he was to be one man in all the million million first and last created; so he took flesh, flesh from a Jewish girl, and he became a certain carpenter in one small Galilean town among many, and in one year among all the yearly cycles of the revolving sun. Yet he had no intention of remaining shut up in the lot of life he had taken; once he had taken it, he could branch out from there. There were, there are, no limits to the distances he could reach from that base, the fields of life he could embrace and could annex; until he should encompass the *universitas hominum*, the whole body of men who walk this earth, or fly this atmosphere.

He took flesh, it was his body; it cried and smiled and sucked, it hungered and thirsted, it laboured and grew weary, it suffered and rejoiced, it lived and died. But before it died, before he died as bodily man, he also took bread, and said *it* was his body.

Well, in a manner of speaking, the bread he took *was* his body. A sculptor might show you round his shop, and pointing out pieces of wood grained suitably for several purposes, might say, 'That is a Churchill, and that's a Victory; that is a greyhound, and this is a leopard.' They are the raw materials of these things; and the food we will eat is the raw material of our body; let us call it our body if we like, by anticipation, or by exaggeration. Yet the bread Jesus took was not his own loaf or roll, that he would eat. It was the bread of the grace, a loaf specially symbolical of the whole company's food: a loaf over which grace was said for them all, and of which everyone present must taste a crumb. It did not stand for the bread or body of any one person there present, it stood for the common food of them all. As St Paul says, writing of this very matter, because the loaf is one, we many are one body, for we all partake of the one loaf. Since food becomes our body, eating from one loaf or from one dish becomes a sort of natural sacrament. As we build up our body from one stock, we feel ourselves tied together in one body corporate; we are members one of another. And to the Jew, this natural tie became a religious bond: the one loaf shared by all was consecrated through the thanksgiving, or grace-before-meat.

This, then, was the bread Jesus took, on the night before he suffered, the bread which was the body of them all; it was this he called his body. The body he took from Mary was no one's but his. From the moment of birth it ceased to be hers; and it was certainly no other man's or woman's. But the bread he took to be his body was the body of the company, of Peter, John, James, Matthew and Thomas: so determined he was, that the effect of his incarnation should not be shut within the confines of his skin. He took their body, but he took it to be made his own, to be consecrated, divinized, Christed; through the oblation of a voluntary death, and the power of a glorious resurrection.

Who supplied the bread which lay on the table at Christ's last earthly supper, and which he took, and held in his blessed hands? We cannot be certain. We hear something of the householder who so providentially and surprisingly offered them a supper-room; we cannot suppose that he also laid on the supper. Judas held a purse, from which the common expenses of the brotherhood were defrayed; perhaps it is right to think that purse purchased the bread. If so, the bread and the body were theirs, were the whole company's, not merely in the sense that the bread was appointed for their use, to be the common substance of their bodies; it was theirs in the further sense, that it belonged to them by purchase and possession; their hands set it on the table. However it may have been with Christ and his disciples, it is at least clear how the case was with St Paul and his friends, say those at Corinth. The materials of the holy feast were neither supplied by the hospitality of a rich householder, nor were they purchased out of a common Church fund. They were brought by the congregation. Every man brought his piece of bread, his little cup or flask; but they were not (it was here that St Paul rebuked them) – they were not each man to eat and drink his own. All was to go into the common stock and be equally shared, after one loaf, picked at random, had been blessed by the bishop and the crumbs passed round; and so likewise with the cup. The remainder would be for the poor.

Christ takes; it is our privilege to bring. Christ takes, through the hands of the priest his representative; we bring the token and stuff of our bodies, no longer in bread and wine, but in the money of the offering, for which the bread and wine have come to be exchanged. It is easily said, that the substitution is bogus; that to give money is one thing, to give ourselves is another. The objection is only valid, if the giving costs us nothing. The only absolute way for us to give ourselves, is as Christ gave himself, in a voluntary death; there is no part of the person left out of such an offering, and we shall all have to make it in some fashion, grudgingly or willingly, when we come to die. Short of that, we can give ourselves only in giving what is ours: our attention, our effort, our sympathy, our patience, our money, our time. Believe me, you are more likely to make a real offering of yourself to God by a decent and costly alms; a bit of your heart will stick to the precious coin, and come away with it, for where thy treasure is, there will thy heart be also – I say that you will probably make a more genuine self-offering in hard cash than by eloquent and invisible acts of the spirit in which you aspire to give God everything – that is to say, to give him what you will take back from him half an hour after; as Peter did, for all his fine words, when he denied Christ in Caiaphas's court.

Dear me, what we give to God isn't much, and our giving isn't much of a giving; so let's be thankful that your preacher is not put up here to discourse on so depressing a theme. No; it is not my text that they gave or presented the bread of the offering (about which, as we have seen, the Evangelists are silent) but that Christ took it into his blessed hands, and said it was his body. He took, and he takes. He takes what we are: he is not ashamed of us, does not discuss us. Peter might deny Christ, but Christ set his eyes on Peter, his eyes and his heart. He takes us, and says we are his body; for his love will make us so. We read of the great St Bernard, that he took some strange monks into his monastery, confident, and rightly, that the love of God in their Abbot's bosom would make Christians of them. But he was only the instrument and copy of his Redeemer. He takes us: he loves us for what we are, and loves us into what we must be; he takes us, incorporate with him through his death and resurrection, and gives us back ourself, that is himself, in the communion of bread and wine.

Now therefore to the living love of heaven, Creator and Saviour of all, who most wonderfully ordained the excellence of man's estate, and more wonderfully has redeemed it, One God in three Persons, Father, Son and Holy Ghost, be ascribed as is most justly due, all might, dominion, majesty and power, henceforth and for ever.

preached in Pusey House Chapel, Oxford

22
Double Thinking

It is a very ancient and mossy platitude, that men throw away priceless opportunities for self-improvement by resenting criticism instead of taking it to heart. And what is true of men is true of doctrines and systems. If only we could seriously consider what the communists say about us, instead of blasting them with cries of 'You're another!' And if only the Church in every age had been as concerned to see what had driven the heretics into heresy, as she was to condemn and suppress them! For the heretics were as serious men as the orthodox, often more serious. Well, it is easy to be wise after the event: our fathers burnt the heretics and we touch up the crests on the Martyrs' Memorial. But cannot we, in our own time, show a little more wisdom and listen seriously to our own heretics?

Two nights ago I was so rash as to let myself be put up in a sort of public match or verbal cock-fight with an unbelieving philosopher. He was to attack theology, I was to defend it. Neither of the birds (needless to say) achieved a kill. I had heard all the arguments before; so, I expect, had he. He argued kindly and temperately. He had no need to get excited, he was so entirely convinced of his own position. But how strange it is, that two men so different inside should present the same placid face to one another, and exchange little neat verbal arguments about the two different universes in which they respectively live! There is no God in his world: he has yet to be convinced that belief in God has any serious meaning or can be discussed on a respectable level. Whereas I – I, like you, make it a rule to spend a certain part of every day conversing with this God, whom my fellow philosopher more than suspects of not existing. I put a good part of my available nervous energy and a fixed ratio of my time into the endeavour to hold my existence in a focus which is for him a spot of moonshine.

Meanwhile, a room full of young philosophers or would-be philosophers watch the cock-fight. If they took it seriously, I suppose their world ought to turn upside down with every apparent swaying of the battle. Fortunately, the young men don't take argumentative dons as seriously as that.

But I must take seriously what my colleague thinks: not, that is, to call my faith in doubt, for since God has shown to me a ray of his goodness, I cannot doubt him on the ground that someone has made up some new logical puzzles about him. It is too late in the day to tell me that God does not exist, the God with whom I have so long conversed, and whom

I have seen active in several living men of real sanctity, not to mention the canonized saints. But there must be much in our teaching of Christianity and our living of it which is at fault, if good men react in total disbelief of it. So let us open our ears to what they say, and take the implied criticism to heart. This chapel is no place in which to argue against the unbelieving philosophers: it would be ungenerous, for this is not a place where they can argue back. But this is a fine place in which to take their criticisms to ourselves, and examine our own consciences.

Let us take, for example, the accusation of 'double thinking' which is brought against us Christians. Allow me to remind you how that accusation comes in. You have to suppose first that the critical philosopher has proved to his own satisfaction that religious beliefs can have no meaning at all in terms of real life. Religious beliefs and ceremonies are just superfluous decorations. In fact all religion in a scientific age is fundamentally of the same character as the religion practised by a couple of sentimental atheists getting married in church because it sounds more comforting. But, you and I object, we are not sentimental atheists: we really do believe. To which the answer is given: You *think* you believe; but you are deceived. You are a double thinker: you have two systems of thinking which in fact you keep apart – you think, as people say, in watertight compartments. And when you switch from one system of your thinking to another, that is, from your religious thinking to your practical thinking, you turn a blind eye to the transition, the passage from the world of reality to the world of fantasy. In the world of reality you think like anyone else (unless, of course, you are a lunatic or a fanatic). But when you turn to your devotions, or read pious books, you enjoy a fantasy picture of the world as subject to God's goodness and governed by his providence. And in this fantasy picture of the world there is a fantasy picture of yourself as a Christian, mysteriously incorporate with Christ and serving his cause, with only occasional lapses and deviations. Whereas in fact you are just an undergraduate or a business man, or some other type of worldly man, a serious man, perhaps a virtuous man, but one who does not take the will of God into his practical calculations, or experience his life as conducted by God. That is just a story you amuse yourself with while you are worshipping or praying or talking pious talk.

Well, now I think you will see what the accusation of double thinking amounts to; and I think also that you will see how deeply the accusation bites into our consciences, and how important it is that we should lay it to heart. For which of us Christians is there, whose conscience does not reproach him bitterly with the crime of double thinking, or, as Christ himself called it, the crime of hypocrisy? For hypocrisy, as attacked by Christ, does not mean self-conscious humbug, it means just 'play acting', that is to say, that the religion of the hypocrite no more enters into the rest of his life than the part the player acts on the stage enters into his life off the stage. In fact, Christ meant by hypocrisy what is now called 'double thinking', the endemic disease of religion everywhere.

Notice that our critics make the substance of religion what we reject as the vice of religion and its most deadly poison. How does this come about? Are not we the men who have brought it about? Am I not, perhaps, the Christian don who is just like any unbelieving don, except that I sometimes talk theology for professional reasons? And are not you, perhaps, the undergraduate who is just like any other unbelieving undergraduate, and proud to be, and whom no one would suspect of being a Christian unless they found you in chapel? Are we just as ready as anyone else to join in the enjoyable game of slander (called gossip), just as determined as anyone else to make our worldly fortunes, whatever the needs of the Church or of unfortunate men may be? I could go on making up a lot more unpleasant questions like this, but I will forbear.

To return to the main point. To the clever logicians, Christianity is an amiable and harmless hypocrisy. But we take the thing more seriously. Christian hypocrisy is not amiable or harmless at all. We are all hypocrites, indeed, because we are all sinners, but God is saving us out of our hypocrisy, if we are faithful to him: he is forcing the two parts of our thinking together. That is the whole issue in the religious life, not to be a double thinker, or anyhow, to be less and less of one.

It is obvious that our blessed Saviour was not a double thinker at all. He just lived God, or God lived him, it does not matter which we say, though the second is better – I mean, that God lived him. And I have known some men – living men, breathing with us a common air, men with whom I have talked and worked – who were single-minded Christians and simply followed the will of God step by step in this life, without any seeming regard for their own fortune or happiness or life, even. But what visible happiness God gave them in this world! and what happiness he has given them in that other world, eye has not seen, nor ear heard, nor has it entered into the heart of man once to conceive the least part of it.

When the logicians say that there is a certain inevitable division between spiritual thinking and natural thinking, they are in a certain sense right. We can't reconcile the spiritual picture of things and the everyday picture of things completely on the intellectual level. If we claimed to be able to do it, we should claim to comprehend the ways of God as well as we comprehend the ways of this world, and that would be an exaggerated claim. We see God in pictures, in images only, reflected in a glass and riddlingly says St Paul: and we cannot fuse our picture of God perfectly with our picture of the natural world. There always remains a certain discontinuity, a certain incoherence on the intellectual level.

The saints confute the logicians, but they do not confute them by logic but by sanctity. They do not prove the real connection between the religious symbols and the everyday realities by logical demonstration, but by life. *Solvitur ambulando*, said someone about Zeno's paradox, which proves the impossibility of physical motion. It is solved by walking. *Solvitur immolando*, says the saint, about the paradox of the logicians. It is solved by sacrifice. I can offer my life to the God who has shown me his face in the glass of riddles. The God who is seen in the sphere of religion takes control in the sphere of conduct, and there he gives me, unworthy, the help of his Holy Spirit.

You can live your religion if you like; you can know the reality of God if you like: for God will rejoice to assist and infinitely over-reward whatever effort you will make. *Resolution* is the crucial point. That is the link by which religious contemplation passes into practical action. From your prayers form simple resolutions – not, like the absurd resolutions of New Year's Day, resolutions for the next twelve months; but resolutions for the next twelve hours. Make them few enough to be practicable, and obey them for the sake of God himself. If you break them, repeat and renew them. What does God ask of me? is a part of every sincere prayer. By resolutions kept, men turn religious fantasy into the substance of living. By resolutions broken, men learn their weakness and are driven back on God. By resolutions renewed and kept they learn to live by him who says: 'my strength is made perfect in weakness' and 'my grace is sufficient for thee.'

23

What is God?

In my hot-headed youth, I thought I would bring about a reformation of the language. Among other refinements I hoped to introduce was the general substitution of 'relative' for 'relation' when referring to one's sisters, cousins or aunts. How could a cousin *be* a relation? I stand in a relation to him, and in virtue of that relation he is relative to me. But 'my relations' – how did so preposterous a usage come about? I suppose it began like this. On hearing Mr X casually remark that he was great-nephew to the Marquis of Bute, 'Sir,' you exclaimed, 'that is a highly respectable relation' – relation, that is, in which to stand. But next day, with that grammatical carelessness which is all too common, you found yourself alluding to 'X's highly respectable relation, the Marquis of Bute'. And so a concrete nobleman came to be defined as a mere abstraction of relatedness to a great-nephew, as though he derived his whole being and function from connection with that unnecessary young man: a very unreasonable description; for so far from exercising the existence of a great-uncle, the noble marquis might be only indistinctly aware of his great-nephew's ever having been born.

To define others by relation to ourselves is a sublime, if unconscious, egotism. It may not matter all that much in human affairs, but when carried into theology it causes trouble. God is my Father. His fatherhood to me is indeed a relation, for it constitutes me as the child of God. But it is not a relation which defines for me what God is. If I begin my theology with the thought of 'a supernatural father for me', I quickly arrive at the much-derided picture of a manlike majesty somewhere up there in the sky. Rational belief in God the Father Almighty has nothing to do with such childishness. God – ah, he is God; how dare I try to say what God is? And *yet* he is my Father, for he has called me into being, and given me just so much kinship to himself, that I can name his name and choose – if only I do choose – his holy will. But in himself, what is he?

Is it right even to ask the question? We are told in a very old and doubt-less very barbarous tale how Jacob wrestled with God in the dark, and tried to make him declare what he was; but as dawn broke God put a wrestler's touch on Jacob, which disabled him while the invisible slipped from his grasp. God had not revealed what he was, but he had told Jacob what Jacob was, and had blessed him. And so it is practical doctrine that if we wrestle with God's holy will we shall find out what we are, and what we are called to be; we shall not find out what God is, for all the assurance we gain that his will indeed wrestled with ours, and that we have his blessing.

The doctrine is good; and it is certain folly to think one will ever say what God is. One must say something, though, however foolish it sounds in the ears of heaven. For we must think something when we think of God, never mind how short we fall of the mark at which our thoughts are aimed. So now let me commit this great folly, and say what is God.

Shall I say he is the prime cause and maker of all things? I shall not err; only I shall still have defined him by a relation, in that all things are *from* him. I shall not have said what is he. But I do see that all things that are made have a hallmark on them, the sign of their createdness; the sign being this, that they are all limited expressions of what a thing can be; any one of them might just as well have been a good deal otherwise; each of them has been shut up to being no more than what it is. Say if you will that each thing and each fact is determined to be what it is by its place in the total universe. Very well; but even this whole great baffling universe of stars is itself just one scatter and spread of material stuff, one arrangement among all the arrangements there might have been. To believe in God is to believe that the ultimate reason why things are so and not otherwise, is that he has willed them to be so. What then is he? God is will, and he is will subject to no such limitations as he has measured out to his creatures. His is the being which knows no barriers; he always is all that he wills to be, and wills to be all that he is.

What have I said? Have I committed the notorious folly of saying what is God? I have not; for I have not pretended to state what sort of a life it must be, that has the scope my words have just attributed to the life and action of God. Let me take a feeble though obvious comparison. There was a time I can just remember when I knew that people wrote, received and read letters, and made themselves understood by that channel; but I had no notion of the principle of the thing, of how words could be scripted, or script convey words. I scribbled with a pencil, and spoilt much paper in my play. Though I wrote nothing, I thought I was writing, for I did not know what writing was. I knew that my elders sent speech through scribbled lines; how they did it, I did not know. And so with my adult knowledge of the life of God; I know that it is a life and action such as to suffer no limits, to be subject to no charter of existence, to be simply sovereign and free. But what must the divine life be, to achieve all this? I do not know.

I do not know; only I find in myself this clue, this vestige of divinity, that my thought climbs out of my skin, and attempts an impartial survey of the universe, with my own body in it; that my will battles against the limitations of character or circumstance; and attempts a sovereign mastery. And so I can at least frame the question, what would that mind be, that saw all things in the very truth of their being, without disguise;

what would that will be, which achieved its whole aspiration without impediment? I can ask the question, I cannot answer it. For the answer is what God is; and that is what I am not.

Enough, then, of this folly. We have looked into the abyss just far enough to remind ourselves of the infinite deep. And that is God. The Catholic Faith in God the Father Almighty is not the belief that we have a relation in heaven, a Father of much dignity and power. It is a faith really consisting of two parts, to be kept distinct and not to be confused. First, the supreme being, cause and good is Almighty God, infinite Spirit. Second, this God is Father, for he has chosen to give himself children.

I don't know whether any of you need to be warned against the more stultifying forms of textbook orthodoxy – because there is a way of so stating the doctrine of the Trinity as to deny that God simply is the Father Almighty, on the ground that God is every person of the Trinity equally. But that is to put the matter badly. God is God, and there is no God but he. He is eternally the Father because he has never willed to be alone; and so it has never been that he has not given himself a Son on whom he everlastingly bestows all that he himself either has or is; the Son of God being so truly God's Son, as to lack nothing his Father possesses. It remains nevertheless that the Father is not only Father to his Son, he is also God to him. His Father's giving him all he has does not make him worship his Father the less. How should it? Why do we men worship God? Because he has given us so little, or because he has given us so much? In worshipping God, we worship a bottomless bounty. We cannot return him a limitless worship, limited as we are. His infinite Son gives him infinite thanks for an infinite gift; and when he appears among us men, for our salvation, he comes as our fellow-worshipper; his Father is ours, his God is ours.

I have called it a sort of folly to say what the divine life is. It's a folly, if so, that we can easily renounce; for to have a practical knowledge of God we need not penetrate the heart of mystery or find the top of being. We cannot ascend unto his height, but why should we attempt it? He comes down into our valley. How foolish was Nimrod, who thought by the hands of ten thousand slaves to rear at Babel a tower reaching the gods! And how blessed was Abraham, when God came to him in the guise of a travelling man, and ate at his table, and called him his friend! In the old tale it is by a special disguise that God comes to the patriarch; but that is poetry. For God identifies himself unrestrictedly with every one of his creatures, he thinks and knows them from within, his creative thought is expressed in their very being; for else, how should they exist? His whole work of creation is a coming down from heaven, an indwelling of his creatures; his heart goes with them, he looks at us out of their eyes. Above all, God becomes human in men; he is met in our neighbour, he speaks in the depth of our heart; not because the heart of our heart is other than we, but because it is our very self, the self God makes, wills and directs. The Son of God came to reconcile us with God in reconciling us with the truth of ourselves; and he it is that leads, that studies, that inflames our adoration of his God and ours, his Father and our Father; to whom through that most blessed Son, by inspiration of the Holy Ghost, he ascribed as is most justly due all might, dominion, majesty and power, henceforth and for ever.

24

Holy Otherness

I live; yet not I but Christ liveth in me.
Gal. 2.20

Perhaps you are all set to hear a terrific sermon about the state of world affairs. If so, you are doomed to disappointment. If we tried anything in that line, perhaps, after a lot of preliminary thunder, we should come round in the end to a simple conclusion: first, that we must be ready to do our duty if called upon; and second, that if the end of all things should chance to be at hand, there is all the more reason, while we have time, to get acquainted with the God who made us. Now I propose to take the international thunder as thundered, and to start from the conclusion, about obtaining the knowledge of God; for that seems more practical. And from the knowledge of God I shall go on to speak of one way in which God makes himself known to us here and now, and that is, through the sacrament.

Now about the knowledge of God. Let us suppose that we really want to know him. That is, of course, an enormous supposition. Really wanting to is far more than half the battle. For although the knowledge of God is not only the last, but also the sweetest, of things, it is the special malevolence of Satan to make it seem harsh and forbidding. We are in love with our own ideas, our own plans and habits, and though falling in with God is the only pure sort of happiness, we do not easily believe it, nor easily act upon it if we do. But I say that I am going to suppose this huge supposition, that we want to know God. Where, then, are we to find him?

Well, doubtless God is infinitely active everywhere and in an infinity of ways: he besets us on every hand. To ask, 'What does God do about us?' would be like asking, 'What is nature up to?' Supposing you were to pause in the middle of a field on a summer day and ask how many natural processes were going on in your neighbourhood, the motions of the air, the evaporation of the dew, the silent growth of every blade of grass, the distinct action of every living thing.

The action of God is not only infinite in the world around us, but beats upon us and affects us and moulds us in endless ways. But for thinking of God and for trying to know him and to worship him, there are two ways specially in which we may see ourselves related to him: *identity* and *difference*. As to the difference, God is infinitely different from us in quality and nature, and distinct from us in being. There is an infinite distance between us and him. Yet on the other hand, God, by his mercy, identifies himself with us, and identifies us with himself.

I do not want to say so much now about the matter of difference; it will be enough to recall how often Scripture speaks of the divine holiness. What is it to talk about the holiness of God, but to talk about his otherness from us and from everything human, and from everything created? To say that he is holy is to say that there is none but he, and that he makes upon us an immeasurable claim, beside which no other claim can even be named.

And this difference or otherness of God is the place from which religion starts. If I try to approach God, to bow myself down before God, I think of him as outside me, in front of me, invisible, somewhere away above the level of my eyes. I call to him, I try to speak rightly to him, as to another person, someone of great natural majesty and unquestionable authority, who knows me through and through, whom I have undoubtedly often betrayed and offended. It is as though I were asking him for forgiveness, as though I were trying to find his face that I might read in it the directions I need for future actions. And then I may think of myself as going away and trying to carry out the directions I have obtained, and to carry with me some memory of the divine presence.

There is no need to continue further in this strain; because it is the most familiar way of thinking about God, thinking of him as a person outside ourselves, different from ourselves, whom we seek, address, worship, and serve. It is the starting-point of religion; and it is a way of thinking, or of imagining, which is common to Christians, Mohammedans, Jews, and Parsees, to name no others.

Now as to identity. That is the more specially Christian thing, that God identifies himself with us, and us with himself. Now that is more difficult to most minds, and he who begins talking along this line will be told by his hearers that they do not know what he means, and that he has stopped talking plain practical religion, and gone off into something called 'theology'. I do not know what the difference between 'plain practical religion' and 'theology' is supposed to be. Does 'theology' in this unfavourable sense mean something which would be no use to us if we understood it, or only something which we have not managed to understand hitherto? Perhaps we haven't understood hitherto how God identifies himself with us, and us with himself. But it would be a serious mistake to think that it would do us no good to understand it. Was St Paul talking mere theology when he said, 'I live, or rather not I but Christ lives in me'; and, 'For me to live is Christ'? And was St John recording a mere piece of theology when he placed the words, 'I in you, and you in me,' on the lips of Christ himself?

If we say we cannot understand such language, the difficulty, of course, is not a difficulty about the sense of the words; the words are plain enough. The difficulty is rather one of imagination. Just now I was talking to you, in a way which you found perfectly familiar, about approaching God as though he were another person, a person outside you and distinct from you. In the same way I could write you a description about the relation of identification with Christ; it would be a story like the other, and if it was obscure to you it would be because your imagination has not learnt to work in that way.

I might say, for example, going back to the same place, here are you, or I, or any Christian making the act of approach to God. But the man we are thinking of is much burdened with his own failures, so that the whole thing seems unreal; much darkened with his own blindness, so that God seems quite hidden from him. But now he remembers the grace of the Lord Jesus Christ. God, through Christ, he says, has identified himself with me, and me with himself. So, he says, I have not got to struggle, or climb, or break through. For Christ is the Son of God, and he is immediately present to the heavenly Father, and the heavenly Father to him. And Christ has identified himself with me, and me with himself. My effort to pray is part of Christ's perfect prayer, my darkness is part of his clear vision, my feeble resolves are carried on the tide of his sacrificial will. There is of course a gulf – how wide and black! – between my mind and the mind of Christ, but that gulf is bridged and indeed cancelled and filled up by Christ's atoning death. He does not reject me or disown me, whatever I am, so long as I believe, and embrace his saving will.

If this were real to you, do you think it would make no difference? You might still hesitate to say with the Apostle, 'For me to live is Christ', but if you could say anyhow of certain acts, 'For me to pray is Christ,' 'For me to obey is Christ,' would that make no difference? Is not that Christianity? Is not that the peculiar grace of Christ, that he makes us to be as he is in this world?

But now suppose we say, 'But I cannot see things that way, I cannot feel things that way'? Is that the end of the matter, and is the end a dead end? No, for Christ himself will be our teacher. To begin with, we can exercise our faith in the grace of Christ when we resolve and when we pray, by taking seriously those words which we tag on to our prayers, 'through Jesus Christ our Lord,' making our prayer as part of his prayer, and believing indeed that he prays in and through us. But then more especially Christ himself has provided the remedy for our trouble by the institution of the sacrament. For, if our difficulty is one of imagination, that we cannot imagine and feel and live our identification with Christ, is it not one purpose of the sacrament to make such identification visible and palpable? 'He that eateth me, even he shall live by me.'

When we were children, people warned us of undue familiarity with the sacrament, and it may be true of children that for them familiarity may breed, if not contempt, at least disregard. But it is certainly not true of us: what sort of a God is this to believe in, if familiarity with him leads grown men into contempt of him? Surely familiarity with the sacrament is exactly what we need: if the sacrament became part of the theme and rhythm of our life, then we should come to experience Christ sacramentally, that is, to experience his identification of himself with us, and of us with himself. Familiarity with the sacrament was unquestionably the way of Christ's first disciples: they received Christ under bread and wine weekly at the least, and many years of such practice lay behind St Paul when he wrote, 'For me to live is Christ'. And the sacrament is always received worthily, if we are sincerely ready, so far as in us lies, to let Christ take us and offer us and our purposes, with his own, to God.

25

The Consuming Presence

It is a fearful thing to fall into the hands of the living God.

Heb. 10.31

We will fall into the hands of God, and not into the hands of men, for as his majesty is, so also his mercy.

Ecclus. 2.17

A learned colleague who shall be nameless was giving me a description of the way in which some Eastern Christians worship God. 'The best way to describe it', he said, 'is to call it a sort of spiritual air-raid drill. The divine presence is the point of explosive danger, and the moment of sacramental consecration is the moment of detonation. The ordinary citizens are protected by a solid stone screen, or rather wall, fencing them off from the altar, and they keep their heads well down to be on the safe side. Then there are the special anti-bomb personnel, the ministers equipped with special protective uniform, and specially trained, who enter the terrible enclosure with fear and wariness and go to the very point of danger. When the incident has been successfully neutralized, the deacon comes out and gives the all-clear to the congregation who get up and move about.'

My friend's description, I need hardly say, is a piece of satire, but satire is sometimes more effective than justice at seizing the point one wishes to make. There *are* Christians in the world who regard the divine presence as above all a thing of dread; and in so doing they are simply returning to the religion of the Old Testament. And my friend's piece about the air-raid drill applies as closely as could well be to certain ceremonies in the worship of ancient Israel.

Moses at Mount Sinai implored God to leave, as it were, his throne on the mountain-top where the volcanic fire blazed and to come down into the camp of Israel and accompany their wanderings. The divine voice gave him many stern warnings before consenting. 'I cannot go up in your midst; for it is a stiff-necked people.' But at length the prayers of Moses, or rather the love of God, prevailed: 'My presence shall go with you, and I will give you rest.' Forthwith the voice began to teach Moses how God's terrible holiness could be housed within the camp without the sheer destruction of sinful men resulting. They were to prepare a special place, a travelling sanctuary, and fence it round with sanctity, and approach it with wariness and ritual precaution. Even then, when the work of the tabernacle was complete, and Moses set it up and celebrated the dedication, the mountain-cloud came down and filled the tent, and Moses gave place and dared not enter where God was.

The presence of God was strength: Israel could not endure to lack him; but the presence of God was terror, and Israel could not endure to have him. 'We are killed, we are killed', they complained, when contagious sickness broke out in the camp as though the fire of God's presence had blazed out from the sanctuary in indignation at their sins. And so they set a fresh barrier between themselves and God. They chose one of their twelve tribes and made its members specialists in holiness: they *only* were to approach the presence; they were to observe all kinds of ritual rules and precautions from which the laity were free; they were to stand between Israel and God's devouring fire.

I suppose you will say that this was all just stupid savagery and craven-hearted superstition: these people knew the fear of God but they did not know his love; the pestilence was not the effect of divine indignation but of defective sanitation; and so on. But I say that they were being taught something of infinite importance; no people can think too highly of the holiness, the majesty of God, and what troubled them still troubles us: how we can live in immediate contact with God's holiness and not be destroyed by it.

Christ did not take anything away from the holiness and majesty of God, he just took away all the barriers which fenced the sanctuary. When he died on the cross, say the evangelists, the veil of the temple was rent to pieces; whether in physical or only in spiritual fact, I do not know. But anyhow the barrier went, and the presence of God is no longer in a safe enclosure, looked after by priestly experts in sanctity: we are all priests and God is lodged in us; the New Testament says, in our actual bodies.

Now this fact of God's immediate presence is a danger to us, not on the physical plane perhaps, but on the spiritual certainly. For if we are the temple of God, and our spirits directly touch his inviolable holiness, our souls are threatened with a sickness worse than the plague that broke out in Moses' camp: I mean despair, cynicism and loss of faith in God. If God were conveniently remote, we could believe in him, but the only God whom we know is not remote: he indwells us. And how can we believe in an indwelling God unless we manifest the effects of his indwelling? Our faith is destroyed, unless we really are the living and moving temples of God. But what are the facts? Our attention fixed nine-tenths of the time on our own selfish concerns; an occasional half-hearted prayer, every now and then a grudging consent to do God's will rather than our pleasure. Such is the life of most of us, and it destroys faith in the indwelling God through flagrant unreality. It might not destroy faith in a remote God, but there is no remote God. God is here in fact, he has taken flesh amongst us, we cannot send him back to the top of Mount Sinai or to the height of heaven so as to be able to believe in him with comfort.

Well, in the end we have got to earn our faith: we have got to become actual temples of God, and we have got to bring our eyes round and keep them on his face – not like the sinners whom God's prophet found in the temple of Jerusalem, with their backs to the sanctuary, worshipping the stars. We have to become God's temples, and his priests. But meanwhile we take refuge with Christ. For the reality of God's indwelling in man is not to be tested by our response chiefly. If we are God's temple where he dwells, we are not so individually only or in mere isolation. God dwells in his holy Church, of which we certainly are parts; but we are not the main substance of it. The Church of God is Jesus Christ and the saints chiefly; it also embraces us, for Christ embraces us. But the reality of God's indwelling is tested by his indwelling in Jesus Christ first, and then by the repetition and continual manifestation of Christ's life in the glorious saints. Here the evidence is plain enough: there is no unreality here.

But Christ and the saints do not stand like the old Jewish priesthood as a screen between the holiness of God and us. We cannot push the duty of being worthy of God's indwelling off on to them. God in his mercy treats us all as one: one body of Christ in which the holiness of Christ, the single-minded devotion of Christ, is found. We are all bound together in that glorious body: Christ's self-sacrifice for us, and his continual prayers for us, hallow us and spread holiness upon us. In like manner the saints pray for us, and we pray for one another. In this whole body of the holy Church God resides.

As for us, the reality of our faith is not tested by our achievement hitherto, but by our repentance now. We have nothing, or virtually nothing, to show in the way of performance: our personal religion is a poor thing. But are we sorry, and are we willing to obey the indwelling God now, with such heart and strength as we have, to identify ourselves with Christ's love of God and Christ's care for our neighbours, to yield to his Holy Spirit? The promises we make to God, though they be sincere, will be forgotten and broken, but the next time we remember, we can repent and renew the offering of our service.

And so it is possible for us to have faith even in a God indwelling us, by virtue of two things: our part with Jesus Christ and the saints in one Catholic Church on earth and in heaven; and our own daily repentance, our constantly renewed submission, our humble prayer and faithful endeavour.

If there are any of you determined to live a more Christian life, there is one resolution you need to make which is, out of all proportion, more important than the rest. Resolve to pray, to receive the sacrament, to shun besetting sins, to do good works – all excellent resolutions; but more important than any of these is the resolution to repent. The more resolutions you make, the more you will break. But it does not matter how many you break, so long as you are resolute not to put off repentance when you break them, but to give yourself up to the mercy which will not despise a broken and a contrite heart. Converted or unconverted, it remains true of you that in you, that is, in your natural being, there dwells no good thing. Saints are not men who store goodness in themselves, they are just men who do not delay to repent, and whose repentances are honourable. The saints have tried God's patience to the utmost, they have explored illimitable mercy; they have found that, through and through and up into the height of heaven, God's terror is the very flame, love burning in a blessed society of equal persons, Father, Son, and Holy Ghost; to whom, as is most justly due, be ascribed all might, dominion, majesty, and power, henceforth and for ever.

26

Walking Sacraments

The Gospel for today shows us John the Baptist under fire. People want to know what he claims to be. They are not content to take his message on its merits. If they rally round him, round whom or round what will they be rallying? Round a man called John, certainly, the son of a priest called Zacharias. Anyone could know that much. But what is this man John? According to Jewish rules he is a priest, because the son of a priest was a priest himself. But all a Jewish priest could do was take his turn at ceremonial duties in the Temple at Jerusalem. And here was John, calling people out from Jerusalem into the wilderness, to consecrate themselves in readiness for a great act of God, a divine event which would involve them all. What right had he to do it? In the past God had given them a King, who had a first claim on their loyalty, being the Lord's anointed; and though the Kingdom had fallen, God had promised to revive the dynasty of David. Was John the promised King of glory? He said he was not; nor was he the promised Prophet, the second Moses; nor yet the reborn Elijah, who must come before Messiah the King. What then? John must say something about himself. He must pin himself down to some fixed position in the great unfolding purposes of God. He must claim some function conferred on him by God's own hand. And so he does, but he makes the humblest, the least pretentious claim which will meet the case. I am, he says, simply that herald-voice which, in Israel's prophecy, proclaims the coming of the Lord. I run, shouting, before his advance, that all may be ready to receive him. But when he comes to his inn, and turns in to lodge, my work is done: I am not fit to kneel before him or ease his travel-worn feet by taking off his sandals. Nevertheless, for all his unpretendingness, John is the heaven-sent herald, he has a place in the scheme of things which obliges all believing men to rally round him and accept his ministry.

John was under fire, he was called on to explain himself: and so it is with the Christian priest today. People want to know what he is, and what he claims to be. Like John, he has a message to deliver, but that's not enough: you want to know why you should pay him any particular attention. Why listen to a clergyman giving you his views on life in general? A student of politics will be more topical, and a philosopher will be more profound. He would be wise, you might think, to stick to theology and Bible-learning. But though he has certainly had some special training there, he has no monopoly. There is nothing to stop a layman from being a more learned and a more penetrating theologian

101

than the priest of his parish; nothing, certainly to prevent a layman from being a much more understanding helper of people in any sort of trouble or sorrow. So when the Christian priest is brought under fire, like John the Baptist, what is he to say of himself? What *is* he when we come down to essentials? What distinctive place does he hold in the mighty purposes of God?

The answer is before your eyes. Here is a new-made priest, and what does he do? He hastens to the altar: he sets forth the mystery of love, the body and blood of Christ, in bread and wine.

You know what is the special mercy of Christ to us in the sacraments. It is, that he just puts himself there. He does not make it depend on anything special in us who receive, certainly not in anything special in the bread and the wine; nor in anything special about the priest either, except just that he is a priest. That's the essential point. Apples don't drop from the sky, they grow on apple trees. And sacraments don't hurtle down here and there like lightning from heaven: they grow on the great branching tree of the Apostles' ministry, the tree planted by Christ when he called twelve men and made them his ambassadors; a tree which has grown and spread and thrown its arms out all through history, to fill the whole earth. Into which tree, by virtue of his ordination, every new priest is grafted.

So, then a priest is a living stem, bearing sacraments as its fruits: he gives you the body and blood of Christ; he gives you, if you faithfully confess before him, Christ's own absolution. And that's not all; the man who bears the Sacrament is sacramental himself; he is, one might almost say, himself a walking sacrament. He is the appointed flag for Christ's people to rally round: the centre of unity to which we hold in every place. Just exactly what a priest is, you can see best in the Holy Eucharist. In a great part of that holy action he is, of course, no more than the voice of the congregation. Some of the prayers we say with him, some we let him say for us: it makes little difference. Or again, in receiving the sacrament, the priest is in the same position as any other Christian, receiving the body and blood of Christ. But there is a moment when the priest steps into the place of Christ himself, to do what Christ did, to bless and to break, to present the mysterious sacrifice before God Almighty. It is much the same in absolution. If you have gone and made your own confession to the priest, you will understand what I say, when I tell you that Christ speaks in him the absolving words.

These moments, certainly, are exceptional in the activity of a priest; exceptional, but still not disconnected with his whole life or character. The man who is as Christ in the Sacrament is not just like anyone else ever: he bears the stamp. He is always, as I said before, a sort of walking sacrament, a token of Christ wherever he is: in him Christ sets up the standard of his Kingdom and calls us to the colours.

It is just this fact that shows up the priesthood so terribly, and makes us, and them too, so painfully aware of their deficiencies. No one's calling or profession shows them up as a priest's does. And indeed, as I began by saying, there is nothing to prevent a priest from being a very ordinary man; most priests must always have been so. Being a priest does not make a man more helpful to his fellow-Christians in matters of wisdom or of kindness; what it does do is give his fellow Christians a right to his services. It might well be (to take another case) that the woman next door to you had greater gifts for teaching small children than the school-mistress; but that doesn't mean you can expect her to teach your little family for you. You've a *right* to the school-mistress's services; she's given herself over to be eaten alive by the children of the place. And so with the priest: go on, eat him alive, it's what he's for; you needn't feel shy of devouring his time, so long, of course, as it's to fulfil a need.

Or again, in matters strictly of religion. Anyone may be a better Christian than the priest, more holy of life, more deeply versed in prayer. But the priest has a special obligation to lead a devout life, to study divinity, to pray; and so to be fit to give some help to his fellow-Christians in these supremely important concerns. Other people may expound the faith, and speak or write in Christ's name, more wisely and more competently than the priest. They *may* do such things, and even do them better; the priest *must*: he must keep the congregation supplied with its staple diet: he must keep giving them some word from God.

I've been talking all this while (have I not?) about the priesthood as 'they', as though I wasn't one of them. But of course I am, and I've been thinking about my own office. And as I talk to you I hope that you will be listening to me as to a priest – that is, you won't just be pulling my (no doubt inadequate) remarks to pieces, but that you'll be listening for something from the voice of God, spoken over my shoulders; for God commends to you, surely, his new-made priest, for you to take him to your hearts; to receive from him the blessings with which he has been entrusted, and to make him your common friend.

There is inevitably something absurd about our priesthood, because what we stand for is so infinitely greater than our poor little selves. But there's the same absurdity, really, about being a Christian at all. None of us can be let off being Christ in our place and our station: we are all pygmies in giants' armour. We have to put up with it: it's the price (how small a price!) paid for the supreme mercy of God, that he does not wait for our dignity or our perfection, but just puts himself there in our midst; in this bread and this wine, in this priest, in this Christian man, woman, or child.

He who gave himself to us first as an infant, crying in a cot, he who was hung up naked on the wood, does not stand on his own dignity. If

Jesus is willing to be in us, and to let us show him to the world, it's a small thing that we should endure being fools for Christ's sake, and be shown up by the part we have to play. We must put up with such humiliation of ourselves, or better still, forget ourselves altogether. For God is here: let us adore him.

preached in Holy Trinity, Northwood,
at Edward Ryan's First Mass

27

You Want to Pray?

'I didn't want a lover yet, but I wanted to want one,' says St Augustine of himself in his teens. When he says this he is looking back after many years, and I suppose he is half aware of making a parable between things earthly and things divine. The teenage predicament which he describes did not last him many months, but all through his young manhood, as he is bound to confess, his spiritual immaturity continued: he didn't want God yet, but he wanted to want him. Well now, it is no use talking about prayer to people who don't want to pray; but before you decide that that rule cuts you out, let me see whether you cannot say at least that you want to want to pray; what a thing it would be, if your heart went out with joy to meet your Maker! If any of you has to say 'I do not yet want' you can still say 'I want to want' and that will do for a start. For God is gracious.

But now what can I tell you? In talking of prayer, we want above all to be realistic; so let us begin with the dead bottom of the subject, and take a ground on which we can all find our feet. To pray is to confront the will of God. Even if you thought that nothing came through from the other side; even if you thought that you had to make all the running yourself; you would still be doing something perfectly real and absolutely necessary, in bringing yourself face to face with the will of God. And sometimes, perhaps, if you are in doubt or despair about prayer, because you start with high hopes and cannot realize them, it might be a help to cut your losses, and be content with simply facing the will of God. It is no trifling thing, surely, to look God's will in the face, and square your will with it, so far as you can. If you had never heard that prayer could be more than this, wouldn't you want to do this, and to do it every day?

A serious atheist might say, 'But now you are simply talking of facing your duty. I can do that; I do it every morning.' Quite right: and what a blessing if he does. But poor man, he thinks of life in terms of duty: we know our lives in terms of God. God is not a prop hitched on to the backside of duty, to hold it up. Duty is merely a bad shorthand name for the mind of God concerning us; and a Christian, on the deeper levels of thought or feeling, has nothing to do with duty. His dealing is with God; and that is why he has the secret of life, and the atheist lacks it. Admittedly we Christians are practical atheists for too much of our time, and see life in terms of duty, integrity, and moral pride: our idea of ourselves, or our neighbours' idea of us. Just so: but since that is so, it is infinitely worthwhile to pray, if only to realize that in all our life it is God's will with which we have to do.

We start, then, with the point of contact: I have to face God. From that point we can spread out in both directions: we want to see to it that what is really I faces what is really God. What is really I! The first thing to get straight here is that I am scarcely real at all. Real enough in one sense, no doubt: look at all this skin and bone, all this largely worthless activity, all this dreaming, all this emotion, much of it bad. But what is that real I which has to meet God's will! It is the willing I, the I who chooses and cares; and *what's* my will? Which way does the current run? The lines of my will are like the tangle of broken and crisscross lines in the palm of my hand, which the clever palmist says she can read; and doubtless God can read the chequered pattern of my unreality. But when I come to pray, I do not come to have my morality deciphered: I come to be pulled together into something more real, and something far more simple.

But if I am to be made more real, I must start from where I am, and with what I am. The only self I can bring to God is the bundle of my choices and desires. Sort the bundle out, and you have the familiar branches of prayer all before you. For what are your desires? They are good, bad, and indifferent. Those that are bad you might have managed to forget (we are all very cunning at that), if they hadn't made their power so plainly felt in yesterday's conduct: examine your life, and you seize them. Needless to say, of bad desires you have nothing to do but to repent, and turn away from them. Some of your desires are good: but they are not nearly good enough, pure enough, strong enough. You have them out before the face of God, and give them some exercise, and acknowledge, with awe, that they are parts of his holy will.

But a great body of your desires are indifferent, neither ignoble nor noble. Do not leave them wholly out, when you come to God, for they are most of you; but talk to God about the things that really concern you, even though they are neither directly to be repented of, nor directly to be made into prayers; but let them find their place, and learn their true proportion, in relation to God's holy will. For he wants you to be a human animal, surely, to play and to enjoy and to realize yourself; only he does not want you to be either a playboy or a drone or an egotist. How do such matters come into our prayers? The natural and happy part of life is for most of us the chief field of thanksgiving to God. Joys we can sincerely give thanks for will not be selfish, nor disproportionate to other concerns.

I say, bring yourself before God, the self of choice, concern, desire. But I have not yet said the most important thing about it, which is this: that yourself, especially in the worthiest part of it, is largely made up of concerns for, and attachments to, other people. Praying for your fellows is not something different from bringing yourself before God: for your concerns for them are half your heart, and you would be a better man, if they were far more than half of it. When you come before God, fix your eyes on him and on those for whom you pray. The more you look outwards, the more you will be yourself. For love is the substance of character, and love self-forgetfulness.

But (I think you will say to me), I couldn't seriously pray for my friends if I thought I was merely exercising my kinder desires, by dwelling on their names with affection. I have to believe that it does them some good. Very well; but you *can* believe it. And now I'm going to surprise, and if possible, shock you. I'm going to talk about spiritualism. What can spiritualistic mediums do? Can they communicate with the departed? No, there is no evidence that they can. But there is so much evidence that it is silly to dispute it, of their receiving into their minds masses of material out of the hearts and memories of the living, with which they recreate the images of departed persons unknown to themselves by ordinary acquaintance. Now spiritualistic mediums are freaks: but they are not absolute freaks. It is very unscientific, indeed, to believe in absolute freaks anywhere in nature. Freaks are special developments of common characteristics. Mind does everywhere flow into mind. How it happens is neither here nor there: it happens. Spiritualism teaches its votaries to make a forced and abnormal use of this power, a use leading to illusion. True religion teaches us the true use of it; and that use is nothing else but intercession. We place our hearts at the disposal of God's will, to spread that influence which he has placed in us in support of our friends' happiness or virtue. We don't have to think a lot of ourselves, or of our spiritual powers, to do that; for influence will flow from us in any case; only, if it is not submitted to God's direction it will be as likely to be bad as good, depressing as uplifting.

I began by saying that prayer would be a great thing, even if we thought nothing came through from the divine side. But you see that in fact you can't believe this blighting negative. As long as your prayers are about yourself, perhaps you can keep it up: *you* repent, *you* face God's demands, *you* resolve, *you* aspire. But when it comes to intercession, it just won't do. Am I to bless my friends? No, God shall bless them, and he shall bless them through my prayers; my little wishes shall become the instruments of his omnipotence. And why not? When I resolve and aspire on my *own* behalf, there is much impurity and darkness in my mind, much adulteration of self-regard in my best endeavours. But when, in the sight of God, you wish well to another, can even the Spirit of God himself get a knife's edge between your wish and his own will? For God is love, and he that abides in charity abides in God.

But when we have seen that God comes through into our prayers for our neighbours, we shall not be able any longer to keep him out anywhere; so, after all, let us pray, with faith that we shall be inspired, for God is in the ground of our hearts.

I must make an end, though I have still said nothing of what may be most important – how we should realize the presence of God and so adore him.

But it really doesn't matter. I meant this to be a useful sermon. But nothing one says from the pulpit on this subject is any great use at all. Only one thing is of use: and that is individual consultation. Are you satisfied with your prayers? Why don't you ask for advice? What can be more natural than to say to a clergyman, may I make a date to come and talk to you about prayers?

Jesus taught his disciples to pray, and his ministry in this regard remains alive in the Church, so long as the Church lives. We must let our Christian friends and Christian pastors help us, that we may worthily perform the first duty of a rational creation, and worship with our heart the Maker and redeemer of our souls.

28

The Day's Work

Family faces was a great game with my aunts. We, their unfortunate nephews and nieces, had to submit to have our features dissected, and given away to various relations we had barely heard of. My nose was not mine, it was great uncle George's nose. My right eyebrow (a bad match to my left) was the property of cousin Hannah Maria – though she was so collateral, it was a puzzle to see how her eyebrow had got on to my head. My aunts might disagree about the true attribution of my several bits and pieces, the one thing they agreed upon, was that none of it was mine – I was a ragshop of patches, I was synthetic to the last drop.

I have heard the same game played with the masterpieces of literature, and even taken a hand in the game myself. St John's Gospel, now, that is a favourite subject for dissection. He got his ideas from the Jewish rabbis – he got them from Greek mystical philosophers – he got them from a sect of half-Christian theosophists – not a bit of it; he got them from the Essenes who wrote the scrolls they dug up by the Dead Sea. The one thing nobody suspects him of having done is think for himself, or turn his eye upon the facts he was attempting to report. But then one listens to a piece like this ninth chapter we have just read, one meets the realism, the shattering force and practicality of it, and one wonders what one has been dreaming of. Here is no repetition of borrowed ideas – indeed, here are no ideas at all, there is just a fact: Jesus heals the blind. The ideas in the chapter are all irrelevances, pushed in by people who cannot face the impact of facts, but cloud them over with words and theories.

The disciples begin it. Here is a man born blind. They want to theorize: Jesus means to act. Was the blindness a punishment for the sins God foresaw the man would commit, or for the sins his parents committed? Jesus says that the blindness is not to be thought of as the effect of guilt, but as the opportunity of grace. It will serve to show the saving love of God. Jesus does not mean that God made the man blind on purpose, so as to have the glory of healing him. What could be more childish? It is more like this – the disciples are trying to relate the man's blindness to the will of God by presumptuous speculations on guilt and punishment. No, says Jesus: this is the way to relate it to the will of God – and he steps forward to heal. Life is too short for such speculation. We must work (says Jesus) the works of the Father who sent me, while it is day: the night cometh when no man can work. While I am in the world, I am the light of the world.

The man is no sooner healed, than fresh ideas are brought in to cloud the issue. The blind cannot now be seeing. There is a confusion of persons. The blind man and the seeing man are different men. And then again: he cannot really be healed, because they cannot understand the method employed, or see why it should work. And then another line of objection – and this is worst of all – Jesus cannot have healed him, for Jesus is not orthodox. Jesus has preferred to heal a sufferer, rather than to keep the Sabbath. Admittedly the man has recovered – it is the inexplicable act of God – but Jesus really had nothing to do with it. In a sense, Jesus agrees. Jesus has no claim and no wish to add anything to the work of God – it cannot be better than divine: he sinks himself in the action of his Father in heaven. But he does sink himself in it: the act of healing is divinely good, Sabbath or no Sabbath. Jesus and his Father are one. If they cannot see that the very thing he is doing is heavenly, then what can they know of God?

Is not God the very Father of light? Uncountable ages (as we now know) before there was an eye to see, light irradiated the field of space, pouring from every star; and the old biblical story, which spanned the whole creative work in the compass of a week, made the creation of light the morning of the first, and the creation of man the evening of the last creative day. So late it was that man came into his inheritance; man, the child of light: for does not man's mind swim in light, as fishes in water, or birds in air? It is true that we have five different senses: but touch and taste reach no further than the organs they employ, smell samples our immediate atmosphere, and sound gives few clear informative reports beyond a range of fifty yards. But sight travels out and back along the paths of light and plots the compass of the universe. Our other senses are chiefly concerned with our fellow-creatures, our food, and our material pleasures. Sight shows us a world of things with calm objectivity, in their own colours and their mutual relations; sight gives us some clue to the survey of that all-seeing eye, which is in truth no eye at all, but the unspotted mirror of an infinite mind, where all things, as well invisible to us as visible, are perfectly discerned and individually loved.

Other creatures beside ourselves have sight, we alone have the mind to enter into our visual inheritance; and though it is truly said that thinking goes beyond seeing, yet it is no mean glory of our mind, or ignoble measure of our scope, that it can stretch to cover the field of light which vision opens to us.

Why, then, if we unlock the doors of darkness, and admit a blind man to the world of sight, is not the work divine? Surely there is no argument; whether it is done by prayer and miracle, or by surgery and skill. I was hearing the other day of a man who, by a sudden infection of his only seeing-organ, went blind in a minute. He could not believe his change; he opened his lids and strained his eyeballs, he groped for the switch and turned on light, but still there was nothing. Imagine it! Or think of the opposite – in our own time living lenses have been grafted on defective eyes, and those who never saw from the day of their birth have, in their grown manhood, possessed the universe of light.

Sight teaches objectivity of view, and steady, appreciative contemplation; we forget ourselves, set aside our prejudices, and let the thing seen passively instruct us. Such is the lesson of light, and yet the lesson is not learnt. The ninth chapter of St John is a sad reflection on human perversity. A man sees: and they will not see it. And so they condemn themselves as blind. For judgement came I into this world, that they which see not may see; and that they which see may become blind, says Christ.

What a reflection on human perversity, and what a rebuke to the Christian disunion, which we are called upon to repent today. Instead of recognizing the work of God where they saw it, the Pharisees applied the test of formal rules. Christ broke the Sabbath. He was no disciple of Moses in the true succession. What example could apply more exactly to the attitude of Christians to those divided from them by empirical allegiance! He is not sound on biblical inspiration. He is incorrect on the doctrine of justification by faith alone. He is outside legitimate Catholic order. And all these things may have their place: but the first thing is the acknowledgement of the work of Christ, wherever it is manifested, in healing sores and making saints. It is divine, it cannot be gainsaid. What can God himself do with us if we will not love, and welcome, and assist the manifest work of God? We can, in the end, commend the doctrines and institutions of religion by nothing else but this, that they are channels appointed to convey, and actually conveying, the efficacious grace of Christ.

The spirit of faction, and of that self-hatred which is the twin of self-righteousness, can so bedevil religion as to make it a form of positive evil, and a blinding of the heart. Where is the man who will see things as they are and allow God to instruct his mind through an unbiased appreciation? He is the man without an axe to grind; and the first thing the world sees in religious believers, is that they are the grinders of axes. They dare not take things as they come, or see things as they are, for fear of disturbing their prejudices or cherished beliefs.

Who can say, surveying the field of history, whether religion, yea, and even professed Christianity, has been a greater cause of blindness and rancour than of charity and vision? I do not think the historical case is worth fighting. But then spiritual truth was never known by counting heads: the saints are our instructors. And it is still true, that the best way to see and to love the work of God in all this world of his is to look for it, and when we see it, to adore. And this, true religion does.

Christ said of the blind man, that his misfortune was an occasion for the word of God to be manifested in him; and that they (that is, Jesus

111

and his disciples) must work at God's work, while the daylight held. How I wish that, every time I am confronted with another man's trouble, or another man's faithlessness, I could remember this truth! It is not something for me to be disturbed by, or discouraged by, still less, annoyed or grieved by. It is an opportunity the heart of God covets, to do his loving work; and he has appointed me, with whatever capacity I have, to be his instrument. So, heaven help me! But the case is really the same, is it not, when I am met by my own faults of character and temper, my failures in religion or in work: a heavenly opportunity for the grace of God! I am not to grieve over old miseries, but submit myself to those healing hands, and give the healer the joy for which he longs.

Above all, we are blind: blindfold in our prejudice, blinkered by our preoccupations, drugged in our self regard: we do not see the glory of God. And above all, God longs to open our eyes. Here at least we know what the cure is. All we have to do is to practise looking through the eyes of Christ: and this is the contemplative art of prayer, when, invoking his aid, we turn over quietly what we know of God or have just read in the Scriptures, and try to see our lives and our neighbours in the light of it, and, what we have seen, to love and to adore.

29

Conscience

So I'm to talk about Conscience. Conscience! What on earth are we to say about Conscience? We can't do with it, and yet we can't do without it. We can't do with it, it's the awkwardest thing. If a man will hear reason, we can hope to make some sense of him. If he takes his stand on conscience, there's no argument possible. It was the custom of a College to which I belonged to admit new Fellows to their fellowships in the College Chapel. But then here was a conscientious atheist. His conscience wouldn't let him promise to be a good boy, or to receive a handshake from the head of the College – not in that accursed building. 'It's all right,' we said to him, 'no one's going to pray at you, and everyone knows you're no Christian. We shall all realize you are merely being agreeable to the rest of us, doing the usual thing.' 'That sounds fair enough,' he says, 'but my conscience is against it.' Surely no one ever took his stand on conscience, if he had a reason to give, for if he had, he'd give the reason. Let us suppose that the Good Samaritan's ass, like Balaam's, finds a tongue. 'Come on, master,' she says, 'you'll be late for supper and I could do with a mangerful myself. What's a roadside accident to do with us?' Can you imagine the Samaritan replying: 'Sorry, old lady, I can't turn the blind eye: my conscience won't let me.' Of course not. He'd say, 'But can't you see the man's hurt? If we leave him there, he'll die.' People don't talk about conscience when they've got a reason. They talk about conscience when they mean to be awkward.

So, as I began by saying, we can't do with conscience. But then, on the other hand, we can't do without it. A man without conscience is too unreliable. He may think very clearly, and even public-spiritedly, when he happens to think, but suppose he doesn't happen to? 'It didn't occur to me that you'd be wanting your bicycle this morning.' 'Oh, didn't it? But didn't you feel a twinge of conscience about pinching it without leave asked?' 'Sorry, I'm afraid I don't go in much for guilty twinges. You see, I was very sensibly brought up.' So if conscience is the very devil, *no conscience* is the deep blue sea. What shall we do between the two? Shall we attempt a cocktail – three of conscience to two of unconscientiousness, with a bit of lemon-peel thrown in? But that's nonsense, surely. Conscience claims absolute authority, if you are to have it at all; you can't tell conscience not to speak out of turn.

No, it can't be a question of *how much* conscience. It's a question of conscience's proper job. It's not conscience's job to do duty in place of reason; what is it, then?

Conscience isn't thought. It's a feeling of guilt or wrongness, connected with ingrained moral habits. And its first function is a warning. It *may* be the right thing to borrow James's bicycle without asking James, but the twinge of conscience reminds you that acts of this sort require justification. Is there sufficient reason in the present occasion for setting aside the general rule? The one thing certainly not justifiable is to set conscience aside without thinking out the case.

Second, conscience comes in at the end of the thinking, to help us judge. Can we feel right, or innocent, about doing what we propose, when we've done our thinking? If not, we'd better think again. Our reasons have got to convince our conscience if we're thinking to ourselves, and they've got to convince our neighbour's conscience if we are appealing to him. That's why we don't state conscience itself as a reason: why should your neighbour feel it right, because you tell him you feel it right? Tell him your reason, and see if he feels it right too, or not.

Third, conscience protects us against self-deception. How easily could Joseph have convinced himself that it would be a charitable action to relieve Lady Potiphar of her frustrations! But still it felt all wrong, and perhaps it was only after Joseph had lost his shirt and run for his life, that he realized why it wouldn't do. Could he betray his master's trust? Could he help the lady break her vows or wreck her marriage? Not to mention his own integrity, or his loyalty to the God of Israel. Conscience is no substitute for thought. It is often a check on superficial thinking though, and on self-deception. And how necessary, for self-deception is a school in which we could all of us take first-class degrees.

But here am I, gassing away like an old Greats tutor on conscience and reason, and forgetting that I was put up here to talk about conscience's witness to God. Well, there are a few minutes still to go, so I'll ask you to wash out everything I've said, and start again, for I'm sure that everything I've said tends flat in the wrong direction. How can conscience witness to God, if conscience is just ingrained moral habit coming back on us in the form of feeling? You can't say, 'There must be a God, for if there isn't, who planted conscience in the soil of our minds?' For it may be quite sufficient to reply, our parents planted it, our infant school teacher planted it. The *fact* of conscience is not an argument with which to convince unbelievers that they have a God – or, to speak less absurdly, to convince unbelievers of the God who has them. Conscience is merely an inculcated rule, a rule which has got under our skin – and who can tell what mayn't have got under our skin? Ah, but that's just it – what may not have got under our skin? And suppose *God* has got under our skin! They will say to us, 'Your conscience, after all, is just a Christian conscience; it's nothing more nor less than faith under the skin'. So they will tell us, and if we're wise we shan't quarrel with that. Faith under the skin! But that's just when faith really is faith – when it gets under the skin. What is more characteristic of faith, than to get under the skin?

There are only two possible testimonies to God. First, that God should testify to himself, and second, that our being should cry out in response to our maker; that our whole existence at every level should give witness of his unique power to penetrate, to possess, and to activate us. Who is to be impressed by God on the lips; by the carefully guarded answers Christians give when they are questioned about their belief? But God under the skin – the divine principle become instructive to the heart – there is a witness indeed.

Not that Christians, any more than other men, are excused the pain of thought, or the exploration of moral dilemmas. The level of conscience or of divine instinct in a saint shows how far Christ's conquest of his heart has progressed. It does not show how that conquest has been achieved. A saint enters into the mind of Christ as alone a mind can be entered or possessed, and that is by thinking; by thinking especially those effortful thoughts of which the expression lies in deeds, not in words, and of which prayer is the nature and the form. But in proportion as Christ's mind possesses his, the conscience guiding a man's immediate acts becomes Christian: the lineaments of his master are expressed in the grace of his conduct, and in the very show of his face. Do we not know what Christian eyes look like? Let us hope we do; if not, we must have moved in a very half-hearted Christian environment.

When you or I attempt to rise above the height of our own heads and to conceive the divine glory, our first thought may well be of the infinite scope, the wealth and variety of that all-comprehending life. But what has impressed the great theologians has been the simplicity, the limpid clarity of God.

Our mind is like the eye of an insect, many-faceted; God's mind is like the eye of an eagle, one clear vision of all the visible. We put together with labour the broken aspects of our ideas; he possesses in one sweep whatever is. So, when our little labouring soul gives witness to God, it goes through separate movements of feeling, speech and act. Feeling is blind, speech is insubstantial, act is cold. But the life is the witness, the life in which they all find their place. The life of a saint is his love for God, which is practical, and warm, and expressive; in tongue, in hand, and in heart. It is not conscience, or reason, or obedience, that is the witness to God. Man is the witness, the saint is the witness; and without obedience, without reason, without conscience, he would not be a saint; for without any one of these he would not be a man.

Such is our life, a prism which breaks the single ray of godhead into partial colours, but such is not God. And where, in the life above all worlds, the Son of God gives answer and testimony to the Father who begets him, there is no difference of heart, hand and tongue. The word which perfectly expresses his understanding is the act of his devotion, which also is the pulse of his being, and the very instinct of his love. He is the faithful witness in heaven, and he is the substance and the bond of our witness on earth, for he unites us with himself in one body by his holy sacrifice.

preached in Pusey House Chapel, Oxford

30

Emptying Out the Sense

Eye hath not seen, nor ear heard,
it hath not come over the heart of men
what God prepares for them that love him.

1 Cor. 2. 9

I was being told the other day about a former Principal of Brasenose who preached to his College once in twelve months, and this is how he would begin: 'The Greek word *allotrioepiskopos*, as I was saying last year,' and so on. It is almost as foolish for me to go on where I left off a month ago, for which of you is going to remember? After all, you are not proposing to do a schools paper on your chaplain's sermons. Nevertheless, I shall commit this absurdity, because we hit on a good vein a month ago, but we did not properly exploit it; so it seems a good plan to revisit the site and see if we cannot dig something more out of it.

The idea, if you remember (but of course you don't) was this. The unbelieving philosphers have been putting up a powerful line of criticism lately against our Christian beliefs, and it seemed that we ought to see what light their criticisms cast either on our beliefs or on our unworthy way of holding our beliefs. We found, for one thing, that they supposed us to be double thinkers, that is, to think one thing on our knees, and something quite different on our feet; and we had to agree that this was only too true, and we spent the sermon reflecting upon that most insidious spiritual disease of double thought. Today we will take up another point of accusation, of which the title is not 'double thinking' but 'emptying-out'.

The point about 'emptying-out' arises like this. You must imagine a theologian – it might be your unfortunate chaplain himself – brought to bay by a ring of savage and keen-scented logicians. 'You say' (thus they begin to bark at him) 'that God is active for your good, that his love makes all things work together for your advantage. But the other day your bicycle skidded and threw you against the wall of a house, and bruised you properly; and today you suddenly got an idea into your head and forgot an important engagement in consequence. Was divine benevolence making the bicycle work for your good when it skidded, or what you call your memory work for your good when it failed you so humiliatingly?' I begin to feel unhappy under such questioning, but (I say) God does work everything for my good, but not in the simple way you seem to expect. He is a very subtle worker, and we cannot always see

117

what sort of good he will achieve for us by his management of events. 'Ah,' the philosophical critics reply, 'God's management of events seems to be management in a highly special sense, almost a Pickwickian sense, mightn't we say? It isn't much like the sort of management we would expect from a good human manager who was really in control. A human traffic manager, for example, who (to suppose the absurd) happened also to be omnipotent, would eliminate nasty accidents. But it appears that God does not do so, either for those who love him, or for those who do not. Some prayer books contain forms for blessing cars; but you do not, I take it, suppose that the proportion of accidents in blessed cars is lower than in those unblessed?' No, I hasten to assure them that I do not suppose anything of the kind. Perhaps, as a matter of fact, I do not hold much of an opinion of the blessing of vehicles. There is a good deal of rust in my car, but none of it is due to the sprinkling of holy water.

'Where, then,' they reply, 'is your alleged faith in providence?' I look down my nose, and wonder how much longer this ordeal is to last, and I say, 'My believing in providence means that whatever happens it will be all right; not that one thing will happen rather than another.' 'Then why', they retort, 'call it a faith in providence, governance, or management? The words sounded quite full-blooded and real when you began, but in the course of discussion you have been emptying the sense out of them bit by bit, until there is no more meaning left; or if there are still a few drops in the bottom of the cup, we could make you empty them out too, if we pressed you a little longer.'

Now I think we have sufficiently recalled what is meant by the accusation of 'emptying-out'. It means that religious language sounds quite full-blooded and ordinary, but when you press the religious believers they empty more and more of the meaning away, until they seem to be saying nothing at all.

Well, I did not do very well against the logicians, because they got me rattled, but you are my kind friends and fellow-Christians so I will relax and take a deep breath and try to explain myself a bit better. After all, it never was much good trying to explain spiritual things to unbelieving men. When I say unbelieving men, I don't mean humble enquirers, whose hearts God has touched. That is another thing.

Well then, about 'emptying-out'. God wants to give us the best thing in the world, a perfect and supernatural good. How is he going to make it known to us? He has to talk to us in the language we already know, the language of earthly things. If he talked to us the language of heaven, how would we ever understand? God takes our words, and uses them: Jesus spoke the dialect of the Galilean peasantry. Inevitably, the earthly words do not fit the heavenly things. The result is a good deal of initial confusion and disappointment. When we begin to learn our religion, we are told that God will answer us in our prayers: that sounds like the promise of a conversation. But when we try to pray, of course we find it is not like that. And how God's Spirit does touch us in our prayers, is a thing no number of words can properly describe beforehand: only God himself can show us that, if we go on faithfully in our prayers, until we find out something of what it is.

Or again, we are promised happiness in our religion. We soon learn to see that we are not assured by religion of the external means to happiness, such as health and wealth. But we may still expect emotional contentment, peace of mind. Yet even these things are not assured to us in the common sense of the words. The greater the saint, the more he feels the burden of the world's suffering and of his own sin; and yet (most strange) in his very suffering, in the opening of his heart to every assault, he is most blessed so.

What shall we say, then? Are the words 'converse' as applied to prayer or 'happiness' as applied to sanctity emptied out by God's actual dealings with men? Emptied out? Are the words emptied out? What was it Christ said of the words of the ancient law? I came not to dissolve but to fulfil. Not to dissolve, to melt away, to empty of sense, but to fulfil, to make full, to pack with all the meaning they could bear.

God promised many things to the Israelites in their ancient religion, things which seemed as human and literal as the promises we give in his name to Christian children now. If they would be good, they should be blest. His presence should go with them, and defend them from their enemies. Their cause was the winning cause, for he was almighty, and in his name they should rule the world.

The Israelite nation outgrew the religion of childhood, but did they pass off the promises of God with bland philosophic indifference? They did not. They adhered to the promises of God, they were crucified upon the promises of God, and in that national crucifixion they crucified the literal sense of the promises in order that God might reveal to them the true and spiritual sense.

The discarding of the literal sense of God's promises is a trivial jest to the unbelieving philosophers, but to us it is nothing less than the crucifixion of Christ. Perhaps that is why we could not answer the philosophers: for how could one say in such a company, 'That's the issue you are talking about: you are talking about the crucifixion of Christ'? Christ did not take the promises of God to be a jest, because they could not be literally fulfilled. He did not say 'In the face of Roman power we can found no messianic kingdom here'. He said: 'In the face of Roman power, which excludes our messianic kingdom in the literal sense, we will see what sort of messianic kingdom God will make.' He kept the words, and God changed the thing, and so we still call him Christ, Messiah, King, but not in the pre-crucifixion sense. He kept the words; and when Caiaphas asked him, 'Art thou the Christ?' he said, 'I am'; and when

Pilate asked him if he were King of the Jews, he did not deny. But God changed the thing. The body of Jesus, first living, then dead, was trussed up and crucified as the guy of literal messiahship, but God placed his true Messiah on the throne of heaven and in the hearts of his believers.

Well, they say, we empty out the professions of our religious faith. And I suppose we do. Not only do we give away too much in debate with the philosophers; we empty away too much in our own minds, we are content to think that God promises us something or other which is good, but there is no need to press very closely the sense of the words in which he gave his promises to us. Not so Christ: he pressed the sense of the words, those words 'Messiah' and 'Kingdom' for example, he pressed them so, that he ran them clean through his heart; and that was how he discovered what they meant, both for himself and for all mankind. He did not empty out the meaning of the words, he lived it out, and found it wonderful; he died for it and found it transfiguring. His fulfilling of the words was not a matter of scholastic exposition, but of death and resurrection.

There is no short cut to the understanding of God's promises. You cannot do it by the wisdom of this world, or by logical sleight of hand. You can do it by active faith alone, by believing in God who has promised, by persevering in purity of life, in constant prayer, in Christ's sacraments, in obedience to every showing of God's will. Then God will reveal to you his excellent things. For, says Christ's Apostle, when in the wisdom of God the world failed by wisdom to know God, it pleased God by the folly of the gospel to save believers. Not but that we speak a wisdom among the fully grown, but a wisdom not of this world, nor of the princes of this world who came to naught. But we speak God's wisdom in mystery, the hidden wisdom which God appointed before the ages for our glory; which none of the princes of this age understood, for had they understood, they would not have crucified the Lord of Glory: but as it is written, what eye hath not seen nor ear heard, what hath not come over the heart of man, the provision God had made for them that love him. And our Saviour says, 'I thank thee Father, Lord of heaven and earth, that thou hast hidden these things from the wise and prudent and hast revealed them to babes, for so it seemed good in thy sight.'

31

Dying to Live

The people we read of in the Bible brought their lamb or their kid to the altar, and there they cut its throat. They held a bowl to catch the blood; they had let out the life, they thought; it was the life they saw pouring red and fast, the life which they took, now the bowl was full of it, and threw against the base of the altar. How merciful was God! By their sins they had forfeited their own lives – God might with all justice claim them in payment – but God had said that he would accept a token payment in exchange; a life, but the life of a beast; a life that belonged to them, but belonged in their flock or in their herd, not in their own pulsating heart. So they cut the creature's throat to let out the life, and that they might signify the giving of it to God, they poured it on the sacred stones. They went away and knew they were forgiven, for God was faithful and just. He had covenanted the mercy, and they had done what his covenant required.

They thought the life was in the blood. Our more exact knowledge of the body teaches us to think otherwise. The blood is a necessary food, an indispensable purifier which replenishes the vital system and carries away the waste; without a steady circulation of the blood life will break down instantly. But the blood is not the life. If by life we mean the feeling, the thought, the action, then if there is one physical carrier of life, it will be a sort of electricity circulating in the nerves, and for ever beating in the headquarters of our nervous system, the brain. We neither think nor feel nor act without the passage of nerve-energy through almost infinitely complicated circuits. What blood was in ancient belief, nerve-energy is in ours. We cannot let it out or spill it on the ground, like blood; though someone might, perhaps, invent a way to drain it off like an electric current, and kill us so. The more familiar method is to let the energy alone, and put the system out of action which produces and circulates it. And there are many hundreds of recipes for doing that. In to-day's lesson Jesus mentions one: 'If any man would come after me, let him take up his gallows-tree,' and carry it to the place where they will hang him on it – hang him until he is dead, and loses his life or his soul; in the language Christ spoke, life and soul being the same thing. For, Christ continues, he who resolves to save his life will spill it, but he who spills it for me and for the gospel will save it.

There is nothing very mysterious about the first half of Christ's remark; it is just hard, cold worldly wisdom. You may treasure and hoard and pamper your precious life as much as you will, and as long as you can, but you will spill it just the same; we shall all come to that last sad scene. He who resolves to save his life will lose it, for death has the last word. Worldly wisdom can see a few inches even beyond this. The resolve at all costs to preserve your life is not merely vain in the end, it is self-defeating all along. Hoarding life is like hoarding money; you get no use of it. It is only by spending your energy with a certain recklessness that you can live at all; if a man lives to a hundred and yet has never *lived*, what shall it profit him? And which of us who reach the age when action is virtually over, will not lament the opportunities which laziness and timidity threw away? Yes, and selfishness too; how infinitely it would have repaid me to have loved the human race with a heroic love, and made the human race in love with me! How can I read the stories of the charitable saints, and not weep to be the man I am?

All this is within the reach of worldly wisdom. Complete unbelievers – Housman for example, the Cambridge poet – quote Christ in this sense, and applaud his insight. It was, says Housman, the greatest of spiritual discoveries that to gain life, to live, we must throw ourselves away; this is what pays. No doubt, but it isn't what Christ means, as Housman might have discovered if he had gone one sentence back in St Mark's text. 'To make a thing of life in this world, live costingly.' You can say this if you like, but what you cannot say is, 'To make a thing of life in this world, take your gallows-tree on your shoulder, come with me to Calvary, and let them hang you there until you are dead.'

When the worldly wise man tells us that it pays us to throw ourselves away, he intends that we should live to enjoy the payment. He knows of course that there is a risk of accidents; live dangerously and you may die suddenly. If you do, it is just too bad; though you can still tell yourself as you lie dying, how reasonable it was to have taken the risk; for after all, nothing venture, nothing win. Worldly wisdom says, 'Take reasonable risks,' but Christ says, 'Come and be hanged'; and that is no sort of worldly wisdom.

In the flower of his youthful age Christ went to be hanged, and he went with his eyes open, inviting his disciples, if they could, to share his fate. An atheist may admire, but he will hardly envy it; and whether he admires or not, he will still not know what to make of the claim, that by so spilling their life Jesus and his followers have gained it. For the life of a man is in the throbbing of his nerves; and though it is an instrument on which a heavenly music may be played; though the music is everything and the instrument in itself nothing; nevertheless, if the instrument is broken, if the nerve-strings are snapped, there is no music; no glory of human life, without a basis of animal existence. And if a man is hanged, he is hanged.

Now we might say that there is a divine compensation; that God makes it up to those who spill their lives; that what is spilt in this world, and soaked away into the ground, and lost past crying for, is treasured in heaven beyond any power of ours to conceive how, and poured into immortal veins, and set to animate the person of our promised glory. There may be such a compensation in almighty power for inevitable loss; but Christ's words do not suggest compensation. It is not like, 'If your house burns down, the insurance company will pay'; it is more like, 'If you want a crop of corn, spoil the grain you have and bury it in the field.' The spilling of life is to be the very means to the attaining of it.

For the life we desire is immortal life, and immortal life must live by an immortal principle. Mortal life lives by a mortal principle, for it aims at the perishable interest of human animals. Immortal life lives by the only imperishable principle there is, and that is the will of God. To have the life of which Christ speaks, it is required that the everlasting will should take the place of the perishable will. And how can a man surrender himself more utterly to the divine will, than by the death of the cross? I try to give myself to God, and so I am sure do you when you pray, and above all when you receive the sacrament. I want to give, and give irrevocably; I do not want to take back what I give to God; but bitter experience tells me that I shall take it back. I promise duties now with a clear desire, but self-indulgence will revive tomorrow and I shall grudge them. I hate my sins now, and promise to forsake them; but my love of them will revive tomorrow and I shall repeat them. If only I could give myself to God past all taking back! But plainly the death of the cross was a self-giving final and absolute; and as it was also entirely free, and gave to the Father a soul unsullied, it was the gate of immortal life.

Here in the middle of the year, with six months either way between us and Good Friday, we are recalled to the memory of the cross; and we may profitably remember how great a part in Christian life, year in and year out, week by week and day by day, the meditation of the Passion has played. Not all the Bible is equally useful to read or to ponder on, and not all parts even of the gospel take us so straight to heaven as do these final scenes. If you have stopped using your Bible to help your prayers, resolve to start again now. Take the Passion of Christ in St Matthew or St Luke, and merely look with all your eyes on one scene at a time. Begin at the upper room; see Jesus give himself away with his own hands to his Father and his friends, in bread and wine that are his body and blood. Go on to the garden, see him give himself again, and confirm his gift in agony of prayer; see him, by standing to the truth of his mission, call death on his own head in Caiaphas's court and in Pilate's. See him, half flogged to death, wear that crown and that robe which assert the kingdom of God's will on earth through mockery and annihilation. See him receive the cross on which he is to die, and see him die on it. Then see if the overflowing mercy which unites you to him will not make something more of your giving yourself to God, if only for a day. We must live one day at a time, but we cannot do that if we do not return every day into the life of Jesus, and above all into his death.

There is a peculiar reason to-day for remembering the Passion. Jesus, as we heard in today's lesson, spread his preaching upwards among scattered Jewish villages, and reached the farthest extent of his northward journey when he reached Caesarea Philippi. From there he turned south, and committed himself to an assault upon Jerusalem which would involve his death – his death, and his resurrection; and he shared his foresight of these things with his disciples. The immediate sequel to his preaching of the cross was a blaze of glory. Jesus took Peter, James and John into spiritual retreat with him on a high mountain; they prayed, and he was wrapped in visionary light. The Godhead shone in him, old saints conversed with him, the Father's voice declared him his beloved Son.

Tomorrow, on 6 August, the Church keeps the feast of the Transfiguration, and learns anew the lesson our lips profess but our hearts forget: that even in the midst of this life the crucifixion of the will is immortality and glory, and the enjoyment of our heavenly adoption through Jesus Christ our Lord.

preached in Trinity College Chapel, Oxford

32

A Christian's Dilemmas

(1) SUBMISSION TO GOD OR MASTERY OF NATURE

The plague broke out at Constantinople. The Christian Emperor consulted the Christian Patriarch and they ordained ceremonies of expiation and of national repentance to avert God's punishment. In saying that the people deserved the divine wrath, the clergy were, of course, on safe ground. The people always do deserve it. No observation can be more safely ventured in any age, than the observation that there is a lot too much wickedness about. But there was a physician in the imperial city who aimed at greater precision of diagnosis. The particular wickedness, he suggested, by which the men of Stanbul had attracted the divine wrath was neglecting the drains: and since it is hypocrisy to confess faults we do nothing to mend, sanitary measures might be more pleasing to God than litanies. Such was the physician's suggestion. Did they agree with him? No, they put him in irons for his impiety. The shafts of plague are the arrows of God. Shall we hope to avert his judgements by cutting his bowstring, or by blunting his darts? No, we must fall on our faces and pray.

The anecdote (which, by the way, is substantially true) puts the matter in a nutshell, and shows that the dilemma which forms my subject is by no means an artificial one. What practical meaning can attach to religion, if it does not teach us to accept the will of God? And once we have got it into our heads that this or that dispensation is the will of God, how are we to set about altering it by our own endeavours, as though it were subject to *our* will, not to his? It was on this point that Karl Marx laid so much emphasis. Religion teaches submission, and what could be more convenient to the exploiting classes? Marx would have liked to say that Christianity was an invention of the bosses for keping the masses down: only he knew too much history to say it. Christianity was then, not so much the device of tyranny, as the expression of servility. Slaves lacking the power or the spirit to revolt conceived a religion, which patted them on the back for hugging their chains.

Was Marx right? He was certainly not plain wrong. Religion as a human phenomenon, like everything human, is good, bad, and indifferent. There has been plenty of bad religion. Religion, as men have conceived of it, has been useful to princes, and consoling to serfs. And superstition, time and again, has paralysed practical action: it has multiplied litanies, and neglected drains.

125

The modern world has turned its back on all this. If we are godless, it is not out of mere pride, selfishness or unspirituality. It is from a practical conviction that there is no rule, but the common good; and no god, but the human will. Admittedly the world is unimaginably vast and largely intractable. But whatever is to be done, we must do; and we have no one to wait for, but for one another. So let's get on with it. Let's plan politics for peace and prosperity; let's harness nature to our safety and enjoyment. An endless task, no doubt, but so much the better. An unlimited prospect, an open hope, an exhilarating aspiration: who can tell where man will stand in a thousand years? In a hundred, for that matter; or, indeed, in fifty?

It must be obvious to you that the substance of this godless view is shared by modern Christians – this godless view, if godless it is. For that is just the point we have to consider. And what are we to say? Is our religion an embracing of God's will? Yes. Does our religion identify God's will with the existing set-up either in nature or in society? Emphatically *no*. Christ came to transform the world, not to conform to it; and the transformation was to be physical as well as moral. It was, of course, useless for Christ or his Apostles to tell their humble contemporaries to set about transforming their physical environment. They had neither the knowledge nor the means. But Christ and his Apostles declared it to be the will of God that the physical world should be transformed – transformed in such a way, as to become the proper habitation and the obedient servant of the spirit. They saw the great change as coming about through some mysterious act of God, which should first shatter the existing order and then renew it.

The author of the Epistle to the Hebrews takes his stand on the principle, that man has been appointed king of the world as viceroy to God, and that all things must be put under his feet. He preaches from the text in which the psalmist says to his God, 'What is man, that thou art mindful of him, or the son of man that thou visitest him? Thou hast made him a little lower than the angels: thou hast subjected all things under his feet ...' The writer to the Hebrews goes on to object that the prophecy is unfulfilled; all things are not subject to the dominion of man. Never mind, he says, they are destined to be so: Mankind, redeemed in Christ, will be the master of the world to come.

Now here we have two prophecies about man's destiny as master in the house of nature: the old Christian prophecy, and the currect secular prediction. They point broadly in the same direction, but they are based on different sorts of evidence. The evidence for the current secular prediction is well known: it is the mounting success of technological science. Since we have done so much, we are confident of doing far more. The evidence for the old Christian prophecy was not any plain empirical fact like this. It was the profound conviction that man, uniquely cast in the image of God, was called to vindicate his maker's glory by mastering all inferior things. The grounds of the two prophecies, then, are certainly different, but they do not stand in any kind of conflict or opposition. Man's power to reason, to understand, and to invent are certainly among those godlike powers which show us to be made in God's own image: the good Apostles, if they visited (and perhaps they do visit) this world of ours, would agree, surely, that it is by our godlike capacities we have triumphed so far as we have over the stubbornness of nature.

Would they say, then, that the movements of material progress now afoot would if realized sufficiently fulfil the hopes with which Christ had inspired his followers then? They would not; they would say that scientific penetration and technical contrivance, though true parts of the divine image in man, were secondary parts of it. The divine image had been branded in their minds by Christ alive, dead, and risen; and Christ was neither a scientist nor an advanced technician; he was a village carpenter, and he was incarnate love. For God was in his flesh. The calling and destiny of mankind is not primarily to rule the lower world: it is primarily to be divinized; to be adopted into union with God, and made one with his heart; and *therefore* to rule with and under God the world which God rules.

Christianity has constantly been digesting new historical situations; there's nothing special in that regard about our own era. The two snakes, Christianity and modernity, are out to see which can swallow which. Faced by such an issue, we are driven back to a scrutiny of our origin in Christ and in the apostolic faith. Again and again we discover that the more true we are to our old title-deeds, the better able we are to meet our present liabilities. And so it is in the immediate case. The gospel which proclaims the triumph of God's image in man can swallow very happily the secular hopes of our time, and assign them their place in a comprehensive faith, which looks for the manifestation of God's glory, the putting of all things under the feet of the Son of Man. The task of our Christianity is to see to it that man shall be truly human, that is, that Christ should have him: for none can be truly human, without being made partaker of the divine.

From so high and splendid a thought we had better descend in conclusion to the practical level. What after all are we to say about a Christian acceptance of God's will? Let us say this. God's will is expressed in two ways: in facts and in leadings. Facts express God's will in the sense that they set us our tasks; and the task is very often that we should alter the facts: our sins, for example, or our neighbour's unhappiness. Nothing forces God's will on me more plainly than your unhappiness or than my sin. There is seldom good reason to accept facts as divine dispensations under which we must simply submit. When it comes to dealing with the facts, we look for divine leadings: we have the words and example of Christ, and of his saints; we have our prayers, by which we seek to touch the living movements of God's present creative work. For he is at work in us individually, and in our neighbours singly, just as he is in the great movements of mankind. And it is men after all, it is the souls he makes immortal, that God supremely loves. What shall it profit men to master the universe, if they have hollow hearts? What shall it profit a man to gain the whole world, and lose his own soul?

preached in Keble College Chapel, Oxford

33

A Christian's Dilemmas

(2) PIETY OR HAPPINESS

I feel myself unlucky to be preaching the last sermon in this series of Christian Dilemmas, for by now, surely, you must have seen the trick of it ... Of course, you say, he's going to begin by pretending there's a dilemma, and then go on to show there's no dilemma at all. Very well then: I give in. Piety *or* happiness? Nonsense. We should enjoy our religion.

Enjoy our religion. I can hardly pronounce the words without a cold shiver running down my spine. I feel the eye upon me – the wicked eye of one of those smooth young professionals who interview unlucky Christians on the air, or on the screen. 'With all due respect, Doctor,' he says, 'I am surprised to hear you admit anything like that. Isn't it just what the critics of your faith say, that religion is an enjoyment, an indulgence in agreeable feelings and comforting ideas, with which believers soothe themselves? No doubt that sort of thing has its psychological value in certain cases, but is not it more important for people in general to be aware of the appalling facts of our human condition? While there are millions starving in Africa,' etc., etc. Whereas, of course, if I'd taken the other line, the interviewer wouldn't have been any better pleased. 'No,' I say; 'religion confronts us with the holy will of God; and the effect is not pleasant at all. It is deeply mortifying.' – 'I realize, Doctor,' he rejoins, 'that what you say is extremely orthodox, but I confess I was hoping you'd give us a fresh lead. To judge from prayers and hymns, there's always been a great deal of groaning about the impossibility men find of being divinely perfect: but doesn't all that tend to discourage us from tackling the vast problems of our human condition. While there are millions starving in Africa,' etc., etc.

As you can see, the young man's trouble is not that he wants tears, and I offer him smiles: nor that he wants smiles, while I offer him tears. His game is, he chooses to assume that religion is bogus: neither the smiles nor the tears are related to reality; and neither of them lead to any useful action.

We might begin, at least, by lumping the smiles and the tears together. No one really believes in impassivity. Great joys and sharp griefs are the healthy reaction of men who expose themselves to life, and open their hearts to their neighbours. The hero of an ancient and famous poem finds himself destitute in a strange city where strange men walk by with impassive faces. He comes to a new building where they are carving on walls – why yes, carving them with scenes from his war, the war of Troy, and carving with a sense both for sorrow and for splendour. They have just cut out the figure of his old king. He exclaims:

> And look,
> Priam! Even here glory her laurel wears:
> Here mortal fates are felt: things have their tears.

The truth is that grief and joy, like hunger and a full belly, have their alternate places in the rhythm of life, and the index of happiness is not found by weighing the proportion between them. The truest evidence of our judgement about happiness may be found by observing whom we most sincerely envy. How can I ever cease to envy that little aunt of mine, the slightest, the least robust of women, who from her youth to her seventieth year carried on her tiny shoulders a weight that might have crushed Atlas himself: the hospital and the whole medical service of a remote Indian town with all the district round it? Shall we pity her the sorrows of her compassion for an evil often too great to do more than touch, or the pains, the dangers of her own body? Shall we grudge her the joys of work achieved, of life saved, of grateful affection outpoured? We may doubt if we have either the virtue or the calling for such a life: but ah, if we had! If we have a calling that is worth pursuing, then so long as we pursue it, our happiness is entire: sorrows and joys can be left to look after themselves.

My little aunt exposed herself to the truth. She was certainly no philosopher, but she was clear on certain points. Christ had died for her, and he had died for the peasants of India no less. The community to which she belonged had missions in those parts, and they were short-handed. She had no need of any more truths than these. She had a call from the living Eternity, which overarches us all; and she had a call from a pinpoint in the Indian map; and the two calls were one. They lasted her her life long. Her hospital did not; as the work grew she rebuilt it twice from her own designs. Her body scarcely did – she nearly died twice from blood poisoning, by operating under impossible conditions, where the proper antiseptic precautions were not available. She survived and her calling lasted her out her working days. She was a humble Christian. There have been more Christians like this than some of you realize.

When we converse in the chilly atmosphere of a BBC studio we are driven to use polite euphemisms, and to talk about 'enjoying one's religion'. No decent Christian wants to talk like that; merely to accept such terms of language is to falsify the issue. What Christians talk about is 'finding one's joy in God'.

We did not see much prospect of joy of any kind, when the aeroplane which should have brought us from New York to London was found to be non-airworthy, and we were faced with a five-hours' delay; nor did we see much mitigation of misery in the second-hand book stall, stocked as it was with manuals of gadgetry, with old chestnuts, cheap thrillers, and bad smells. There was only one paperback I thought I could read, and that was St Theresa's *Interior Castle*; how it got there, goodness knows. And so, in sheer desperation, I found myself opening a spiritual classic. And there it all was, the old plain monastic virtue, set out in the homely phrases of that no-nonsense Spanish lady. It is the same theme essentially as Thomas à Kempis's *Imitation of Christ*; only the style is less biblical and more down-to-earth.

Do you read Thomas à Kempis? You might do a lot worse. You will be moved and awed, but also a bit perplexed. For Thomas and Theresa put the issue of life and death before you in an unfamiliar form. It's a choice between seeking your happiness – your consolation as they put it – in created things, or in God alone. And this sounds like a religion not for a monk, merely, but for a hermit. What is the use of your or my reading a book which forbids us to find our happiness in one another? Thomas à Kempis seems actually frightened of friendship: he is afraid of loving his neighbour better than his God. That, surely, is as unchristian as it is fantastic. What is the use of reading such a book any further? And yet – and yet Theresa and Thomas refuse to be thus set aside: as we read them, we cannot resist the urgency of their plea or the force of their rebuke.

May I tell you my recipe for dealing with these authors? It is to ignore the negative part of their teaching. Never mind the advice about turning away from our fellow creatures. Whoever it applies to, it doesn't apply to me. Let me stick to the positive. My soul must perish if I cannot find happiness – consolation as they call it – in the will of God. How long am I to go on saying: 'I suppose I must do God's will. What a bore! Never mind, I shall still have some time off to console myself with light reading, or games, or social pleasures.' I do not want to learn to do without relaxation: I want to learn to find a delight in the service of my Creator. If I do, perhaps I shall need less relaxation: but that's a secondary point. The main thing is to delight in God and not to be a reluctant, slavish worker in his service. God's will is God himself: it is his love, for he is love. One thing at least I can do when I pray: I can remember that the duty God lays upon me is the means of union with his most glorious life.

If we look further into the writings of our old-time saints, we shall see that their achieved delight in God brought human happiness with it. Theresa's God-given duty is to govern her convent and direct her sisters: and of course she cares for them with all her heart; how could she do otherwise than share the care of God's heart for them? It is another case of 'Seek ye first the Kingdom of God, and all these things shall be added unto you.' Only Theresa has reached this position by a path of abnegation which few are called to follow. It will be enough for me, if I can find consolation in God, and not in creatures alone.

'Happiness or piety' is, certainly, an absurd dilemma. We all set our hearts on something, and there is our happiness: piety is the name for a life which sets the heart on God. Theresa is only developing the saying of Jesus. 'Where your treasure lies, there will your heart be also.' And what a treasure that heavenly treasure is! Once get the lid of that box open, and out flies a very different throng than flew out of Pandora's box: the angels of God's will, leading us through the paths of all good purposes, and so by way of our appointed quests back to our meeting place with God.

preached in Keble College Chapel, Oxford

34

Responsibility for Our Friends

In the year of grace 1929 (always allowing that I remember correctly) I dropped my spoon into my soup. I dropped my spoon into my soup, a fault I do not commonly commit: but then the circumstances were peculiar. I was attending an Old Balliol dinner a couple of years after going down, and was swopping news with my left-hand neighbours. 'How's Philip?' I said, 'I hoped he'd be here.' 'Oh, haven't you heard,' my neighbour replied, 'he put his head in the gas oven a couple of months ago.' I dropped my spoon into my soup. 'Sorry!' said my neighbour. 'Now I'm afraid I've spoilt your dinner.' – 'Oh, goodness,' I said, 'nothing will stop me eating.'

I am going to talk about this, little as I approve of preachers making confessions from the pulpit or using themselves for examples. I am going to talk about it, because I saw the inside of it; and because it was a long time ago. Also because, to get the practical truth out of the business, there will be no occasion for me to squirm about on the pulpit-floor or ask you to judge me as an out-of-the-way young sinner. God knows about that: but the errors and stupidities I committed in the matter were simply those of any well-meaning, would-be pious young man: it might just as well have been one of several of you sitting here. So I will talk about it.

I picked my spoon out of my soup, but though I ate my dinner, I did not greatly care for it, because I kept saying to myself: Oh, why didn't I ...? Why couldn't I have ...? Philip (whose name, of course, was not Philip) had not, as I was well aware, suddenly and inexplicably gone off his head and killed himself; nor was he in the least liable to brainstorms. He had a naturally happy temperament, and a genius for companionship. He was a clever man, who went down with a very poor degree, and without any clear aim or purpose in life. He tried a job he didn't like, and then, defeated by it, went home, did nothing much and saw no one. He was reported to be getting queer. I broke in on him once, and we played chess; played chess and staved off conversation. He cheered up a bit, and said that sometime soon, when he was feeling better, he'd try another job. We left it at that. What was the matter with me, that I couldn't obtain his confidence? What was the matter with me, that I couldn't help him? Lots of things, no doubt, were the matter with me: but it was too late, then, to ask about them. I was asking the wrong question, because I was thinking about myself. Being what I was, I couldn't help him much in an afternoon's visit – and I was tied up

133

elsewhere: I couldn't sit down and lay siege to him day after day, even supposing that would have done any good. But why, for heaven's sake, didn't I talk to Philip's father? I could have told him a lot about his son that could have helped. Why didn't I stir up Philip's other friends to come and see if they couldn't draw him back into life? If your friends are in trouble, you can always do something. You must not shirk your own part of the job; but ten to one it isn't you by yourself who can do what's needed. Very often you and your dons, parents, or other seniors can do little good without one another. If we notice a young man lonely or unhappy or unable to work, very likely our only useful move is to let him alone, and encourage a few of you to take a bit of trouble to befriend him. On the other hand, when you are worried about one of your contemporaries, often the most useful thing you can do is to go to your tutor, college doctor, or chaplain. They can be trusted to be discreet. They are people whose profession it is to be so. I remember I felt a residual schoolboy detestation of sneaking to one's elders; but the price that you may pay for respecting that bit of the schoolboy code is often excessive: Philip killed himself.

But naturally my mind ranged further back. Maybe, by the time we played those games of chess, there was nothing to be done. But Philip and I had been close acquaintances for three years. Why, we had even lodged together for one of them. We were naturally attracted to one another, we had common studies, common hobbies; I should say as a Christian that God had given him to me for a friend. Yet I had watched him drift into a useless way of life. Couldn't I have helped him at all? Well, perhaps I wasn't a very strong character; and it's no use talking about that. But I can see – and this, surely, is deplorable – that religion got in the way. Philip was very nice, and he respected my faith, though he scarcely shared it. He regarded me as a pious innocent, whose ears should not be vexed by hearing what would grieve them; and I acquiesced in this provision for my mental comfort: with the result that whatever it was that was eating out his heart, I wasn't going to know. I thought that if I was to help him, I ought to come the Christian over him, and convert him to a lively faith; but in that mutually sealed-off relationship in which we stood, nothing was more unlikely than my being able to help him in such a way.

How plain a lesson this is, and how hard to bear in mind, that our concern is not with our own holiness, but with other men's happiness, health, or well-being. That is the common pattern. Of course we have sometimes to testify to our faith; but it's an opportunity which springs out of a care for our friend's happiness. I suppose that, in my immaturity, I felt the need to expel from myself certain evils by condemning them in him; but we are not going to preserve our integrity by judging our neighbours: we are going to preserve it by the indwelling of the Holy Ghost.

I suppose (I cannot well remember) that I prayed for the man; but it is not much use in such a case praying for people if your prayer consists in telling God to make them good Christians. We should do better, if we were telling God all the good and delightful qualities he has put into our friend, and were thanking him for them with all sincerity. When you have blessed God for your friend, you can go on to pray for his blessing by God. This is the sort of prayer that breaks down barriers: it is the way to accept our friends as God's good handiwork, and to delight in them. And then, when we talk with them, we mustn't be constantly forcing their thoughts into the mould of our own moral orthodoxy: we've got to take them as they are, to go with them in working out their own way. And that need never mean that we help them in going to the devil. There is good somewhere in every heart, with which we can sympathize: it may not be a good tailored to the pattern of our ideas. What a good man Philip was! Not wise, of course not prudent in making a job of his own career or keeping himself in hand; but how kind, how available, how generous of himself to his friends.

I do not want to suggest to you that you are living in a society of potential suicides or that you are the specially designated instruments of Providence to turn some threatened soul back from perdition. Not at all. But we are all responsible for one another's happiness; and we are bound, as Christians, to pay regard to the providences by which God puts us in one another's way and makes us one another's concern. When Jesus was asked 'Who is my neighbour?' he did not reply with a philosophical generality; he did not say, 'You are a man: mankind is your concern.' He told the story of the traveller, who had a half-murdered man thrown in his path. It is not commonly in such dramatic fashion that God puts us in one another's way: but he does. And now I recall one of my clearest memories of that man Philip, when we lodged together, lecturing me in his very gentle style. 'So and so', he said, 'likes you a good deal. Oughtn't you to take a bit of trouble not to disappoint him! You could be a bit nicer to him, really.'

These are very plain lessons. But they are the foundation of great virtues. What is the greatest height we Christians think to climb? Can we climb higher than the blessed Trinity, to find our place in that movement of mutual devotion which is the pulse of being, and the life of God? And the school of divine love is common charity. He that loves not the brother he has seen, how shall he love the God whom he has not seen?

But now I am sorry I said that we have to climb, for love has come down to us, the heart of heaven is here: and it is with the impulse of the Holy Ghost, and by the leading of the Eternal Son, that we give the Father of our lives our hearts.

preached in Keble College Chapel, Oxford

35

Grace and Resurrection

Last week, when we had given a party, I admired the politeness of our guests, who, occupied as they might be, found time to write us an acknowledgement next morning. So it occurs to me that it is time I thanked the Worshipful Company for the dinner they gave me forty years ago, and which, graceless youth that I was, I never acknowledged in such a manner. That was the last time I was at Mercers' Hall, and the only time previous to this that I had the honour of addressing the Worshipful Company. I still have the dress coat which I got made for the occasion; the moths have had their meal of it, but still I have no other. This I do remember, you gave the very kindest hearing to a boy speaking on behalf of St Paul's scholars; and you will need to be just as indulgent to a man who speaks to you on behalf of your Creator. For I do not need to tell you that all preaching is folly: no one can speak worthily of divine themes. Those who judge a sermon, will always find plenty to criticize; those who listen for divine wisdom, may receive hints of it even from the mouth of a man so unwise as to claim that he speaks in the name of the Father, and of the Son, and of the Holy Ghost.

I will take as my subject, the power of God. Let me explain what I mean by such a title. I do not propose to roll you out sounding sentences on the almightiness of the Creator's will, that will apart from which there would *be* no world at all; apart from which I should have no voice to address you, and you would have no ears to hear me; for neither you, nor I, nor anything would have any being, but for the will and the power of God. A fine subject, no doubt, to preach upon; but not, perhaps, a very practical one. The practical question about the power of God is this; what can we look to him for? If we trust him, what do we trust him to do? No doubt it is very pious, and very proper, to say, that the whole system of nature expresses God's creative will; and that the more we discover about nature's laws, the more reason we have to admire both the consistency and the intricacy of God's ways. That's all very fine; the God of nature can be worshipped, in a dumb and distant sort of way; but how can he be prayed to? And how can he be trusted? If we pray to him, what can we ask him to do? And if we trust him, what can we trust him to perform? Is not he committed by his own consistency to the rules of the system he has created? How can we ask him to act out of order, that he may answer our prayers? How can we rely on him to save our children from disaster, if the disaster is coming to them?

When we pose the practical problem about the power of God, we are not questioning his almightiness. He need not have made this world; he made it: nothing resists his will. But, in view of his commitment (so to speak) to the world-order, what can he wish to do for us, except to let us be swept along in the great process of nature? Suppose a musical composer were conducting his own newly written symphony; and suppose the little man who does the drums were suddenly to put up his hand, and ask to have the score altered – he hadn't a sufficiently interesting part. What could the composer do, but explain to him the structure of the piece? And what answer can our prayers or wishes discover, other than this – to be told to study the way the world goes, and why?

There is the problem, and of course it's extremely familiar: you are already wondering why I should waste so many words in expounding the obvious. Don't we all know that this is where science has got faith into a corner? Yes, no doubt. But there's an odd fact about the scientific position. We think that the success of our great scientific enterprise has tied the hands of God, by committing him to his own laws. Yet in tying (as we think) the hands of the Almighty we have been freeing our own. In one sense, this is obvious: everyone recognizes that a knowledge of nature's laws is a mastery of nature; our knowledge sets us free to do, within limits, what we choose, even if it is to fly to the moon. But not only does science set man free from a thousand age-old shackles; science is also itself a vast enterprise of man's free initiative. The laws of nature do not disclose themselves; they yield their secret to the free endeavours of investigators; to clearly thought-out soundings, and to cleverly thought-up hypotheses. Science is the work of wit, and wit is ours, wit is free.

So here is the puzzle, here is the paradox: the further we explore the law-bound regularity of things, the more we experience the free power of exploration. We, the explorers, are free, however tied up the forces of nature may be. And what are we? We are certainly parts of the world, whatever else we are besides; and if God made the world, he made us, too. It would seem, then, that God cannot be tied down by the pattern of a world-plan he has himself adopted; for look, he made us, and in some of our doings we are as free as air. So God's plans must allow for free operators, after all.

What is more, God's plans do not simply leave room for free operators, they employ free operators in carrying them out. The hand of God is most clearly seen in what is highest and best; that is, in the free flowering of the human spirit. We shall have the whole of religious insight against us, if we attribute the works of nature to God, and the works of the spirit to ourselves; what is more divine than the charm of character, the fire of genius, the steadfastness of virtue, the unselfishness of love? These things are not merely the masterpieces of God's hand, they are the sole revealers of his nature. No one can think that God is any sort of radiation, or of energy, or of physical structure; but if he is not some sort of wisdom, some sort of loving-kindness, some sort of free creating power, then I have no notion what he is, and even the mention of his name is sound without sense.

It is what man is, then, that most clearly shows the print of God; not, however, what man is by nature, but what man freely achieves. Serene wisdom, heroic charity, inventive cunning, these are the principal and most revealing works of God; but none of us has these glories by nature, they are achieved by choice, effort, and freewill.

I want to press upon you the whole force of the paradox, that what is most freely our own is most truly God's, what is most fully our achievement is most entirely God's creation. We make ourselves what we are; but God makes us make ourselves what we are. Men can make dolls and machines: God alone can create creators, yes, and create through their hands.

The highest piece of wisdom which the world knows on this subject is the Christian faith in Christ. The Christ of faith is not some figure remotely supernatural about whom ingenious doctrines have been propounded by theologians. He is the very heart of the present matter. For consider; what do we mean, when we call the man Jesus, Christ and Son of God? We mean that the action of Jesus was simply the action of God. But what was Jesus? Was he a divinely mesmerized sleepwalker, a jointed doll pulled by heavenly wires? Was he a painful pedant, carrying out with pharisaic exactitude a part which had been written for him by a divine hand? He was all the reverse of this. Never was there a man whose words and actions were more utterly his own. The spontaneity of his compassion moves us to tears. The blaze of his indignation shocks us; his speech is an unforced poetry, the coinage of his heart; the sacrifice on which he spent his blood was a decision personally made in agonies of sweat. If any man made his own life, Jesus did; yet what was the impression he left on his friends? That his whole life was the pure and simple act of God. What Jesus did was simply what God did to save us all.

Now what I am saying is that this belief is no extravagance of religious fantasy; it is the most serious established conviction of twenty centuries, that if the action of God is anywhere to be seen it is in the free, the human life of Jesus Christ. The more human it is, the more it is divine; the freer it is, the more it is the will of God.

When we try to think about the mystery of God we inevitably become the victims of our own imaginations. We think about God in pictures or in figures of speech; and presently we find ourselves taking the figures for facts and the pictures for portraits. For instance, we find it natural to think of God as being above us; and this *above* is indeed expressive: it

138

speaks of the height and glory of the godhead, outsoaring our fullest reach of thought. But God is not literally above us, nor need the picture of height become a tyranny in our minds. From another point of view it is useful to think of God as beneath us, his life everywhere underlying us: we are rooted in him, he is at the ground of the heart, at the springpoint of our freewill: we draw our life out of him, as water out of a well; or, better still, we clear the channel of our mind, that the fountain of his goodness may freely rise.

Here, anyhow, is a way of thinking, or of picturing, which may help us to see the life of Jesus as both human and divine: the creative power of God came out in the spontaneity of his freewill. But this is not just something we have to gape at, and worship from a distance in the person of Jesus Christ: it is the model and pattern which we have to follow. The divine power underlies our being also; the wellspring of life is in the ground of our heart, even if the channel is blocked with mud. We pray; that is, we lay our heart upon the heart of God, we surrender our resistances; something of the divine care for our friends and for our own perfection becomes our care; we love a little what God greatly loves and resolve, though feebly, what he firmly wills. This is the grace of God, and everyone who has ever received it knows this: the grace of God does not remove our own initiative. Far from it. The man who receives the grace of God says: Now I am really myself; now I am caring about what I really care about; now I am making a genuine decision. The more it's God, the more it's I: and the more it's I, the more it's God. And it's no use telling us that such a state of affairs is contradictory or impossible. For that's the life of religion: everyone who has tested it knows it to be true.

Is not it about time that we turned back to our original question? I think it is. We asked where, in a world bound (as it seems to us) by natural law, we may trust the power of God to act for us? Well, we have got some sort of an answer. The power of God will act for us in making or inspiring our freewill. In the language of theology, God will give us his grace. If this is a miracle, it is a miracle which is repeated every day in the lives of humble Christians, who repent and throw themselves back upon the sources of life. God will give grace; and if to us, then of course to our friends, and to thousands for whom we are free to pray.

We can leave it to philosophers to puzzle out, if they can, how it is that the system of this law-bound universe allows for God's grace, and for our freewill. We do not know *how* it is so, but we know that it is so, and the knowledge of the fact is enough for plain men to go upon. And if we begin to doubt the evidence of divine grace our humdrum lives afford, then we look to the shining examples of heroic saints, and beyond them, to Jesus Christ himself. Christ's life is the proof that God's power is not bound by laws of physical functioning.

When we have seen that God acts thus for our salvation within the world, we become brave enough to believe that he will also act for our salvation beyond the world. Because Christ's disciples saw that Christ's life was the act of God, they were able to see his death as the act of God, and to see the completion of God's act in Christ's resurrection. I do not know how the life of Jesus, broken and destroyed by crucifixion, was restored. It was not, anyhow, an event contrary to nature: it was beyond and outside nature. Christ's resurrection was revealed within the world; it was no part of the world. And so with the resurrection which God has promised us. It is neither contrary to the natural order, nor in accordance with the natural order: it is clean beyond the natural order; it is a next stage after nature has run her course. The God who made us and all things can continue, renew and enrich our being in another sort of life if he chooses; and he chooses.

If nature cannot stand in the way of God's action within nature, still less can she stand in the way of God's action beyond nature: if God is able to give grace in this present world, he is able to give resurrection in a world to come. So we have two answers, not one answer, to our original question. What does God do for us, in spite of natural order? He gives grace; and he raises the dead. These are the two focal points of Christian faith, the two basic assurances; and if we had nothing else but these, we should have enough.

Yes, if we had nothing else. But this is not all we have. In posing the problem, we accepted for the sake of argument the suggestion that God is so committed to the laws of physical nature, that in the direction of physical events he has tied his own hands. There is no good reason, in fact, to believe that the grid of natural law is as rigid as this, or the mesh of physical necessity so close. The whole world is subject to the infinitely subtle leadings and persuasions of God's good providence. There are many physical blessings for which it is perfectly reasonable to pray: for health, for deliverance from pestilence and famine. Only that such blessings are to be prayed for with submission, and under correction; we do not know whether it is in the good pleasure of God to grant them or not. But for grace, and for everlasting life the disciples of Jesus may pray with assurance; the generosity of God has placed these best of good things ready to our hands; we have only to want them with all our desire, and we can carry them away.

Grace and resurrection are the best of good things: and why? They are a sharing in the life of God himself. By grace, he fills with the inflow of his Spirit the leaky narrow vessel of our heart; by resurrection he makes that heart a lasting and a fit receptacle to catch the overflowing glory of his presence. There light spills evermore from the fountain of light and streams from soul to soul; the more they hold, the more they give away, and all are rich by what each one of them receives; and none keeps back the unforced voice of thanksgiving and joy, the praise most justly due to God in Trinity of persons, Father, Son, and Holy Ghost; to whom he ascribed all might, dominion, majesty, and power, henceforth and for ever.

preached in Mercers' Chapel, London

36

The Bells of Heaven

I remember when I was an undergraduate, browsing about in books which were no proper concern of mine, coming across this phrase in a late mediaeval text: *ad septem horas de clocca*. If that was Latin, I was prepared to eat my hat; but Latin or not, it was the obvious origin of our phrase: at seven o'clock. But how, I wondered, did it come, and what was a *clocca*, anyhow? A little research showed that *clocca* was a bell; and 'seven hours by the bell' may even go back to a time before mechanical clocks: someone being detailed to watch a sundial or an hour-glass, and pull the bell-rope in the steeple when the hour was up. Many of the early clocks were literally *cloccas*, i.e. time bells: interest was still centred on the bell, rather than the dial. I am the proud possessor of a seventeenth-century piece which I may well call a grandfather's clock, since it stood on my grandfather's stairs, as now it stands on mine. It has only one hand, and the face is hard to read; but the hour bell is so strong and clear that it might wake the household if we had not learned, with subconscious cunning, to discount it. But if we should lie awake, there it is, shattering the silence: one; one, two; one, two, three. Alas, the hours are overtaking us, and we are not getting our sleep. Or in the day – there's that bell already and I am still dawdling over my letters; my work is still untouched. The voices of bells impose on us the tyranny of an alien measure, measured to us by the revolutions of the earth through light and darkness. Left to ourselves, we should have our own rhythms, our own periodizations of life: the beating of our pulses, the cycle of hunger, search for food, eating, and round into hunger again; the cycle of curiosity, finding out, delight in discovery, peace of mind, and round to curiosity again. Such are the cycles which life makes for itself, measuring itself by its own rhythm. But no, it will not do, we are not content with these: we put ourselves under the tyranny of an alien measure, and force it upon our own consciousness by these accursed and accusing bells.

But if bells number our hours to us, we cannot really object, for our hours are numbered. I cannot hear the bell more than just so many times, as many as my seventy or so years allow; and then they will ring for me the bell which gives a shorthand or summary of all the bells I have heard, but shall hear no more: one stroke for every year of my life, counting me out, when I am dead. But meanwhile, here I am, alive, and how little use I make of the time which the bells ring away for me, hour upon hour.

The stroke of the hour bell makes us seem impotent and small, in face of the infinite and inexorable procession of measured time; makes us see our mortality and our guilt, as we fail to meet the challenge of the passing day. But not all bells humiliate us, by imposing on us an era not our own. There are bells which have the opposite effect. I remember the armistice day of the 1914 war, when sirens began to blow, and bells to ring. Those bells did not, like a conqueror's curfew, impose an alien time on us. The victory was a new era we ourselves had made. The steeples shook, the bells rent the air, as though to impose our achievement on the world. They did not tell us that we had been overtaken by an era, but that we had created one.

They did not tell us of time relentlessly pacing us, they suggested almost that time, war-time, that is, had ended; as for the peace which spread before us, it was not a race to be kept up with, but a liberty to be enjoyed. So when bells are rung to announce an heir to the throne, the royal mother hears the air humming with the new era to which her body has given birth. In former days, when the priest had consecrated the sacrament on the altar, they rang a bell, so that the busy people in the town might know that the sacramental presence had been once more vouchsafed, and so they might adore. And it is so with Christmas bells, Easter bells: they do indeed mark times and seasons, but their message is not that time has overtaken us, but that our salvation is born. They ring the bells when the bride comes out of church; and it must be a half-hearted bridegroom who reflects – time has overtaken me, my bachelor days are ended, and little I have to show for them. He has his bride to show, and that's enough: let everyone within sound of the steeple share the achievement, the glory.

A carol tells us that all the bells in heaven do ring on Christmas Day; and though it would be childishness to take such language for literal truth, yet symbolically speaking, it seems right. There are glories enough in heaven to rock the tallest steeples; our difficulty might be, to see why they should ever cease to sound, though they would not always please, nor even mean much, without intervening silences. But setting that aside – if marriage, if the consecration of the host are joys and achievements reaching on into eternity, what shall we say of that bridal day, which shall unite our souls for ever to the life of God, and to the company of the saints?

For the other sort of bell, the bell of time, cannot be thought, even by the most wayward and picturesque of poets, to toll in heaven. For, says St John, night there is none, there: no place, then, for bells, tolling out the divisions of day and night, where they have no use of lamplight or sunlight, even, for the Lord God lightens them; their lamp is the Lamb.

The thought of everlasting life often perplexes, or even dismays us: we think we are called upon to concern ourselves in a state where nothing happens, except that, perhaps, we feel ever more deeply, and understand

143

ever more clearly. There is no warrant in Scripture, nor, I make bold to say, in right season, for such a picture. Our immortality cannot be the timeless eternity of God, who infinitely transcends us; but an everlasting-ness suitable to our own nature, such as will permit us, while remaining ourselves to hang on the skirts of God's eternity, and drink the fountain of his peace. Nothing will *happen*, if you like – nothing befall us, or overtake us, like nightfall and the striking hour: we shall not run a race against the ebb of time. Nothing will happen to us passively, but much will be actively achieved: the life we shall draw from the Countenance we shall behold, will inspire us and carry us to splendid actions, glorious creations, happy partnerships: and why should not such works, brought to their perfection, merit the ringing of golden peals?

St John (1.5) says that Christ is a light in the darkness of this world, a light which the darkness never overtook – not, I think, never *comprehended*, as our old version has it: that is not the point in this place. In a sense, Christ was as much overtaken as any of us, by nightfall and the striking hour. Very often, we must suppose, since he was the type of that good Samaritan, who turned aside from his scheduled journeys to heed the cry of need. Darkness overtook him, he fell short of his inn, and camped by the wayside. And yet, it did not *overtake* him, as an alien thing: for he was himself, says St John, the Word by whom the world was made, and through whom light and darkness were both appointed. He was no more *overtaken* by the darkness, than I am *overtaken* by the words I freely speak. His earthly mission, his charitable action, were one with the cycles of the sun and moon; they all went together to compose the single but manifold purpose of God. He did not fret at the passage of time, it did not accuse him of negligence, nor did it mock him for his impotence. He had taught, he had healed, he had journeyed, he had prayed as the time allowed. That his planned journey should fail, all this was carried in the higher plan by which, human choice and heavenly providence concurring, he moved forward to the redemption of mankind and the marriage of heaven with earth. He never watched time running through his fingers: when he still had more than thirty years in hand, he spent them at a single throw, and bought the pearl of infinite price. You can say that, in the end, he embraced darkness: he never let it overtake him.

When I was a boy, my father, wishing to encourage me at once in Greek and in handicraft, and to edify himself at the same time, caused me to carve him a little wooden plaque, with the words, *ERCHETAI NUX*, night cometh; the night, that is, in which no man can work. And this he put under the clock in his study, to discourage him from idleness, a warning, it seems to me, he of all men least needed; and yet, when he came to the end of his life, he would lament how little he had made of it. And so we are all likely to feel. Time accuses us, time, and those awful words, 'We have left undone what we ought to have done' – for God knows what that is. And when we are most triumphant in the sense of having overtaken time, and imposed our achievement on the day, we may have most cause to rue, in our supposed success, the failure to have done the only thing that would have been truly worth while.

If we have to suppose that any souls are condemned to everlasting misery, surely a striking clock will not be left out of the equipment of their prison: the sound of time relentlessly passing, and never occupied to the hearer's content. A life on earth continually overtaken by time, and by remorse, is a pattern of damnation; but if we suffer such a hell on earth, it is only for lack of taking hold upon the redemption so freely offered to us. The Light, which darkness overtaketh not, has shined on our heads: he who commits his soul to Christ is one with the will which made both night and day. He puts himself into the hands of Christ, to live in his will. He will not be perfect, and so he will have many repentances for time misspent; but he will be humble and believing, therefore he will feel no remorse. He will say: I missed this or that from a fellow-being, I followed my pride, or my pleasure, I did not do as you, my Lord, would have done. But you have let me fall into these errors to show me my heart, and you, in your mercy, will use them for my discipline, and turn them to account in the designs of your loving kindness. You have undertaken my life, and you will bring it to good. While we are yours, we shall never be overtaken by darkness; work out in us the purpose of your perfect will and bring us to that day, which will marry us to joy, and ring every peal in all the city of heaven.

37

The Hidden Spring

The Holy Communion is not a special part of our religion, it just is our religion, sacramentally enacted. Of course God is not served only by his celebration of sacraments, but much more by an obedience to his practical commands. But in so far as our religion receives sacramental enactment, it is all summed up in the Eucharist, no aspect of it is left out. For the whole of our religion is summed up in Christ, and the sacrament presents Christ, his birth, death, resurrection, and his present existence: his manhood and his godhead, his being in himself, and the service of his Father.

Since the Eucharist is so many-sided, almost anything may be a fit theme for a meditation in preparation of it. Through Christ we are to approach God, and so we shall make a better communion if we come with an enlivened idea of the God we are to approach. Let us take this most fundamental point. Let us reflect together on the being of God.

I want to find God, to lay my hands, as it were, on the reality of God, to know him not in idea, but in substance. Where is he, then? I am taught to say, everywhere. But how 'Everywhere'? Not like the atmosphere; not like a diffused ghost being flowing through the veins and interstices of things. Rather he is present in the things themselves. The stones of this church exist and are present by the continual effect of God's will. This body that I am, these feeling nerves, this beating heart, this vital breathing, continue and perform those rhythms of process by which my life persists, not of themselves alone, but as the perpetual expression of creative will. Let me pause and collect myself and quieten my busy thoughts, and feel in my own actual being the impress and expression of almighty Godhead. Each moment of my being, added to the last, is a further message to me, a soundless voice of the all-creative act. Let me feel, and listen, and receive in my own existence the bounty of God.

But now, to receive the effects of God's presence and power is still not to know God in himself. I see what comes out of the fountain: I cannot dive back into the hidden spring which is the divine life. Not, anyhow, so long as it is my body to which I attend. It is opaque, a dead end, I cannot look back through it into the power out of which its life constantly arises. Let me turn from my body, then, and think of my mind. And let me think, not of any and every state or act or thought, but rather of this present thought by which I am trying to know God. I have prayed God to guide and assist me, to show me himself: surely he has forgiven me my sins for Christ's sake; surely his goodness is actually here, supplying that thought by which I try to know him. I go on thinking, stringing words, shaping images. Where does all this come from? Out of a hidden depth of mental being, and down at the bottom of the well once more is God's creative power. My thought arises no less than my bodily existence out of the infinite reserves of God's will. O my God, let the waters that spring up be the waters of truth, let them arise out of your predestinating, prevenient grace, for otherwise they will be nothing worth. How can I think truly of you unless you give me the thought?

If, then, this rising fountain of my thought could be very clear and still, like a pool, could I look back into the depth of it, and see the open view in the rocky bottom out of which the living waters rise? How hard, among the stones, to mark and single out the crack from which the overflowing pool is born! But even if I can see it, I can see no further. Everything on this side is me, mine, my thought in its familiar quality and nature. God in the purity of God is all that is below, on the further side of the deep fissure. Even if I can see as far as the springing point, I have only reached the point of transformation at which God's creative act ends and my created action arises from it.

But now let me yield to fantasy. Let me suppose that I can borrow the nature of one of those thread-like transparent creatures of the water which seem only less liquid than the water itself. Let me suppose that I can dive into the vein of the spring and swim upwards against the current into the head of living waters, out of my thought into the will and mind of God.

Let me then swim and pass among those living waters which are life itself. Here I am amidst them where with scarcely moving weight they are passing towards the outlet up which I have come, the spring of my human mind. What are these waters? They are the divine will which underlies my will. Here I find, with penitence and amazement, my own thoughts, thought for me beforehand by God, in all the minuteness of their detail – nothing is too small for him to have forethought it: here are all my acts and ways. But how pure, how sweet, how clean they are in the predestinating grace of God. O my God, you have willed all this for me, and how I have muddled it with my sins! Here I find all the lovely archetypes of what my life has caricatured and distorted, and many noble, saving things so spoiled by me that their effects were never seen on my side, even to myself! O my God, clean out the passage of my fountain, let it be so no longer, O my God.

But let me swim still on beyond God's forethought of my thought and predestination of my ways into the very love from which they came, and explore that ocean of constant well-wishing and inexhaustible patience of mercy which overflows in all these divine intentions for my good. I will let this water flow over me and through me, to be joined with it, to share some part of your care, O God, for my friends and neighbours, yes, and for my own true good.

Can I go still further – can I come to the place from which the whole lake is filled, where a great cataract of waters flows soundlessly down and spreads without foam, falling from no cliff and issuing from no cavern, but constantly self-supplied as out of nothing, out of a bright clear air? God's being is sheer creation, he is all he wills to be, and wills to be all that he is.

But here I will shake myself from my dream, and repent my presumption. All this is vain fancy: what am I, to be able to explore the secrets of the divine abyss? I cannot dive through my fountain into you, O God, from whom I rise: I am condemned to remain here with myself. If there is any traffic between us it must be because you come through to me, not I to you. We cannot come to you, you are beyond our reach: but you can come to us, we are not beneath your mercy. With thee is the well of life, and in thy light we shall see light. The well of the mind is indeed dark, but is there not a thread of light, so fine that it is scarcely visible, rising at the bottom from the fissure of the spring? Let me be still, attend and watch, and see the lights gradually spread and extend, as the light of a candle does in a dark room into which we have newly entered: at first one sees nothing but the single thread of light upon the wick, but gradually the walls and features of the room lift themselves out of the darkness and are more and more clearly seen. So the dark well into which I am looking is mysteriously lighted from below, revealing – and this is wonderful – not the sides and bottom of the well itself, but other images. At first I see, of course, the reflections of what is above the well, perhaps the mass of my own head and shoulders looking down. But no, it is another face, and what is that on the head! I do not wear – no certainly I do not wear – a crown of thorns: sometimes you have given it me to wear, for a while, but I have always pulled it off and thrown it away. What is this pool? Is it not the magic mirror spoken of by St James, into which a man looking beholds the face of his new birth, the image of Christ which he is to be by grace, not the image of what sin grafted on nature has made him? Here is the mirror-image which forms the face that looks upon it, instead of being formed by that face. O my God, to think that I may thus look into myself, and see not that cursed reflection of my own vanity which haunts me, but the likeness of Christ which thou has predestined me to wear! Can it be indeed that if I will faithfully meditate and be still, if I will give my thoughts to thee to shape and govern, thou wilt prefigure Christ in them?

But let me wake from this dream too. God, you are not present to me by any images, any pictures. All pictures lie, all images distort. Why should I strive to figure and represent, when it has been said, Thou shalt not make a graven image? Is it not enough that you, more bright than any image, more full than any fountain, more alive than life itself, are actually here, feeding my soul with your grace? Let me be quiet while I can, and in naked faith receive him who is perfectly invisible and clean outside my range of thought or power to conceive. What does it matter what I tell myself? How am I the better for picture-making? You whom all pictures falsify are here.

And, last, from all dreams let me awake, and act. Do you only feed me while I think of it? Are you not my perpetual, my inseparable, life? Let me thus go, and live out your inspirations. The best way to assure a constant supply is not to gaze into the bottom of the pool but to draw water out and scatter it on the garden, so as to make room for more to flow in below. Be with me, O God, and help me to obey thee in using and spreading abroad thy grace.

preached in St Mary the Virgin, Oxford

38

The Commander's Love

We know an old naval officer, a huge and splendid man: to hear him
blast an incompetent navigator out of his water would be an experience
for the student of invective. I have heard him say – he likes to say it – he
is a man who feels that if a point is worth making, it is worth repeating.
So a parson is not likely to talk to him for long, without hearing
something like this. 'Our chaplain isn't a bad fellow, but he will preach
about the love of God. This sort of thing does a lot of harm. Makes
religion sound so unnatural. A man can't love God, I mean to say.
Perfect nonsense. I love my wife, I honour God and I hope I obey him:
as I do the Admiral, and the Queen. If only the parsons would stick to
commonsense, the men would pay a lot more attention to what they say.'
So says the commander, and one can't help feeling sorry for his chaplain:
the commander is so large and authoritative, and has such a bridge to his
nose, that nose under which the chaplain has to preach, has to preach,
poor man, the gospel he has been ordained to deliver; has to tell the
men, whether they like it or not, that fornication kills the soul; and to tell
the commander, whether he likes it or not, that (since he says he means
to obey God, if he can) the first precept laid on him is this: Thou shalt
love the Lord thy God with all thy heart, and all thy soul, with all thy
mind and all thy strength.

Poor chaplain, he's got to preach the word of God, whatever the
commander says: but how is he to persuade the commander? How is a
man to love the Great Cause of all, the mind behind the universe? He'd
find it hard work to love his wife, if she hadn't got a mouth, and a pair of
eyes. Make her invisible, reduce her to a speaking voice, and she'd be a
queer object to love, even though she had a human mind like her
husband, and sympathies attuned to his. Love goes by kindness, that is,
by kinship. How shall we love a God who is not only invisible, but
inaudible, and at the same time infinitely wise, and great? You would
scarcely have the nerve to tell that hard-bitten old commander that he
can draw a picture in his mind, and fall in love with that: the picture, let
us say, of a fatherly man with a majestic forehead sitting on a throne.
That is just the sort of thing that the commander reckons to be nonsense,
only fit for parsons and schoolgirls. And if you say, but what about Jesus
Christ, he replies, that he respects him very much; that he taught us how
to live, and backed his teaching by his example; but that to us he's a man
in a book, and you can't love a man in a book. At least, ordinary people
can't; it may be different for these literary fellows. And as for imagining

him in the room with you, when you've read what he said, surely tricks like that can't be a necessary part of a sensible man's religion. So says the commander. And now I find my sympathies veering round from the chaplain to his officer; for there is something very straight and candid in what he says, and I feel that we ought to be able to meet him on his own ground. But how can we, since it is written: Thou shalt love the Lord thy God, and not only so: but, 'with all thy heart'.

It does not seem likely that the chaplain will persuade the commander. After all, commanders are unpersuadable, almost by definition. But perhaps, as Isaiah said to his unpersuadable young king, the Lord God himself will give him a sign. The commander, as he quite truthfully boasts, loves his wife, and he might have added, his four children no less. Now it happens that one of these dear beings falls ill, and is in some kind of danger. Then, not by any miracle, but by the ordinary processes of nature and medicine, the patient comes back, as though from the other side of a thick mist. The commander goes to divine service, and they begin saying one of those psalms about the great things God has done for us, and how he brings us back from the gates of death; and that high bridged and venerable nose is filled with tears. It seems one cannot sufficiently love a God who does such things for men; how foolish, how stubborn one has been, to keep him at a distance all these years.

But that is only the moment of sentiment: the hour of reflection follows. If we cannot help feeling the hand of God in the recovery of a dear endangered life, but overflow with thankfulness; why not be equally ready to feel the direct stab of divine cruelty in the boy's falling ill? And suppose – for boys do die – the boy had died? And anyhow we all do die in the end: so what's the odds?

The commander may leave it at that. I must say I should like to think that the chaplain would be at his elbow in that moment of reflection, that he had the commander's confidence, and knew what to say. But how seldom, alas, anything of that kind happens. The commander will probably have to sort it out himself, with the aid of an occasional verse from the psalms. No, says the commander to himself, it's an odd thing: they look the same, but they aren't the same. The bad things and the good things look as though they ought equally to be credited to God: but they don't make that impression. Acts of life-saving belong to him, they come straight from his heart; disaster and destruction are not his in the same way. We find ourselves asking not, why does he do them, but why does he let them happen? Bad things don't reveal a cruel God; they hide us from the God of love. I wish I could make sense of this – the world's such a mixture of bright and dark. If I could see the whole thing from start to finish as a process by which God is saving us, as, in the last three weeks, he has saved my young John, why then – why, then – how I wish the ship's chaplain were there, he would never have a better chance than this to preach the gospel of saving love. For Christ's life, and death, and resurrection, show us this, that through all our existence, and all the circumstances of it, God is drawing us up from destruction to everlasting life. And progress in the Christian way should mean this, that we learn more and more to experience our life as the saving work of God.

The commander could not love God, we remember, because God was great and distant: it was otherwise when the hand of the Almighty touched him. But to the eyes of an enlightened faith, we are never out of the hands of God; every friend is a blessing, every duty a guidance, every necessity a call, every task a divine service. Taking these things right, we are saved from corruption and death, we are lifted to everlasting life, and into union with God himself.

I don't know whether you ever try to read the Book of Job. If so, what do you make of it? It is the description of a mental agony; as for the solution, and the happy ending, one can't help feeling that it has been clamped on by violence, like a happy ending added to *Hamlet* by an old-fashioned film producer. But what of Job's mental agony? For modern taste, it seems too much concerned with a worry about wicked men escaping their punishment, and righteous men failing of their reward: and most of us don't care whether the wicked are punished or not (except of course when the wicked attack us) nor yet whether the just are or are not rewarded (except, of course, when we see ourselves in the role of good men lacking due recognition). But really the whole question of kicks and halfpence is very superficial. It is, of course, meat and drink to Job's comforters, but Job has a deeper concern. Job has loved God, and wants to love him still; even more, he wants to have God loving him. But how can this be? God's love was shown in flocks and herds, in sons and daughters, and no less in the good and useful life he gave Job to live, as a magistrate and a patron of the poor. But one day has carried off the herds, killed the children and brought Job down from the seat of judgement to the dunghill. We can love no other God but a God revealed in his acts; and the love of God to us is itself action, no mere sentiment. Job is as a man whose friend has stabbed him – *Et tu, Brute?* – even now he would love God, if he could see any sense in it, if someone could shown him why God should have done it.

It is no accident that the solution of the plot is no solution of the problem: without the revelation of Christ, there is no escape from Job's dilemma. If we are to love God, we must feel him in the whole substance of our life: we cannot love disembodied ghosts, and the whole world pressing in on us is the body, or better, let us say, the hand, through which God upholds, directs, checks and caresses us. And without Christ's revelation of redemptive suffering, and everlasting life, we should lack the voice which interprets to us the action of God's mysterious hands.

I have asked you what you make of Job – and now I am going to ask you about a New Testament puzzle. Have you noticed how many of the texts about love of God or love of Christ are ambiguous? To take one at random – St Paul prays for his Ephesians 'that they may know the love of Christ, which passes knowledge'. What are they to know? What is this mysterious depth, which can be dipped into, but never plumbed? Is it the love of Christ for us? Or is it the blessedness of loving Christ? Or is it the Christ-love, that is, the love with which Christ inspires us, so that we love all things and all men somewhat as he loves them? Perhaps in this or that text careful reflection will enable you to decide – here it is Christ's love for us – there it is ours for him – and here again it is a Christ-love towards all. But other texts are hopelessly ambiguous. Ambiguous, yes: but why 'hopelessly'? What does it matter, after all? If the sacred writers were content with the ambiguity, it is because they feel no need to distinguish. These three loves are bound together: but the love of God for us comes first. Herein is love, not that we love God, but that he has loved us, and given his Son to be the propitiation for our sins. Once this love is present, and seen, and accepted, our love for God can scarcely fail, for it is his gift; and what form shall our love of God take – we soon come to an end of oh! and ah! – if it does not take the form of sympathizing with his love towards his whole creation, and especially towards those of our fellows to whom he has bound us? There is no great need to distinguish between these three loves: to St Paul or St John divine love is the element in which the Christian lives, and of which the currents flow downward, upward, and outward on every hand.

39

Soul-making

Dons, or anyhow literary dons, are much too interested in words. Sensible people don't think about words except when they can't find the words they want. Otherwise they see straight through the words into the things the words convey. But from time to time we hear a phrase which astonishes us by its oddity and gives us pause. Maybe the speaker has no notion of saying anything beyond the ordinary. What is a cliché in English may be a paradox in French, and *vice versa*. If you remark to an old-fashioned Frenchman that he has, in his later years, got more serious than he used to be, he may reply, *'Il faut enfin faire son âme, n'est-ce pas?'* – As one's day declines, one can no longer put off making a job of one's soul. I should think *make one's soul* to be a mistranslation. No Christian, not even the most ironical Frenchman, can talk about *making his soul*; it goes too near to blasphemy. I take it *'faire son âme'* is more like *'faire les cheveux'*: 'doing your soul' is like 'doing your hair', or, if you are a woman or a certain sort of American, 'doing your face'. You didn't make your features, God made them, but it is up to you to present them in good order. And so with your soul. You must get to work on it.

A limited, down-to-earth point of view, perhaps; but one that has the merit of being practical. There is to be no nonsense about this sort of religion, no waiting for the tide of feeling to flow or the light of inspiration to break. Your soul's a job; get on with it. When I was confirmed there came into my hands a little book of Tractarian provenance containing lists of things one should know for one's soul's health – the three parts of penitence, the four last things, the seven deadly sins, and so on. Among the rest there was the day's spiritual *menu*, which ran as follows:

> Remember, Christian Soul, that thou hast this day
>   A God to glorify, a Christ to imitate,
>   A soul to save, a body to mortify,
>   Sins to repent, virtues to acquire,
>   Hell to avoid, heaven to merit,
>   Eternity to prepare for, time to profit by,
>   Neighbours to edify, a world to despise,
>   Devils to combat, passions to subdue,
>   Death maybe to suffer, and judgement to undergo.

Well, even if I am let off death today and judgement tomorrow, it's certainly an assignment; and when I look through it I don't see which of the items I can hope to skip. So when I do my teeth and do my hair, let me not be negligent to do my soul.

But it's a puzzling task, surely. If a girl does her face, she does it to the satisfaction of the eyes which she glues to her looking-glass; if she can please herself, it is enough – herself, and the mob of friends or acquaintances of whom she is vaguely aware, as looking through her eyes. 'It'll do' means 'It'll do for them' or more narrowly, perhaps, 'for him'. But if I am to do my soul, it is no use making it up to meet my own eyes, still less my neighbours'. I have to meet the unfathomable eyes of God. Merely to look that way, merely to uncover myself to those eyes, is half the business of doing my soul. And then, as to the other half – how am I to do it? What am I to do about it? Does my Maker want me to make up a face, or to put on an act? To profess before him virtuous intentions not grounded in my heart? I cannot make myself as God would wish to see me; I can only, under the look of his eyes, hope to see myself somewhat as he does see me. And how does he see me? With perfect truth, and with all the kindness in the world.

I must do my dressing (*faut faire sa toilette*): I must do my soul (*faut faire son âme*) – if such language is to be endured. And is it to be endured? Am not I unfaithful to my commission in talking so? I should be expounding scripture, not drawing out a Gallic parallel which is popish, profane, and utterly unbiblical. Do you think so? If you do, you put me on my mettle, and you drive me to a text. With the Apostle too it is getting-up time: 'The night is passing,' he says, 'the day is at hand: let us put off the works of darkness and put on the accoutrements of light. Let us go about in good order, as in the day.' – 'Put on the Lord Jesus Christ,' he adds, 'and stop working out how to get the things you happen to feel like.' St Paul's text is very far from standing alone: it is a commonplace of the Epistles, that we have an outward person to array in clothes, and an inward person to clothe with virtues. St Paul does not say *'Fais ta toilette et fais ton âme'* because he doesn't happen to be writing French. But he does say, 'It is the daybreak of the world; put off the night and put on Jesus Christ.'

To put on Jesus Christ is not like dressing to please yourself; it is not like putting on the suit which the shopman persuaded you to think was *you*; it is more like putting on an academical gown, or the vestments of a priest; like accepting a character assigned you by your status, the character of a Christian. But that is not all; for Christ is not a set of lifeless habiliments, only brought alive, as our daily clothes are, by our living ourselves into them. Christ is his own living self; indeed, Christ is life itself. Even when he sees this most strongly, St Paul can hang on to his figure of speech. But it means that the clothes we put on must be seen as magic clothes. Instead of a live man putting on dead clothes, a dead man puts on living clothes which grow into him, transform him, and bring him to life. 'We that are in this tent of flesh,' he says, 'groan under our oppression – not that we wish to throw off our mortal raiment, but to be clothed over, that the mortal may be swallowed up in life.' That is what it is like, to put on the Lord Jesus Christ.

Language here has been stretched until it is tortured; and while the result moves our awe and our amazement, it does not perhaps help us very clearly to answer the question. What do I do to be saved? For how do I put on the Lord Jesus Christ? Try turning back a page from the text I quoted last. You have St Paul already at his spiritual toilette, but this time he is looking into a looking-glass. Here too there is magic. 'We all with unveiled face gazing into the reflection of the Lord's glory are transformed into the same image from one glory to another.' The glass shows us no face of ours; it shows us the face of our glorious Lord. And the relation of looking-glass to gazer is reversed: instead of the mirror-image taking form from the gazer's face, the gazer's face takes form from the image, changed from glory to glory under the radiance of the Lord's Spirit.

After all, then, we do not have to 'put on the Lord Jesus Christ', for he puts himself upon us. When we have found the eyes of God in the magic glass, there is nothing we have to do, so as to 'do our soul' in front of such a mirror; the mirror itself will do our soul.

And now suppose we try to answer the practical question, 'How is a Christian responsible for his own sanctification – for the making of his soul?' What are we to say? From one point of view he is as responsible for it as he is for keeping his bodily man in good order. Unless I do my soul as regularly as I do my hair or my teeth, nothing much is going to happen towards my sanctification. But I am not responsible for my sanctification in the sense that I can sanctify myself by direct action. A woman can do her face, a Christian cannot do his soul like that. He can look into the magic glass and be transformed by the Spirit of the Lord. But once again – if that is all, nothing much will happen, either; mere gazing will not do it. The vision in the glass, as St James reminds us, issues in practical inspirations or commands; and these we must go forth and obey; we are responsible for our obedience. If prayer issues in no resolutions, and if no resolutions are ever kept, little will happen towards our sanctification.

And now, before I end, I ought to say something more about that gazing into the glass of God; for so to talk may sound high faluting and mystical and not for us. Let me explain. We use such high-flown language to do justice, if we can, to the divine reality. This, we must confess, is what is really going on. It is not what we commonly see to be going on, blind as we are. But faith cannot bear to measure God's glory or his grace by our blindness in perceiving it.

We see no magic glass, and attempts to conjure up visual pictures of our Saviour's face are of limited value. The plainest thing I can say is that to look at our Lord just means to talk to him in all seriousness about himself. You might think of him at this season as he actually is – the Ascended Christ who sends the Holy Ghost. You might talk to him about that perfect union with his Father which he now enjoys – union of mind, as well as of heart, of knowledge as well as of will; and the overflowing happiness of simple oneness with the living Truth he had always devotedly served. By talking to him about himself you let him come into your mind – I do not say, into your soul, for he was there already. But as you employ your thought about him in speaking to him, he will become your thought, and you will adore him. Presently you will see what he would have you do, or not do. Make your resolution, and next time you pray, see if you have kept it.

Even now what I have said sounds too ecstatic. Prayer can seem dull or difficult; though if we give ourselves to it, commonly ends up less dull and less obstructed than it began. Only what is dull or dark or laboured on our side is not so on the side of God, who rejoices in every least motion of our good will towards him; and where we see the merest vestige of his presence, there with cherubim and seraphim and all the host of heaven is he.

preached in Little St Mary's, Cambridge

40

A Churchman's Duty

His disciples remembered that it was written
THE ZEAL OF THINE HOUSE WILL DEVOUR ME

John 2.17

I remember once talking to a man who had written a successful play for the London stage. It seemed a miracle to me: I wanted to know how it was done. 'You can't *do* it,' he said, 'just like that. It comes together, somehow, between the writer and the actors: it's half what the author wants to say, and half what the actors feel they can put across. Put an actor in an armchair, and as likely as not he's a rotten critic of your play: all an actor can be trusted to do is act. Give him the lines and start him rehearsing; he'll try the words this way, he'll try them that way, until he gets them how they want to be said. But sometimes, after trying every way he can think of, the actor turns to the author, looking pretty miserable, and says: "I'm sorry, I can't say it. You must alter it." And (said my friend) if he's a decent actor, he's always right. There *was* something false about the lines, they weren't in character, they hit the wrong note, they wouldn't do at all!'

Reading the Bible in church isn't play acting, the last thing we want is stage tricks here, but it presents some of the same difficulties. The reader, like the actor, wants to say the words as they need to be said, and sometimes he gets a mouthful which he doesn't know what to do with. If any of you had been reading this evening's lesson, which is the text of my sermon, and if you had the author (that is, St John) at your elbow, wouldn't you feel inclined to protest: You've given me an impossible task. I can't say these words right. How do I make Jesus Christ drive the market out with a whip of smallcord? It's not in character. My Jesus is all patience and compassion: how is he to flame with intolerance, to act with anger, to throw down the tables, to reach for the whip, to drive the cattle out? It is bad enough (you might say to St John) that you expect me to speak with the lips of Christ at all: to say words which, properly heard and felt, are to break down the heart of man and let God into the world. It is bad enough, that I have to say such things at all: it is altogether too bad, when they just won't say.

If you made your complaint to St John, would he change the lines for you? He would not. He is not writing a play, he is recording a fact, which the other evangelists also record. He won't change a syllable. Very well then, it's only fair he should help us with the interpretation. In what

158

spirit does Christ act? Is he staging a protest against the doings in the Temple? No, that's too artificial: he cannot have planned it all, he cannot have resolved beforehand to register spontaneous indignation. But then, is he caught out, overtaken with anger, carried away from the kindness in which he meant to remain? That seems even less credible.

'The trouble with you,' St John might say, 'is flying off into theories. Stick to the words I have written, and say them just as they come. TAKE THESE THINGS HENCE. MAKE NOT MY FATHER'S HOUSE A HOUSE OF MERCHANDISE. Turn it over on your tongue. Does not it taste right?' Why, yes, it tastes divinely right. It's just – LOYALTY. This is my Father's house; I am his son. I cannot stand by, and see him dishonoured. It must not go on a moment longer. Take all this stuff away. What, you won't? Then I will!

If you and I have not the same sort of loyalty towards our human fathers, or towards our friends, so much the worse for us if we stand by and hear them ridiculed; still worse, if we join in, and add our contributions to the slander. It is extraordinary how we betray our friends, and how we expect them to stand up for us. Or (as we think in our conceited minds) it's not extraordinary at all; for we, of course, are superior persons, viewing mankind from a great height, and awarding our acquaintance praise and blame with poetic justice, or if not justice, anyhow with such charm, that even malice ought to be forgiven us. Whereas if they presume to exercise their wit on us – well, it's a scandal, isn't it. Aren't they our friends?

In our better moments, all the same, we can shed tears of shame for our treason, and see that a grain of loyalty is worth a bushel of malicious wit, or non-malicious wit, at that. It is ignoble to dishonour our friends, and scarcely less ignoble to let others dishonour them. Here's a proverb for you: It is magnanimous to bear insult against ourselves, it is pusillanimous to bear insult against our friends. Jesus was magnanimous, he pardoned insult to himself. They struck him, they spat upon him, and he said not a word. They hammered through his hands, and he said, 'Forgive them, Father; they know not what they do'. They taunted him for hanging on the cross, but he did not reply. That was his magnanimity. But pusillanimous he was not: he did not tolerate insult against his Father, not for a moment. Here was a temple, administered to his Father's name: here the tribes of mankind were to be welcome to their Almighty King. But here, in the place where men of non-Jewish race should have made their devotions, the noise, the profanity of a market; here the priests of God making so much per cent on selling beasts for sacrifice: beasts on which, when they had been sacrificed, the same priests were to feed. Jesus plucked a whip. 'Take these things hence,' he said. 'Make not my Father's house a house of merchandise.'

He did it, and he died for it. And if you had asked him, was it politic?

Mightn't it be mistaken for rebellion? Mightn't it take the bread out of dishonest (or even fairly honest) men's mouths? I do not think that any of these questions would have moved him. There are times when a good man does not deliberate long, or weigh remoter consequences. How could he go wrong, to vindicate the honour of his Father?

Jesus was pre-eminent in the virtue of religion. Religion, properly so-called, is not the whole of our spiritual life: it is not faith, for example, nor is it obedience. Religion is a practical concern for the honour of God: it is in some ways the purest, the most unselfish part of human duty; it does not aim at human advantage, but gives honour where it is most due, and glorifies the King of Glory. If it were possible (which it certainly is not) for a man to know that he would surely die and be everlastingly damned tomorrow, he could not make a better use of today, than in glorifying God, for then, when his light was quenched in misery and darkness, it would at least have shone a moment, before it went out.

And you – you whom he has not damned, but predestined, and called, and justified, and made partakers of his glory in Christ Jesus – what will you do for the honour of God? It is my duty tonight to set before you the obligations of a Churchman; and this is the light in which I ask you, for the present, to view them: as the acts of religion, the claims of God's honour on our loyalty.

The Jesus who threw the traders out of the temple foretold that *that* temple would fall, so that one stone would not remain upon another. After it had fallen in fact, he came to St John on Patmos, and, in the vision of the Revelation, delivered judgement on the new temple which God had raised up in place of the old. For the gospel is everlasting. What Jesus does in the gospel he always does: he still visits, and purifies, the temple. He stands in our midst; and what does he find? Not cattle here, but cobwebs; and by which is his Father more dishonoured? By corruption, profanity, and noise; or by neglect, emptiness and disobedience?

The new temple is not wood or stone: like Jesus its foundation, it is alive. Hear what St Peter says: 'Coming to him, the living stone, ye also as living stones are built up into a spiritual house: for ye are a chosen race, a royal priesthood, a holy nation, a people of God's own possession, that ye may show forth the excellencies of him who hath called you out of darkness into his marvellous light.'

Why compare a mass of people to a temple? What is the sense of it? A temple is rigid, square, clear-cut, a visible block, bearing its purpose on its face, unmistakable for anything else: and unless it has these characters, it cannot witness to God. Pull the stones down and pour them back into the quarry; they may be excellent stones, they will not be a Church. And so with us, whom St Peter calls living stones. As a point of history, let me assure you of this: from the first moment of its foundation, the

Church was hard, clear, visible, and firmly knit: nothing mossy about its edges. Its members professed one truth – they would not have risked death for religion, if they had not been convinced of the gospel. They submitted their lives to the congregation, under the leadership of the ministers whom Christ's Apostles had given them: if they were judged to have given scandal by their disloyal lives, they accepted penances from the Church, they fasted and wore mourning until they were readmitted to communion. They paid for the upkeep of the poor. They were present every Sunday at the Holy Sacrament; if they were absent, they were assumed to be sick, they were enquired after and the Holy Communion was carried to them. Their heathen friends divorced their wives if they were tired of them; the Christians did not. Their heathen friends could make money in any profitable line; the Christians were forbidden a whole list of dishonest or indecent occupations. Their heathen friends rose in the government service; not so the Christians, because of the idolatrous oaths and other ceremonies attaching to public office under Caesar. The lines were clear enough, sharp enough, and costly enough, which silhouetted the living temple of God against a heathen sky.

This was the Church which Christ's Apostles built for the honour of God, and if they did not know the mind of Christ, it is useless indeed for you to think you will ever know it. These were your masters and fathers in faith, whose prayers from heaven you invoke. And what are you? Church of England men: members of a body whose peculiar glory is to combine the form with the Spirit: to say with the Churches of the Reformation what Christ said to Nicodemus: You must be born again; and to keep with the Catholic Church the form of that visible temple, from which Christ expelled the traffickers, and which he rebuilt with living stones, to the everlasting glory of God the Father.

We have the form: bishops, priests, deacons; baptism, confirmation, eucharist; Bible, creed, catechism; commandments, excommunication, absolution; the Christian year, Christian week, Christian day. We have the form of the temple; the outline, the skeleton stands. And Christ comes to visit it. He finds the roof tiles slipped away, the windows broken, and in the walls great gaps everywhere, filled with cobwebs. Where are the living stones – the stones which Jesus himself put in their places to abide? How can God be honoured here in England, with such a universal treason on every hand?

What can we say to the complacent Anglican, who thinks it a matter of private convenience, whether he should even stand by his fellow Christians in Sunday worship? Who calls the creed of his Church in question, and that before unbelievers? Who has never bothered to ask the vicar of his parish, whether there is anything he ought to be doing to help? Who will think he does a very Christian thing, to let the Church marry him, and a very reasonable thing, to let the state divorce him?

Some arguments dry up in the mouth, because they are too obvious to plead. What would you do, if you were told to argue for fifteen minutes that black isn't white? And how am I to spend a sermon in arguing that treason is no true loyalty?

But it is no use, is it, my being one-sided? People who declare with passion that there is no argument on the other side confute themselves: for if there is nothing against them, it's a walk-over; and if it's a walk-over, what are they shouting about? And of course there *is* an argument on the other side in the present case: an argument which embodies a tragic mistake, but is no less powerful for that, to influence men's minds. There is the argument which opposes the form to the spirit: which says that, anyhow in religion, action must be the expression of previous inspiration. I must not profess the creed, because I may not have been inspired with a lively faith in all the articles. I must not accept rules, for fear I should carry them out in the spirit of a slave or of a Pharisee. I must not make it my law to worship God, because it may turn out on any given day, that I have no more prayer in me than an old squeezed orange.

That is how some argue. It is not, of course, how they act. On any given occasion, they do not really say: I lack the inspiration to worship God today; they say, George is driving down to Bognor and he's offered me a place. But then they say: I should indeed lack the inspiration to worship God every week. If I worship him when there's nothing else to do, it will come out about right: in fact, God probably laid George on with his little MG, to save me from trying to worship him too often.

Well, but if I go to church, I'll be bored, and I shall scarcely pray. True enough, you'll be bored; and I dare say your spiritual resources are very limited. You'll be bored: but God will be publicly honoured or – put it negatively – at least he won't be publicly insulted: and you, for his honour, will have endured to be bored. And what will be the effect of your being bored? Don't you see that the effect of it is to throw you back on God? Why are you bored? Where are your spiritual resources? This is to make you know – I must be born again: or rather, since you have been born again, in the fount of your baptism – I must dig away the stony rubbish, and let out afresh the fountain of living waters, which God has opened there, that it might spring up to eternal life.

We are loyal to the form for the honour of God, because he is gracious, because his mercy endures for ever, because there is nothing better that a man can do, than glorify him. But the keeping of the form drives us back upon the Spirit; and the Spirit fills the form with life. Then God walks in his temple, and the house is peopled with cherubim; then heaven descends to earth, and earth is exalted to heaven, in the praises of him from whom all things everlastingly proceed, and to whom they unfailingly return, glory above glory, light beyond light, life uncreated, love immortal.

preached in St George's, Bloomsbury

41
Always Beginning

Shakespeare's foresters, you will remember, found 'books in the running brooks, sermons in stones, and good in everything'. There is a (I suspect legendary) German commentator who remarked how obvious here was the corruption of the text: the words had got transposed. The poet could not have written such nonsense. It must have originally been 'stones in the running brooks; sermons in books' and so forth. There has, I am afraid, been a good deal of emendation of this variety inflicted not only on Shakespeare but on the Bible. Here is the writer of Ecclesiastes saying 'God has made everything fair in its season' (has, that is, in Shakespeare's phrase, put good in everything): 'moreover he has put the world in men's mind, so that man cannot find out the work God has done from beginning to end.' Nonsense, the commentators have said. If God puts the world in men's mind, that cannot be the reason for their *not* tracing out his handiwork. If that were God's good pleasure, he would have taken the world out of men's mind, not put it in. It's all right, though; we have only to give a flick to the tail of a Hebrew letter, and hey presto, the word 'world' becomes the word 'ignorance'. That must be what the author wrote. Though God has made everything fair in its season, he has put nescience in men's mind, so that man cannot find out the work of God from start to finish. Splendid, a resounding platitude. Ignorance leads to ignorance. The sermons are tied back into the books, the stones into the running brooks, and we can all go to bed happy.

But I wonder. Wasn't Shakespeare, and wasn't Ecclesiastes, being a bit more subtle? If God had dumped a simple piece of knitting into our laps, we might hope to see how it goes from start to finish, and go on with the job ourselves. But he has thrown the world into our laps -- and what an assignment! No wonder if we can't unravel it, nor make out the handiwork of God from start to finish, or see what hand we are to take in it. God might not have put the world in our mind. He might have made our minds a perfect blank to everything but a few simple little matters directly affecting us; as is the case, we may suppose, with the beasts of the field. But no, he had to put the world in our mind, and hence comes our bafflement.

It's a stock theme, of course, with the Hebrew prophets and especially the book of Isaiah. The man of God cracks off at us a whole series of rhetorical questions: what do we know? Can we track the wind? Can we weigh the earth in a balance? I get somewhat hot under the collar when these passages are read out in chapel because the reply to so many queries expecting the answer 'no' is now 'yes'. I, Austin Farrer, cannot track the winds, but it's no great mystery to the meteorologists. I cannot weigh the earth in a balance, but an astronomer (or would it be a geophysicist?) is ready to state its substantial mass, which is, I suppose, what the prophet means. I listen to the reading of the prophet's eloquence, and wonder how many of the bodies in chapel will go away with the impression that the scientists have taken over the job of being God.

It is certainly a propaganda nuisance that the unanswerable posers of the Hebrew prophets are physical commonplaces now; but that's all it is. No reflective person can doubt that the puzzles we are aware of are far more numerous and more baffling than theirs were. The more we know, the more we see we don't. And that may be taken to be the point of Ecclesiastes' remark: God has put the world in men's minds, so that man is baffled to find out the work God has done first and last: and the more world he has thrown at us, the more baffled we are. If a modern Isaiah wants to point the lesson of our ignorance, he has only to mention the confines of the universe, or the ultimate constituents of matter: as Pascal said, the infinitely great, the infinitely small. If we go to the moon, we have gone, perhaps, further than the roof of Ecclesiastes' imagined world; but in relation to the ceiling of things, as we now see it, we've done no more than lift our hand to scratch our own heads.

God has put the world in our mind, and so it is that we are always on the threshold of knowledge. The decisive advance is the next step forward, or the step after that; then we shall really have things under control. Even more, God has put God into our mind, and therefore we are always beginning, always on the verge of possession. For here the case is, in a way, even more extreme. Science can cut off bits or aspects from the world and master them: the steps that really matter may always be the steps yet to be taken, but the steps of our previous progress are at least real and our results assured. But God is all of a piece: you cannot take pieces from God and master him bit by bit. And so in our pilgrimage to God we never seem to have made even an assured beginning. All's to do afresh and we have to stretch ourselves for the embrace of the infinite every day anew. The most advanced of saints commonly think that they have got nowhere. Looking back, they see with thankful amazement what God has done in or through them; they see themselves as far as ever from laying hold on God.

Christians must wish to be able to edify their less believing friends by claiming some fruits of religion, some experience of God. But take care; it's a dangerous proceeding and may end in professions very destructive to the person who makes them. It would be better to say, Don't take me for anything more than what you find me: I'm not much of a man, am I?

I'll tell you about a real Christian I once knew. . . . Some undergraduates have made me talk three times this term about how one can pray. Well, thank goodness that's over. It's a fine thing, indeed, for two Christians to talk together about praying. But if one is put up to pontificate about it how can one avoid being put in the absurd position of talking like a man who can pray? And no one can pray, or at least not I, for to pray is to embrace that infinite godhead which God has put in our mind. We are always on the threshold of prayer, and indeed it is a marvellous thing to have been admitted so far, to have a crack of the door open, and half a foot on the sill; but it is always in the future, that we shall make something of the beginning which has been so mercifully allowed to us.

Even the dear Christ who saves us was never in this mortal life further forward than a beginning. I do not say that he made no more than a beginning of knowing God our Father. Indeed no, I do not say that. But Jesus had set his heart on the Kingdom of God – that God's infinite goodness should infinitely and in all things prevail – God's will be done on earth, just as it is expressed in his heavenly mind. And Jesus could make a beginning of it, there and then – the dawn was breaking, the sun would presently arise; things took a mighty move towards the great consummation, when he died on the cross, and rose from the dead. There was opened up a new and living way to God – but still it remained for God's creatures to find it and march up it.

There are people now who profess the Christian name, and who are nevertheless ashamed of heavenly hope. The cry is raised, 'A this-worldly religion'. There *may* be a bonus hereafter – only better not count on it. But I tell you that Christianity cannot for any length of time survive the amputation of such a limb as life to come. For God has put his infinity in our mind, and if we cannot stretch out for him beyond the little beginnings here allowed us, we must let go of God and loose him wholly. For we can only have God, if God has us: and if he will not make a job of us and bring us to union with his glorious infinity, how can we believe that he has taken hold of us at all? What is our salvation, but that we are in the hands of God? And what are the hands of God, if they are weaker than animal death?

This life is always a beginning, no more – and therefore it's heaven or nothing for us. But again – for the same reason, because of the infinity of God – heaven itself is always a beginning: a beginning, indeed, which for those that are there has really and firmly begun: the exploration of a Paradise of which more will always be before us than what we have seen. So that the loveliness we have known always increases our desire for the delight to which it points and leads us on; as we walk the way we are drawn into the very thought and action of God. We sing all too Jewishly of heaven, as a perpetual Sabbath: but the Sabbath was the seventh day; the closure of the week. Shall not we call heaven Sunday, an endless

165

beginning, ceaseless wonder, perpetual resurrection in the unexhausted power of him who everlastingly makes all things new? Be sure of this, there is no coming to the end of God; the more we know of him and his ways, the more avenues will open for futher exploration, or revelation, rather: we may explore God's creatures, but God is known as he bestows himself.

To return to earth – it's the end of the Church's year, and we may well do some self-examination and see how we have spent our time and how we have served our Creator. We shall find that all is to be begun again – who can say we have advanced? But we must be patient. God shapes us by his providence and by our very failures, if we will keep looking to him. He knows that the beginnings he has made with us are not in vain. For it is his good pleasure to give us the Kingdom.

preached in Keble College Chapel

42

The Old Rosewood Desk

Some of you are philosophers, and others of you, when you overhear your philosophical friends discussing, get as far as wondering what it is about. Philosophy seems to be a mental disease which makes people passionately dispute what they perfectly well know; for instance, whether a man is the same person now as he was five or ten years ago.

Still (if you won't mind going philosophically mad with me for a moment) there is something in this question of personal identity which we can all appreciate. Sometimes we get sudden shafts of light on our own past which amaze us, and make us ask 'Was that me?' There is one of those old rosewood desks in my study; I was given it as a boy, but it is so hideously inconvenient to write upon that I have not used it for years. I opened it some little while ago, and shot the spring of that secret compartment which would scarcely baffle the most guileless of pilferers; and there I found a piece of birchbark painted with a fuzzy and ineffective landscape by a childish hand. The hand had been my own. It came back to me suddenly; in a flash I saw the tree with the silver bark peeling off, and felt again the sudden idea I had of painting on it, like a real wild Indian.

That was me. What has it to do with me now? It might just as well have been any other child; nothing runs on from then till now; I no longer try to paint in water colours; I no longer regard it as a prime concern to be a wild Indian. Nothing comes through into my present, except something very general and scarcely personal at all, like a tendency to have sudden foolish ideas, and to act upon them.

But suppose you or I are rummaging, and we put our hands on something rather different. Suppose the hidden compartment in the old desk reveals a card they gave you at your confirmation, where you yourself have signed your name to certain resolutions: to fulfil your baptismal vows, to receive the sacrament every so often, well prepared. Here is something rather different from the painted piece of birchbark. True enough, the handwriting of the signature is scarcely recognizable for yours, and the fact is symptomatic – the way you thought about yourself and your world was different, very different, then. But the undertaking that you then made was not a blind alley leading nowhere, like my birchbark painting. During the moments, the days, the weeks, when you have since been faithful to God any time in these many intervening years, you have returned into the line on which you set your course when you signed your name there. That act was not something broken off short; it stretches an arm forward across a long oblivion, it grasps, it claims you now.

167

Faithfulness, then, is the thing which most forcibly convinces us of personal identity. If we rely on a friend's words, we know that he will not become a different person; for if he did, he might change his mind and let us down. He may become a different person in many ways; he may change his tastes and occupations, many of his opinions; but he will not become a different person in this particular way; not, that is, in respect of his faithfulness to me.

We commonly say that those who have no faithfulness have no character, no constancy of person at all; they seem to hang together by the mere fact of attachment to a single body; that body being destroyed, what is there, what thread of real being, on which God can bestow a share of his own immortal life?

God said to Moses at the bush, expounding that mysterious name by which Israel invoked him, 'I am what I am; thus shalt thou say to the Children of Israel, I Am hath sent me unto you'. Theologians have disputed, and do dispute, the meaning of that oracle. To our modern ears it sounds philosophical and profound; 'I am,' says the Lord, as though he alone had changelessness and eternal being, while of us it would be true to say, not that we are, but that we come to be and change.

But then, again, other theologians say that it is hardly likely Moses should have received so abstract and philosophical a revelation; for what would he have made of it? The Israelites were not metaphysicians. More likely, then, that God's 'I am what I am' was practical, and meant 'You can trust me through and through. What I am, I am; I do not become a different person, I do not desert my undertakings, I do not change my mind about my friends.'

In view of what we have been saying about personal identity, the two ways of interpreting the oracle of the burning bush may not differ so much after all. It is through God's unbreakable fidelity that his changeless eternity of being is experienced by us. He could not be eternal and be faithless: his eternity and his faith are all one thing.

We were thinking just now of the childish token, the card of resolutions we signed at our confirmation; or let it be a page of a notebook that we filled in at the turn of the year (or was it on our birthday?) many seasons back, when we wrote down our repentance and duty to God for the future, and meant to do it. Since then we have changed in so many ways; I do not think now as I thought then; I behave in many ways differently; it is a very different job to me now from what it was then, to attack an intellectual puzzle, or to carry out a piece of personal diplomacy, or to try to fit suitably into a social party; all such things are different jobs from what they used to be. But being faithful to God is still the same endeavour; the thoughts which lie behind those old written resolves and heart-searchings show us in the same posture before God as we stand in to-day. The same words will serve us, the same motions of the heart. This part of us is permanent, this is the immortal soul in us, for this is our fidelity to our faithful God, to him who changes not. Something in us is, not merely comes to be and passes, but is and abides, through virtue of our fidelity to him who thus reveals himself, 'I am what I am.' Having spoken of all the things that change and pass, the childish things and thoughts which grown men discard, St Paul speaks by contrast of what abides: faith, hope and love – faith in God, hope towards God, and love for God. And of these three, that which most directly expresses permanence is that which the Apostle puts first, faith. If love abides, it is because it is a faithful love, as in a worthy marriage. Indeed Christ's teaching about sexual love amounts to this, that without the undertaking of fidelity love lacks the nature of love.

One of the earliest histories of Christian heroism outside the pages of the New Testament is the martyrdom of Polycarp, the old Bishop of Smyrna, on whose head men said that the Apostles themselves had laid their hands. The police took him and brought him before the Governor. The Governor was a humane man and did his best to save his life, moving him to recant. 'Consider your many years,' he said. The persuasion was ill-chosen. 'These eighty-six years,' said Polycarp, 'I have been the Lord's servant, and he has never let me down; and shall I revile him now?'

We do not know what the Governor made of that; but I think if I had been in the Governor's place, and an unbeliever like him, I should have thought poorly of Polycarp's logic. 'Your Lord has never let you down, you say? Well, he has let you down now; you are caught and you are going to the stake.' Having imagined a speech for the Governor, let us imagine one for the old man. 'Let me down! He has not let me down, he is upholding me against my enemies, and he will see me through my torture and my death. He is letting me be tested, indeed; but what would fidelity be without trials, under which to show oneself faithful? There has been testing on both sides, but far more on the other. How many times have I tried his faithfulness by my laziness and self-will! But he has never abandoned me; he has brought me to repentance by his providence, he has assured me of his pardon again and again, he has renewed to me the power of his grace. His faithulness has undergone trials enough; and now mine is to be tried. He has borne with me eighty-six years, and I will not renounce him now.'

Man, knowing that without faithfulness he cannot be anything, looks for a loyalty to which his whole existence, and not part of it only, can be pledged. And who deserves this measureless, this all-embracing faithfulness, except the faithful God? Those childish undertakings, those writings on cards, confirmation professions, have grown dim and somewhat unreal. It is now that we must make up our minds, and pledge our obedience to the faithfulness of God. If we do so, we shall be bringing our former resolves to life by our new decisions. We shall, indeed, bring to life something older than our youthful resolutions – that is, the grace of our baptism, when the resolution was not yet ours, but our parents'; and we shall bring to life something older even than our baptism – Christ's will for our salvation when he died on the cross; and older than that, the everlasting faithfulness of God on which the world was built.

Religion is not self-improvement, or decent conduct or emotional worship. Religion is fidelity. 'Promise unto the Lord your God and keep it,' says the psalm. But the fidelity which is the soul of religion is not our fidelity, it is God's. We give ourselves to him in no reliance on our own trustworthiness. Experience has taught us what we are. Our confidence is that God's faithfulness will prevail over our faithlessness, that he will recall us, that he will not let us go. Our broken resolutions witness against us, but he renews to us daily the miracle of his forgiveness, beause he is faithful to his friends. 'What,' says St Paul, 'if some have proved faithless? Shall their faithlessness frustrate the faithfulness of God? It shall not be.' And he thus expresses the unchangeableness of God's mind towards us. 'If, being enemies, we were reconciled to God by the death of his Son, how much more, being reconciled, shall we be brought through safely by his life.'

preached in Trinity College Chapel, Oxford

43

How Can We Be Sure of God?

There is something absurd, or almost indecent, in the task I have been given this morning. We are here before God's altar, pledging our souls to him: we are considering what his holy will lays upon us, to make our self-oblation an actuality; we are to receive at his appointment the body and blood of his incarnate Son under a mystery of bread and wine; we are to give thanks to him for infinite and inexpressible acts of mercy in our creation and in our redemption. And now in the midst of this we are to pause, and ask ourselves how we can be sure of God at all. What is our predicament like? I will tell you what it is like. Yesterday I had to replace a lamp at a height of fourteen feet in the clear middle of the ceiling; and my stepladder wouldn't reach. For the first time I found a practical use for the bound volumes of the *University Gazette* bequeathed me by my predecessors in office; and balancing a pile of them on top of the steps, I reared myself gingerly up. I had just unscrewed the globe when I asked myself whether I was securely placed. No sooner the question asked, than I trembled at the knees, and came near to losing my balance by thinking of it. Pull yourself together, I said, get on with the job, that way safety lies – and so I did; and so I remain in one piece, to come and address you this morning. I hardly need to draw the moral of the comparison. It is not in looking at our faith that we have conviction of God, but in looking at God, and in obeying him. God can convince us of God, nothing else and no one else can: attend the Mass well, make a good communion, pray for the grace you need, and you will know that you are not dealing with the empty air.

Think of my mother, now – you have known women like her, though few, perhaps, as good – a more unphilosophical thinker it would be difficult to find. Now suppose that in the heyday of my adolescent intellectualism I had told her that she had no right to her fervent evangelical faith, not being able to put together half a dozen consistent sentences in justification of her mere belief in God. What would she have said? She would have told me that admired intellects had bothered themselves with such enquiries, and been able to satisfy their minds: for her part, God had given her faith, and God had never let her down except it was by her manifest fault.

Well, but surely the Warden of Keble isn't going to preach you sheer anti-intellectualism – no, he isn't: you are perfectly right. The centre of your Christian conviction, whatever you may think, will be where my mother's was – in your exploration of grace, in your walking with God.

But faith perishes if it is walled in, or confined. If it is anywhere, it must be everywhere, like God himself: if God is in your life, he is in all things, for he is God. You must be able to spread the area of your recognition for him, and the basis of your conviction about him, as widely as your thought will range.

And now today, on Septuagesima, we think of God's illimitable creation; so let me say something about that. Can I honestly claim to see this mighty spread of galaxies as God's handiwork – as needing him for their existence? I think it is best here to be very modest in one's assertions. I will even begin by something with which a candid atheist ought to agree. It is this: the world raises a question which the world doesn't answer: you can't find within the world an explanation why the world's the way it is. All explanations come back to the laws of nature: but we can't account for the laws. We must say they are what they are, and there it is. Again, all explanations of a present state of affairs carry us back to a previous state of affairs; we never come to a state of affairs which explains itself, or has to be the way it is. Why are nature's laws as they are? And why are brute facts the way they are? There is no answer within the world.

I say that a candid atheist should agree with us. But only up to a point – he will say that the question the world raises and the world doesn't answer is an empty and fantastic question, since it admits of no answer, and we can do nothing with it: it is like those silly questions little children go on asking beyond all meaning and all sense: Mummy, why is that a dog? Don't be silly, darling, a dog is a dog.

So the atheist thinks, poor man, because he is an atheist. Not that we are to pretend that we believers can get behind the scenes of nature, and see God making things be the way they are. Of course we can't. Indeed, if we *could* press behind the scenes of nature, there'd be nothing for us to see. God acts by simple will; and we cannot see the will of God except in what that will has created. There is only one point at which we can possibly touch the nerve of God's creative action, or experience creation taking place; and that is in our own life. The believer draws his active Christian existence out of the wellspring of divine creation, he prays prayers which become the very act of God's will in his will. Because we have God under the root of our being we cannot help but acknowledge him at the root of all the world's being. So it is that, where the atheist sees the search for an ultimate explanation of things as a meaningless 'Why', we see it as the searching out of God's creative power.

I will tell you how to disbelieve in God. Split the evidence up, and keep it apart. Keep the mystery of world's origin carefully separate from your experience of God, and then you can say that the cosmic facts are dumb: they raise a question, they give no answer. Keep the believer's experience of God by itself, and away from the general mystery of

172

nature; then you can say that it's so peculiar, so odd a little fact in this vast indifferent universe, that to attach universal importance to it is too absurd. Then on the other side, be careful to keep the barriers up between the God in you and the God in Christ. Then you can say of your own Christianity (as you must indeed confess) that it's too slight a thing to support the towering edifice of faith. Meanwhile, shutting Christ off in a separate compartment of your mind, you can say that the idea of a God-Man is a mere erratic streak, with nothing to support it in the whole range of experience.

I have told you how to disbelieve. Now I will tell you how to believe. Just do the opposite: pull all these mental barriers down. Where can I be sure of God? In Christ, yes, of course, in Christ: if Christ was not the breakthrough of God showing his hand in a part of the world, where are we to look for it? But is not God-in-man too great a stretch of miracle to be believed? No indeed, for God-in-man overflows from Christ and shows many shining tokens in the saints; and even the clue to what it is, it reveals in our own poor lives. Poor they are, and too thin to bear the weight of evidence: but then they do not stand alone. We see clearly enough that what we have an inkling of, the saints apprehend, and Christ simply achieves. Ah, but is not this whole phenomenon of life invaded by the divine a mere freak in the vast material solid of the universe? Nonsense, the universe isn't solid at all: it is, as a totality, unexplained and subject to the appointment of creative will in all its infinite detail.

We believe in One God, One not only in the unity of his substance but in the unbroken wholeness of his action. All the work of God is one mighty doing from the beginning to the end, and can only be seen in its mind-convincing force when it is so taken. It is One God who calls being out of nothing, and Jesus from a virgin womb, and life from the dead; who revives our languid souls by penitence, and promises to sinful men redeemed the vision of his face, in Jesus Christ our Lord.

preached in the Cowley Fathers' church, Oxford

44

A Share in the Family

– for All Saints Day

There is an Indian story which I suppose everyone has heard – the story of the wolf-children. From time to time a shewolf who has lost her cubs picks up human infants from a village cradle, carries them off and suckles them. Years later they are found again by the villagers, running with the wolfpack and behaving like wolves. There is nothing human about them except their shape. So far the story is always the same story: from this point on the several versions diverge. Sometimes the tale is, that the wolf-children can never be humanized; sometimes it is, that they are slowly and with difficulty educated into being men.

The story of the wolf-children is an unsolved puzzle. Our learned doctors say the thing's impossible, because human infants cannot survive a week on a diet of wolf's milk and raw meat. On the other hand, there are plenty of witnesses to the fact, among others a pair of much-respected Christian missionaries. It's a strange business. Never mind; even if the tale is an invention it's an intelligent invention: it expresses the truth, that without other people we just can't be human. We all lay like idiots in the cradle; and idiots we should have remained, if no one had smiled us into smiling back, or talked us into talking. And if we could have been brought up by wolves, they could have made nothing better than wolves of us.

Christians sometimes talk about Jesus Christ, as though he had walked down from heaven a readymade man, with a complete outfit of true ideas in his head; as though he had only pretended to be a babe in the cradle. But he made a more thorough job of being human than that; he needed a mother to smile at him, a father to talk to him, if he was ever going to be a man. Without Mary and Joseph he wouldn't have been anyone on earth. The divine life came to earth in Jesus, he was the heart and centre of it: but the divine life could not live or act in Jesus alone. The divine life had to use his parents, his kindred and his friends, to make Jesus a man; and had to use his disciples and associates to keep him being a man; for we cannot go on being human, any more than we can get to be human, without other people. What is a painter without colours, brushes, or canvas to use? What is a teacher, without pupils or disciples to pull the wisdom out of his heart? And what can a Saviour be, without souls to attach to God, by attaching them to himself? Jesus could only be Jesus, by having Peter, James and John to be himself with; and he would have been a different Jesus, if he had had different associates, just as you would be a different person, if you were married to a different wife or husband. Jesus became the saviour of his friends, by attaching them to himself: but that attachment was mutual. When it came to his hour of trial, he did not want to be alone; he took them with him when he prayed in Gethsemane, he begged them to keep awake and see him through his agony of spirit. Some of them tried to get near him in the court when his case was heard; Mary and John even stood by his cross. Yet his death, like everyone's death, was solitary: no one can take that last step along with us. Our friends may stand around us, but we shall very likely neither see nor hear them. The moment when we cease to be what we were is the moment which cuts us off from company. But the moment when we become what we are to be, the moment of new life, of resurrection, restores us to fellowship with the living; and Jesus was no sooner risen from the dead than he was among his disciples. He was the first to die of the divine fellowship. Since none of his human friends were in heaven, no wonder if he came to find them on earth.

Jesus was more of a man, not less of one, by having died and risen; he needs men not less, but more, if he is to continue his divinely human life: for now his range of fellowship is unlimited, he spreads himself over mankind.

It was only a matter of months, it seems, until Stephen followed Jesus, and died a martyr; then James – and Mary died, we do not know just when. And so the friends of Christ in Paradise built up to a great company, and meanwhile his friends on earth did not decrease but constantly added to their numbers. Still Jesus is only Jesus by what friendship does in human souls, whether those souls are on earth or in heaven. In heaven – for naturally, those who are joined in one life and action with the Son of God cannot die. How should they die? As Jesus said to Martha, distressed for the death of her brother Lazarus, 'I am the Resurrection and the Life: he that believeth in me, though he die, shall live; and he that liveth and believeth in me, shall not die eternally.'

St Paul, seeing that the friends of Christ are one life with Christ, used a very bold figure of speech; he said that Christ and we are all one body, Christ the head, we the various limbs of it. Sometimes he used a bolder figure still, and said that we are all one Christ. And yet St Paul knew well – no one knew better, that he was a sinful man, a victim to pride and to wayward desire. His part in Christ's body of life – our part in it – is by the overflowing generosity of Christ, who treats us as being what he makes us. We are not the body of Christ because we are good men, but because Christ works in us to make us so.

There is a question I would like to put to you. If ever you come to Holy Communion on a Saint's day, what do you make of it? The collect mentions the saint, and, if he was a martyr, recalls his heroic death. But then, as we go on in the service, we set aside the martyr and his martyrdom; we commemorate a death in bread and wine, but it is the death of Jesus that nourishes us. Where does the martyr come into it? Wouldn't it be better to commemorate him by himself in a different sort of service?

I answer, No. A martyr is only a martyr because his sacrifice was the act of Christ in him, and a saint is only a saint because his life is the life of Christ in him. All the feast days of the saints are feast days of Christ – of the Christ in Francis or the Christ in Bernard or the Christ in Paul. They are what they are by feeding on Christ, just as we feed on Christ; having union with Christ in the Holy Sacrament we have union with all his people, all his mystical body.

And above all, the Feast of All Saints is a feast day of Jesus Christ, the feast of all his glorious actions in the whole of the people he saves. Sometimes we hold a feast in honour of a public performer – a great singer or dancer. We seat him or her by the head of the table, we hear handsome speeches, we drink the toast in wine. It is all very well, but it's an indirect sort of way for showing the distinction of a dancer or a singer. Oh, for heaven's sake, says somebody, let him stand up and sing! Let her stand up and dance! Then in the perfection of the action, in the delight of our ears and eyes, the glory of that person would appear.

So if we are to feast the glory of Jesus – let our imaginations place him in the high seat of heaven, let us raise anthems in his honour. Yet it's an indirect sort of way for showing a Saviour's glory: for heaven's sake, let him stand up and save! There is no need to bid him to do so: see how the vigour of his saving love works through the length and breadth of earth and heaven, how countless lives live by the bonds that tie them to his heart, how the Spirit stirs their minds, his love looks out of their eyes!

Where Jesus is, there is the Communion of Saints: his life never lives, his action never acts, alone: he gives his saints everywhere a part in all of it. Jesus gathered his disciples round him in Gethsemane to pray with him, and they fell asleep. Unsleeping, his saints pray with him in glory, where their whole life becomes a prayer; a holy desire, strong and efficacious, for the fulfilment of Christ's redemption, and the accomplishment of his kindgom; a perfect union of heart and mind with the society of love, of Father, Son and Holy Ghost, three persons in one God.

45

Made to Order

The sermon I am going to preach to you came to me readymade – it drove into the Front Quadrangle where I happened to be standing – drove in on four wheels, and came to a stop in front of my nose: a brisk little van with this inscription painted on its doors, 'Crosses and wreaths made to order.' The driver jumped down, opened the doors, and began getting out all the stuff that had been ordered for the College Ball; and it struck me that a preacher might act in the same way – might play the part of a delivery man, and simply open out what is concealed behind these extraordinary words, 'Crosses and wreaths made to order.'

Crosses and wreaths can be made to order, and that is a very comforting thought; for when something so *un*-made-to-order as death turns up, it is a pathetic sort of consolation for us to switch our attention on to something that can be made to order. Death cannot be called to order, or got under control by us; the souls of the righteous, and of the unrighteous too, are in the hands of God, not in our hands; but we can get crosses and wreaths supplied to our order. So what shall we order? We think a cross of violets would be just right, to express the modest fragrance of a sacrificial life. And for a wreath, what could be better than white roses; the noblest of flowers, in the purest of colours? For the wreath is a symbol of everlasting reward. We make our own choice of shapes and flowers; and floral emblems will be made to order. The florist's girls will do overtime, rather than be late for the sudden event; but the things for which wreaths and crosses stand, those things cannot be made to order. It is too late for us to supply crosses in death, if the crosses supplied by providence were shaken impatiently from the living shoulder; and it is premature for us to order wreaths, if the word has not gone forth on high, 'I give thee the garland of everlasting life.'

All this is obvious enough; the moral of *crosses and wreaths made to order* is sad and evident, if we place ouselves at the fatal moment which the florist's advertisement is intended to exploit. But how if we place ourselves at an earlier moment, the moment which is still our own, we that are alive and have every intention to live? Can we not still hope to have our crosses, and our heavenly garlands, made to order? Put it like that, it sounds ridiculous; every one of us would deny that we ever dreamt of ordering our own crosses on earth, or our own garlands in heaven. But I wonder if we are as innocent of this monstrosity as we suppose we are? If you are at all like me, there are many occasions on which you do not let the right lobe of your brain know what the left lobe thinketh. Let us try to help the human mind – yours, or mine, or anyone's, to overhear itself for once. I only ask you to listen and see whether what I am going to say is your mind talking, or not.

Well then, here you are, ordering your own garland from the heavenly store. 'I am sure,' you say comfortably to yourself, 'that there are crowns above of the highest splendour, a glory round human faces filled with God. But not for me. I am not called to be a saint; I am called to be a decent, godfearing person, hurting no one, helpful here or there, and keeping the rules. They will not shut the door of heaven in my face; they will acknowledge my solid, though unpretentious merit with a slight circlet of gold, and give me comfortable, busy things to do at a convenient distance from that intolerable gulf of light which opens in the heart of heaven.'

If such is indeed your unspoken thought, then are you ordering your own wreath, or are you not? What you would wish to say, perhaps, is that you are merely telling yourself the facts about yourself; but are you sure you didn't make up the facts? Who assured you of your limited calling, your mild and unexacting reward? When people order wreaths from florists' shops, it is observed that, after much show of choice and personal decisions, they ask in the end for what is conventionally reckoned good taste: the very thing that Mrs Jones ordered last year, and not much different from what Lady Smith sent a fortnight ago. So with these modest wreaths, these limited ideals of achievement and reward we design for ourselves: what do they represent but the prevailing taste, the way of the world? And what, in fact, is that wreath like which, beyond and above our fashions and choices, has been chosen for us by him who died for us, and held out to us by nail-pierced hands?

One of the chief points I bear in mind when I am so modest in choosing a wreath, is that my wreath must not put my cross to shame, they must look well side by side; for of course if there is one thing I am clear about, it is that I can't afford myself an expensive cross. And the wreath mustn't look more splendid than the cross deserves. You can't be too careful about ordering your crosses; plan your little heroisms, and carry them out to your own admiration; but keep out of situations in which you are liable to be caught off your guard by unexpected trials, by crosses too heavy to bear, or, what is even more humiliating, by crosses too light to be borne: little undignified crosses, supplied unexpectedly when handsomer ones had been ordered: nasty little 'heads I win, tails you lose' sort of things; for there is not visible dignity in bearing them, and a terrible loss of dignity in failing to carry them with gentleness.

Well, but can you really choose your crosses? From whose hands, in fact, do crosses come? And for whose sake are you going to bear them? For your own credit's sake, or for the sake of him who lays them on your shoulder? And if for his sake, must they not be what he assigns? We cannot, surely, be so childish as to do to God what children do to us, and imagine we are helping, while we work at the tasks we want to do, not at the tasks he wants to have done. All too often this is what children call 'helping mother', but it is not what Christ calls either loving God, or obeying him; for as to 'helping God', that is scarcely an expression we should ever dare to use.

Crosses are never what we ordered, but always either greater than we ordered, smaller than we ordered, or other than we ordered – and it does not matter which; for God measures the love with which they are carried, and not for the poundage of each particular weight. Wreaths are never what we ordered, either; but, unlike crosses, the wreaths all have the same fault – they are all ridiculously big and splendid; because God's thoughts are not as our thoughts, and he prepares for man such good things as pass man's understanding. So the wreaths he orders for us throw into the shade all the crosses he assigns us, and it becomes painfully obvious that our crosses will never deserve our crowns. If you want to see a wreath and a cross to match it, you must go as far as the empty sepulchre outside Jerusalem; and there you may see the great garland of glory, with, lying beside it, a cross not unworthy of it: a cross which lately stood upright on Calvary, but now is laid beside the crown of fadeless flowers. Look closely at this cross, and there you shall see like a jewel laid over the intersection of its arms, whatever cross you have faithfully borne for God's sake. Alone, it would not be measurable against the glorious crown; but the great arms of Christ's cross extend the spread of yours, and fit it to the heavenly scale.

The very heart of the Christian mystery is this, that there is a wonderful interchange between Christ and us, both of crosses and of crowns. Our little crosses are no more than token payments for our crowns, no more than farthing damages for our sins; and yet Christ unites them with his own cross, he takes them up into the great blood-price which redeems the world, and which purchases heaven. What happens when you come to the Holy Sacrament? Christ makes you partake of his death: that is, he gives you his death to taste, and you cannot taste it only in the wine of the sacramental chalice; you have to taste it in the crosses, the sacrifices of yourself which you make in the strength of the sacrament; or rather, which Christ himself makes through you and in you, in your daily life. And so, when you have received the chalice, you offer and present yourselves, your souls and bodies, to the Lord, to be made a reasonable, holy and living sacrifice, and to be taken up into the one sacrifice of Jesus; for you are his members, his body, both in life and in death.

In life and in death; in death and in resurrection. I have heard that a Christian soul, released from the flesh, was shown a shining crown high above, and told to fly upwards to it. But on nearer approach, what had seemed a wreath for the head now appeared as a wide circle of light, such as we sometimes admire in the clouds round the moon. Still more nearly seen, the clouds were revealed as hosts of heavenly witnesses, blessed saints, on whom rays from the centre broke, and were reflected in the form of a shining crown. The newcomer thought with relief: 'After all, I do not have to wear this crown; I may lose myself among the myriads who make it up.' He dropped into his place among old friends, and was at peace. But he was no sooner there than his mind slipped away from him, and flew into the heart of that glory which sat throned in the midst, a glory in whose body there were five wounds, like sun-spots in the body of the sun. United with the centre from which all love goes forth, and to which all love returns, he felt the whole wreath of light, the company of the saints, pressing round him; and so he wore the crown, the crown of which he was himself a part, and which no cross of his had merited.

We are all called to be saints: our place on high is appointed, and there is no reward short of union with the heart of Christ. God has only one thing to give: he gives himself. We cannot aim lower; and so may God have mercy on us all, through Jesus Christ, who died for our sins and reigns for our reward, with the innumerable company he has redeemed; to whom with the Father and the Holy Ghost, be ascribed as is most justly due all might, dominion, majesty and power, henceforth and for ever.

preached in Trinity College Chapel, Oxford

46

Committed Christians

It is generally thought that preachers should be allowed to get away with vagueness. Preachers ought to bang about with resonant words, and to ask them what precisely they mean is to misunderstand the business. For preachers are either speaking of divine things, or moving us to virtue; and in neither case is it sensible to ask for precision. If they speak to me of divine things and I ask them, 'Now what exactly do you mean?' they can fairly retort that the God about whom his creatures can be exact cannot be the God who made them, only an idol they have made for themselves. Whereas if the preacher is not talking about God, but moving us to virtue, it is pointless to ask him exactly what he means; for the object of the exercise is not to instruct us, but to move us; and if we are moved, we are moved.

Fair enough; but in due course there comes the inevitable question on the part of those who are moved, 'What must I do to be saved?' and at this point we must have some precision in the answer, and we can scarcely have too much of it. If I am told to do something, I had better be sure what it is; or else I may follow the lamentable example of the cavalry officer who misunderstood General Raglan's orders, and caused six hundred men to do and die, without achieving any valuable object. So when the preacher tells us what to do, that is the point at which it is appropriate to demand precision.

And what does the preacher tell us to do? He tells us, as often as not, to commit ourselves, to be committed Christians. There are, it seems, Christians, and again, there are committed Christians; these are distinct; you can tell them, perhaps, by the set of their jaws, but certainly by their godly conversation. Now I want to know what this is about being 'committed'; and my desire to torture the word is neither frivolous nor negative. I want to wring the truth out of it, since I am sure that those who talk like this are saying something vital for my salvation; and for my part I want to be saved, and not to be lost; I want to know what to do to be saved, and so I seek for precision in my orders. 'Be committed.' Well; but how?

There is an obvious sense of the demand which does not apply to me, and I think – I certainly hope – it does not apply to you. There are people who, out of laziness of mind or lethargy of will, and not through any earnest intellectual perplexity, refuse to make up their minds. They keep in with Christianity for some sort of emotional comfort, while being perfectly prepared to side against it in a conversation, or to reject its authority over their actions. They run with the hare and they hunt with the hounds. They tell themselves that some day, of course, they will have to make up their minds. Shame on such men! Do we need even to reason with them? Their own consciences, and the very religion with which they toy, convict them. They must commit themselves, and if to-morrow, why not to-day? If this is what the demand for self-committal means, then it is something very obvious and gross. To be uncommitted is to be playing with damnation in the most unmistakable way.

But I do not for a moment suppose that this is all that is meant when we are told to become committed Christians, and I ask what more. And I see that one of the things meant is a criticism against the Church. In the days of persecution, to be a Christian and to be a committed Christian were the same thing. If you committed youself to the visible Church by receiving baptism and attending mass, by that very act you took up your cross. Whereas now I may commit myself to the visible Church, and not commit myself to anything much. Well then, what? Shall I improve on my committal to the Church by committing myself to some visible holy party or brotherhood other than the Church, of whose members more is expected than of mere Christians? Are committed Christians to be party members of some sort? Heaven forbid! It may be an excellent thing to belong to a religious society for mutual encouragement in our Christian life, or for the joint undertaking of good works; but only as a help to our fundamental committal, which is our committal to Christ in the Catholic Church. If many are lukewarm Catholics, that is no reason for us either to imitate them, or to seek our committal in something else. Our committal to the Church is enough; it is what we shall never be worthy of; for what is it? We receive Jesus with our mouths, Jesus in our hearts, that we may go and be Jesus in our place and calling, and in relation to all those with whom we have to do. When you have achieved that, come back and ask for more.

Now we are coming near to the heart of the matter. For it is said we must commit ourselves to the service of, or to faith in, Jesus Christ. Well, yes. There are no half-measures possible here. Woe to the man who dare approach the knees of Christ, without in that moment intending that his homage to his King should commit him entirely, body and soul, now and for ever, to do whatever his King and his God lays upon him to do. True, when we come into that presence, we are moved to confess our imperfect desire, our divided heart. But we come asking for grace to have the divided heart healed; or if you prefer to say so, for grace to throw away the worser half of it. We cannot dare to come, refusing to receive such a unifying grace.

And so we never come to God without committing ourselves to him entirely, so far as in us lies, and in the present moment. It seems sometimes to be preached, however, that by a decision once for all made, we can commit ourselves irrevocably. But if this is preached, then it is not true. To-day's decisions cannot tie to-morrow's hands. What I give to God to-day, such is my frailty, I may take back or withhold to-morrow. It is through this that God disciplines me, through this that he breaks my pride. The heart is sick and desperately perverse, even the redeemed heart: what it gave God yesterday it takes back to-day. Our wickedness is so great that we fail to do promised actions, which we had perfectly envisaged at the time of promising. But even if we had the virtue to keep our promise with God when the circumstances are foreseen and remain unaltered, we should still lack the power to commit ourselves on issues which cannot be perfectly felt or foreseen in advance. He who promises to be chaste, does well and may be perfectly sincere; but he has not by that promise dealt with the temptation he will face when he falls in mutual love with an actual woman, and cannot marry her. Our fences cannot be jumped beforehand, nor our battles won before the enemy appears. You promise fidelity to Christ to-day, and you are sincere; but it will spare you none of the agony of decision, if a day comes when political brigands hold to our heads the pistol of absolute power, and say, 'Your religion or your life.'

No, we cannot commit ourselves in a day, because we cannot, merely by saying we will, put our whole trust in God. To trust in God is a thing which has to be learnt. We may stand up and make our profession of faith, clasp a missioner's hand and say, 'I have taken Christ for my Saviour, I trust him for all'. But we shall still trust ourselves to do our part in the new covenant we have entered. For we do not learn what dependence on God is, except through having our self-dependence broken in the mill of life, slowly and painfully. Many tears, much shame, continual repentance, this is the lot of those who pledge themselves to God. A paradoxical pledge; we learn to keep it by breaking it. True confessions, bravely and sincerely made to our confessor and absolved with the word of Christ, these are the means by which we learn distrust of ourselves, and trust in God alone. On every such occasion we reaffirm our self-committal. We firmly purpose amendment, when we humbly ask pardon of God; we bring to life every promise we previously made, back to our confirmation, back to our baptism when others' lips promised for us, back behind that to the cross, on which Christ committed us to God by dying for us.

A Christian who knew his own heart might pray in some such fashion as this. My God, I wish to give you the gift you so much desire; I wish to commit myself to you once and for all, so there shall be no taking back. I cannot commit *myself* into your hands, O God, *I* cannot do it; but yet I can commit myself into *your* hands; for though I cannot keep myself there, your fingers can hold me there, your strong, gentle fingers always giving way and never letting go; your wise, subtle fingers, wrestling so gently against my puny rebellions, that I tire myself trying to climb out of your hands, and come to rest at last in those wounded palms. You will not let me go; for though I have not the virtue to commit myself to you by an irrevocable act, you have had the love to commit yourself irrevocably to us. I cannot nail myself to you past breaking loose, but you have nailed yourself to us, witness these wounds. Your voluntary self-oblation, begun by free choice, hardened into unalterable necessity when they sentenced you, when they nailed you, when they lifted you into the air alive yet fixed, incorporate with the dead wood, and stiffening through agony into the irreversible fixity of death. You gave, beyond taking back, you were committed, when you gave your spirit into your Father's hands; and so I am content to know that I am committed into yours. For you are our everlasting shepherd, with the Father and the Holy Ghost, one God; to whom be ascribed, as is most justly due, all might, dominion, majesty and power, henceforth and for ever.

preached in Pusey House Chapel, Oxford

47
Narrow and Broad

Living in a university as I do, and even venturing from time to time to hear essays from beginners in philosophy, I cannot help being aware of the sort of tortures faith suffers from contemporary criticism. No doubt it would be more suitable for a theologian to be absolutely pickled in devout reflection and immune from all external influences; but wrap ourselves round as we may in the cocoon of ecclesiastical cobwebs, we cannot altogether seal ourselves off from the surrounding atmosphere. A tail protrudes from the envelope for the twisters of tails to twist, and it hurts a bit sometimes. But it must be confessed that one gets used to it, and it does not hurt so much as it did. After twenty years of having one's tail twisted into several variations of the same knot, one begins to appreciate how the tail is constructed, and why it is that, though twisted, it does not break. I will venture to offer a few observations based on experience of the anatomy of this resilient organ. To speak without metaphor, I will mention two characteristics of spiritual truth, which those who criticize it seem sometimes insufficiently to notice. I will call them its narrowness and its breadth.

The narrowness of spiritual truth is seen in the field of evidence. It is very wicked indeed to call saints (as people will call them) by the boastful name of religious geniuses. But there is this point of truth in the comparison between sanctity and (let us say) poetical genius, that it is rare, and that the instances which most fully reveal its nature are the rarest. Is there such a thing as poetical creation? Then produce me an instance under laboratory conditions. Well, I find you a verse-maker who will do his entry for the *Sunday Times* competition epigram under laboratory conditions; though I fear that under those conditions I cannot hold you out much hope of his winning the prize.

What do you mean by the evidence of divine presence and action? Where will you look for it? In the field of prayer? Though how we are to pray, when we are watching ourselves to see what happens, I really don't know. By good luck, however, we forget about the laboratory conditions, and we just pray. It is almost sure to be one of those days when we can do nothing but remember our God and our friends, put the two together, and identify our will with our duty. But perhaps it is an exceptional day. 'Sometimes a light surprises the Christian while he sings'; the world turns over in our heart, like a capsized boat recovering its true position; the throne of Mercy is seen, planted victoriously upon it; and the rays which stream from there kindle our dead affection for heavenly things.

Well, but even so, isn't that just a dream? What importance attaches to such a scrap of abnormal psychology? While you were praying, it looked to you as though the world had turned inside out; but is that a reason why I should turn my world inside out and (what is even more serious) turn myself inside out? That instead of drawing my life out of the well of my own decision, I should strike the shaft deeper, deeper than the brain can think, deeper than creation, and draw my life henceforth out of the fountain, from which all things always have their first unimaginable origin? You must give me better reason for that than the dream you dream, the prayer you pray, for half an hour one day in twenty. Are the foundations of the world uncovered then? Does omnipotence look through? How am I to know it?

If you address such questions to me, I fear that you will merely throw me into the unfashionable posture of repentance. By my fault, by my great and inexplicable fault, the God whose face is unveiled in my heart is obscured in my life. The almighty lovingkindness shapes a fragment of my thought; I do not let him wield the engine of my action. My assurance of him is in my repentance, in the miracle (as it is to me) that he renews my fresh beginnings with inexhaustible patience. But how are you to see that? I must give you better evidence. Somewhere a life wielded by God in a way that could not be mistaken, a life lived out of God, not out of self.

And indeed I knew a man whose name, though uncanonized, I shall always silently mention when I recall at the altar of God those saints whose fellowship gives reality to prayers; a man who sacrificed in the prime of his age a life which he had never lived for himself; a man whose eyes sparkled with all the passions, pity, indignation, sorrow, love, delight, but never for himself; unless it is more proper to say, Yes, for himself; since he had made God's loves and God's concerns his own, and had no others you would greatly notice.

Such a life, then, is evidence; and what other evidence could you hope to find? We have no inspection, no insight into the works of nature, which could conceivably let us through them to a vision of anything that lies beneath; all we can study is the diagram their movements draw in space. The only being we can know from within is our own; we are forced, however inadequate it may be, to take it as a sample of the rest, and judge the world from man. And man knows God only by yielding to him; we do not know the fountain of our being, so long as we are occupied in stopping it with mud. So the saint is our evidence, and other men, of course, for the glimpses of sanctity that are in them.

There, then, is something about the principle of narrowness. The unknown God reveals himself; but revelation is not something which tends to occur; apart from heroic charity, it is something that tends not to occur. Jesus Christ rose from the dead, but men do not tend to rise from the dead, as water tends to reach a level. Neither do men tend, deserted by their following and rejected by their nation, to die, with their eyes open, for a cause which they alone are left to sustain, praying for their assassins and offering themselves for their friends. Men do not tend to do so, but Jesus did. And I hope that when you next hear spiritual reality discussed as something which must be generally diffused if it is genuine at all, you will not be greatly moved. The evidence of faith is incorrigibly aristocratic.

But now something about breadth. Those who scrutinize evidence like to chop it into convenient slices, so that they can slip it on a slide and put it in the microscope of exact inquiry. This saint of ours now, what can you do with such a confused lump of data? Good heavens, the very unity of the human person is an unsolved logical problem. 'Give me something manageable, some single proposition he enunciated, some single decision he made, some single act he performed.' Well, you may take your specimens if you like, but I am afraid you will learn nothing from them. How much can you learn about dramatic art from half a line of Hamlet? Nothing, unless the half line carries the overtones of the whole drama; and how will you pile those on the microscope-slide? There are those who rub the texture of verse between their fingers, like women at a handkerchief counter; but there are many things that such criticism is incapable of testing.

The acts and words of saints will not fray between your finger and thumb, but you will not take God between your finger and thumb, the supernatural will have escaped you. The acts of saints are but brush-strokes towards a picture; and the picture is not even to be found in the rest of their own biographies. The picture they are painting is God expressed in mankind, God entirely and worthily served and adored. The saint paints his picture over and over, effacing his former work and aiming at perfection; and just when he has painted everything out and prepared for a fresh delineation, he dies. And in any case the piece he is busied with painting is only one corner, in itself meaningless, of a picture where Christ born, living, dying, raised and glorified holds the centre. That friend of mine, for example – except as serving the divine mission of Christ, his life was meaningless; and it was meaningless except as directed towards that great goal or consummation, where all things shall be fulfilled in the light of the countenance of God.

Here then is the principle of breadth, to set beside the principle of narrowness. Spiritual truth is narrow, in the sense that the sort of spiritual evidence which will carry weight fills a minute area. But again, and in another sense, spiritual truth is broad. For no piece of this most rare and precious evidence can be understood by itself, but only as a detail in the vast divine action it subserves. Our weak prayers and weaker virtues are understood in the saints, and the saints on earth are understood in Jesus Christ; while Jesus Christ, the saints and our own Christian existence are understood in that end alone towards which they strive, and in assuring which the love of God to us is love indeed.

There light spills evermore from the fountain of light; it fills the creatures of God with God as much as they will contain, and yet enlarges their heart and vision to contain the more. There it is all one to serve and to pray, for God invisible is visibly portrayed in the actions he inspires. There the flame of deity burns in the candle of mankind, Jesus Christ; and all the saints, united with him, extend his person, diversify his operation, and catch the running fire. That is the Church, the Israel of God, of which we only exist by being the colonies and outposts, far removed and fitfully aware; yet able by faith to annihilate both time and distance, and offer them the only pleasing sacrifice to God Almighty, Father, Son and Holy Ghost; to him ascribing as is most justly due, all might, dominion, majesty and power, henceforth and for ever.

preached in Trinity College Chapel, Oxford

48

Craggy Doctrine

Your preacher of a fortnight ago was not allowed to get away with it; the interceptors were out, they caught him between the screen and the door, and asked him what he meant by preaching predestination. Why, it is even rumoured that his doctrine was discussed in hall at the scholar's table. When I heard this news I was green with envy. Why don't they ever intercept me, I said, and have it out with me? The answer, 'Oh, because your sermons are irreproachable,' did honour to the social training of the Wykehamist who made it, but gave little comfort to the college chaplain who received it. Who wants to make irreproachable remarks? But I must not waste time on lamentation. If your chaplain hasn't the skill to create in your minds that mental discomfort which is so salutary for you, the best thing he can do is to pick up a crumb of discomfort from a former preacher's feast, and help you to indigest that. You want to hear about predestination? Then you shall hear about predestination.

But remember that indigestion is the object aimed at. If you will have such a craggy doctrine on the table, you can't expect smooth conclusions. I am not going to make you see how difficult it is. I am going to make you look into the unfathomable abyss of God's will; and if you turn away with a dizzy head, you will at least have looked beneath the surface of things.

First, a mere preliminary. Divine predestination has nothing to do with a scientific determinism. People who discuss determinism may discuss whether men really act by choice as they think they do, or whether they are worked by their nerves, as puppets are worked by strings. Alternatively, they may discuss whether men are fooled into acting by a sort of Guy Fawkes conspiracy, a gang of subconscious wishes under the floor of the mind. Whereas people who discuss divine predestination take it for granted that we do make real free choices. They are theologians, quite often they are saints; and they are so impressed with the help God gives them in choosing right, that they feel the absurdity of making a fuss about their own part in the business. Clearly it all depends upon God. He has, by an act of unspeakable mercy, decided to bring them through to glory, and has so overwhelmed them with his goodness as actually to bring it about. If we had such an experience of God's grace, we might see predestination in that way ourselves. But as we are far from such a position, we had better begin from another place, and from something that is more readily intelligible to us.

Anyhow, if we believe in God at all, we must believe in his wisdom and foresight. God does not push his creatures into existence like ducklings into a pond, to sink or swim and to fend for themselves. He has a plan for them. Ah, you say, this is better, we can understand this. Stalin has a five years plan for the Russians. Lucky Russians! all they have to do is carry it out. There is no conflict here between predestinating wisdom and individual free will, for of course the plan may not be fulfilled. It's up to the Russians. Lord Attlee and Sir Stafford Cripps brought out a plan for our economic salvation; but unluckily we did not tighten our belts enough, or sufficiently increase our export quota; and so, although (as a minister felicitously phrased it) the target was only just round the corner, we never managed to hit it. Sir Winston Churchill and Mr Butler came forward with another plan. In like manner, perhaps we may say, a divine plan was put forward through Moses and Aaron, which the chosen people didn't live up to. And so in due time we find Peter and Paul more divinely and directly commissioned to proclaim a new and better plan. And we seem to have been making a fair mess of it ever since.

I must say that the further I go with this comparison, the less I like it. To begin with, there are so many reasons why government plans fail. It is not only because of the stupidity and non-co-operativeness of the public; it is very largely because statesmen, like the rest of us, are fools; they make demands on public virtue of which they ought to know public virtue to be incapable. And they leave a multitude of factors out of their reckoning, which then proceed to turn round and bite them in the leg. Very likely it is the best that they can do; but it is not the best that God can do. God leaves no factors out of his reckoning, nor does he plan for an imaginary virtue we haven't got, he plans for the very men we are. His plans for us are what perfect wisdom suggests to infinite love; his plans for us are his love, they are all the good that his love can see for us; as a parent's plan for his child would ideally be – he looks at the child and loves it, and in loving it sees what opens out before it.

The plans of governments are concerned with statistical charts, with something highly general and impersonal, with persuading the curve on the economic graph to sweep handsomely upwards and, in short, with giving contemporary history a streamlined look. But God's plan is not concerned with streamlining, let us say, the ecclesiastical system, it is concerned with the living body of mankind in all its warmth and variety; not from the point of view of its rationalization, but from that of its eternal salvation. New every morning is the love, and new every hour the loving foresight, which sees the openings for our happiness, and sets the opportunities of good ready to our hand. Reach out and take them, for now is the appointed time. God's plan is not a five years plan, but a five minutes plan; or, again, from another point of view, neither a five years plan nor a five thousand years plan, but a plan for our eternity, starting here.

But that is not all. Not only does God's wisdom continually open our path before us, God's grace is continually offered us for strength to walk in it. To the sluggard, says the book of Proverbs, there seem to be lions in the path; and to the self-indulgent there are sirens luring him aside from it. But if the pilgrim invokes the name of God, and makes the sign of Christ's cross, where are these demonic phantoms? They have vanished away. So indeed it is our fault, if we have not walked in that path. The Chancellor cannot give the industrialists the vigour they need to fill their export quota, he can only exhort them or threaten them. *Extrinsecus tonat*, he thunders at them from without, as St Augustine says of Moses and his law; but what says he of Christ? He pours the love of God abroad in our hearts, by the Holy Ghost that he has given us. So when the industrialists have failed, they can say to the Chancellor, 'We were weak and quarrelsome, we could do no better,' and there is really nothing he can reply. He can swear at them, but he cannot contradict them. But when I say to God 'I was weak,' he says 'Why did not you ask my aid?' I could have done that: he reads my heart, and I have no answer, except that Christ has died for me to be forgiven.

Well, where now have we got with the question of predestination? There is a divine intention for me, a path under my very feet, and there is divine grace by which to walk in it; and none of this is anything foreign or harsh, nothing forced upon me; it is all my own happiness, my only true good; so if I turn aside, or if I stop and sleep, O God, what am I but an utter fool, and ungrateful, disloyal besides? How fortunate it is for me that God is merciful, that his patience knows no end.

'And a very harmless doctrine,' you may say. 'All's well, for free will is secured. So far as you have done any good at all, *you* have co-operated with God's grace, *you* have consented to invoke his aid and to use his inspirations.' Yes, I have not always been an utter fool, I have sometimes allowed God's goodness to persuade me; but what are you proposing to deduce from that? Are you trying to make me accept some such statement as this: 'God put his grace at this man's disposal, somewhat as the Bursar of the college laid him on the electric light. He can't generate either electricity or divine grace. Still, it's left to his own sweet will to turn or not to turn the switches.'

But I can't have that. My life hasn't been like that; the life of no Christian ever was like that. Divine goodness has persuaded me, hedged up my path, headed me off, driven me back into the road; that is why I am here. I suppose it is abstractly conceivable that I could have been a greater fool than I was, but that is no reason for saying that I have been brought here by my own wisdom. 'You, O Lord, have wrought all our works in us,' the Christian must say.

My failures, foolishnesses, vanities, cowardices, these have been mine. Here are two angel-recorders, and each of them shows me a scroll. On one is written the evil I have done, and the attempted good I have misdone or scamped. It is quite enough for an Advent penitence; what can I do but read such a score and weep, except that God's predestination has better things for me to do than weeping? He sets the good path at my feet, he gives me the grace to walk in it. But here is the other angel with his scroll. 'No,' I say, 'take it away; I know I must read it on the day of judgement, but I will not read it now. Not now, not here in this world, the vision of all those good things God predestined me to have done, and I did not do them: the men unhelped, the prayers unsaid, the sadness uncomforted, the sin unrebuked.' 'No, not in this life,' says the mercy of God. 'And on the day I show it to you, I will also show you my face, and the thorns on my head, and the wounds in my hands.'

But as to those good things which God has predestinated for us, and we have achieved, let us so speak of them that we may give him the glory alone. For whom he predestinated to be conformed to the image of his Son, them also he called, and whom he called, justified, and whom he justified, glorified. To him, therefore, with the Son and with the Holy Ghost, be ascribed as is most justly due all might, dominion, majesty and power, henceforth and for ever.

preached in Trinity College Chapel, Oxford

49

On Religion, Natural and Revealed

The founder of this sermon directed us to consider the excellence of revealed religion. I take it that 'excellence' in his vocabulary meant 'superiority'. He was not asking us, that is, simply to utter encomiums on divine revelation, but to institute a favourable comparison. There was natural religion, and there was revealed religion. Many people said that natural religion was good enough for them; but we were to urge the contrary. We were to display before the eyes of a not sufficiently appreciative public the superior advantage of revealed truth.

In the time of John Hulse, the distinction between natural belief and a faith supernaturally revealed was familiar. A comparison between the two had been the whole stock-in-trade of Butler's admired *Analogy*, a book which it is easier now to praise than to read. Our trouble is, we find the very idea of natural religion artificial; it smacks of oracular conscience, copybook metaphysics, and the noble savage. One thing at least is clear to us, when we look back on the age of Butler and of Hulse. What was taken by them to be natural religion was deeply indebted to Christian faith. It was supposed to derive from a view of the world and of man, simply as we see them to be. But these natural realities had been looked at so long with Christian eyes, that they had taken on a Christian sort of look. People could not distinguish naked fact from inveterate inter- pretation. An old man may find it intolerable to revisit his college, because (he says) the staircases are full of ghosts. The ghosts are not there; but he cannot see the walls and banisters, without expecting the footfall of friends long dead. In some such way the vaunted Age of Reason could not see a natural world, unhaunted by the ghost and echo of ancestral faith.

What I have just remarked would be too trite for repetition, if we were proposing to leave it at that. But our historical platitude places us in a situation in which we can scarcely hope to sit down, and repose. If the old natural theologians were listening to the reverberations of a Christian thunder, muttering on among the rocks of natural fact, we still do not know how we ought to handle the issue which they too credulously defined. Perhaps the obvious course to take is that which has commended itself to the austere philosophers. Banish the Christian echoes, lay the ghost of positive religion in any form, strip the facts of nature and of man down to a naked objectivity, and then see if there is anything of a theological tendency which, in contemplating them, you cannot but believe. If there is any such inescapable and residual theology,

193

you may speak of natural religion – not, that is, a religion natural to Hottentots but a religion natural to that level of mentality and culture, which the graduates of our more respectable universities have attained.

The project sounds laudable; it positively bristles with intellectual integrity. Unhappily it is as sterile as it is aseptic. Strip the facts down to what no one with a head on his shoulders, and eyes in his head, can dispute, and they will yield you no theology. If you want any, you will be obliged to let in the ambiguous test: 'What is there more, which, in contemplating the bare facts, I cannot but believe?' – or rather, *could* not but believe, under an unreal supposition: the supposition that I had received no illumination and felt no influence, whether direct or indirect, from any mouthpiece of revealed truth, or any tradition of positive faith. Unluckily, the proposed experiment in hypothetical believing is impossible to make. I can experiment in scientific reasoning, under the artificial condition that I use no premises introduced into European thought later than Aristotle. But I cannot experiment in reacting to the realities of my situation, as I should have reacted if Moses, Buddha, Christ, Augustine, my father, my schoolmaster and my nurse had never opened their mouths. I can only react as I do react, being the man that I am. And what man am I? The man that these I have named, among many others, have made me to be.

Even if, by a miracle, I could do it – could make a reaction to the world, unaffected by any inspired or revelatory utterances ever given – it is still not clear what the value of such a reaction would be. For we commonly think that, whatever the great prophets and revealers have or have not done, they have brightened, purified and refined our reaction to nature and to life. If there can be said to be such a thing as a true and proper response of the heart and will to this shared human existence of ours, and to its several situations, will a man be more capable of it who has learned nothing from Christ, and nothing from Buddha? In looking for natural religion, as we said, we are not looking for the religion of Esquimaux and Hottentots; we are looking for something which results from the unbiased use of civilized faculties. But civilized faculties, like civilization itself, are a historical product; and the history which produces spiritual faculty is spiritual history; a history in which Christ, the Buddha and others we have named or not named, play decisive parts.

What follows from the considerations we have advanced? Are we to conclude that the eighteenth-century distinction between natural and revealed religion was meaningless? We should be rash to conclude so, without first hearing the defence of those we criticize. – But the men are dead. – Never mind: since we have talked of ghosts, let us raise a ghost: let us pose our eighteenth-century deist with our twentieth-century question. I bar table-rapping; I propose straight mediumship, and I offer myself as the medium. Listen, then, to the voice of a spirit in a powdered wig.

'You tell me, Sir,' says he, 'that what I took to be the mere motions of our rational nature are an acquired habitude, which the prophets and lawgivers of former generations have largely formed in us; that because we look as they have taught us to look, we see what they have instructed us to see. I will be so candid as to confess, that your arguments convince me on this head. And indeed it must be acknowledged more in general, that the powers of our human nature attain neither maturity nor use, without teachers to cultivate and to develop them. I myself, in the idleness of my youth, amused many hours with drawing and painting; and for such poor skill as I had, was entirely indebted to several masters. They taught my eye to distinguish a beauty in the scenes of nature, and my pencil to delineate it. Yes, Sir, they taught me; for (not to flatter myself) I was not born unteachable. But here lies the point – they taught *me* to see, and *me* to draw. They taught me not what they saw, nor what they drew; they taught me to draw, and to see; and it was by my own acquirements that I measured the value of their instructions. They had several theories and systems, some of which seemed to me fantastical, and all superfluous, except as they served to foster in me the pictorial art. All was but scaffolding to raise a house. The house once finished, the scaffolding is carted away, and no more accounted of.

'Now, Sir, I will confess that the sages and, since you will have it so, the prophets of former times, have taught me to think, to feel, and to act. Very well; I will do these things, and I will thank them for the ability. I will use my faculties to the best of my powers, and reason as I may on what I perceive. But I will not trammel myself in the systems of ancient philosophers, or in the visionary metaphysick of the prophets. Indeed, I will propose to you a pragmatic test for distinguishing the grain of antiquity from the chaff. Whatsoever in these old oracular teachings has become, as it were, incorporate with our faculties, and passed into the very ideas we have of the objects about us, so much is of worth; the rest is nothing to us. The teachings of antiquity have been called the food of the mind. But I will beg leave to observe, that the evidence of nourishment lies in the assimilation of it. What passes into our physical being is food. What does not is at the best an encumbrance, at the worst, a poison.'

Return, Alphaeus; the dread voice is past ... our deistical ghost vanishes as suddenly as he came. But surely he has left us something to think about. Has he not expressed, with the hard clarity of the Age of Reason, a view more vaguely and less consciously held by many of ourselves? Christianity, such people will generously admit, has given us new eyes for the qualities and claims of personal existence: qualities so rich and claims so stringent, that we cannot but take them for the gifts of an infinite bounty, and the requirements of an absolute will. We may refresh the Christian lesson, and kindle anew our perception for these things by

195

reading the Gospels. But we can make no approach to reality save by throwing ourselves upon these things. We cannot know God or his will save as we find him expressed in the beings we encounter; in their virtues, their needs, their potentialities, their aspirations. Or if we can know more of him, it is not through any record of the past; it is by a direct wrestling with an ever-present eternity in the difficult practice of mystical contemplation.

Such, we may fairly say, is the general shape of a natural religion widely prevalent. How many people do we know, who honour Christ and repudiate atheism, but believe no supernatural creed, no mystery accepted on the credit of any revealer? And the first thing we are moved to say about their religion is, that there is much virtue in it. What a refreshing contrast it offers to much, if not most, dogmatic belief! Do we not approach the fully-practising, orthodox Christian with the sickening fear that we shall find a being prejudiced and profoundly insincere, unwilling to trust his eyes, his reason or his heart, anxiously substituting a world of cardboard maxims, for the glorious and terrifying universe which God has made? How infinitely more wholesome the lapsed but unresentful Catholic, still instinct with natural reverence, while his heart beats freely in a blessed new release from believing things other than they seem!

I am put up here to preach the excellence of revealed religion, so I must not allow the beautiful candour of natural piety to carry me quite away. But I will say that unless the virtues of natural religion find a place in the life of orthodoxy, orthodoxy becomes the caricature of itself, and the bugbear of honest minds.

Hail, holy light, offspring of Heaven first born!
Or of the Eternal co-eternal beam
May I express thee unblamed? Since God is light,
And never but in unapproachèd light
Dwelt from eternity –

and in his light we are to see light. The evidence of light is that it illuminates; and if by the light of faith we do not see more colours in the world, more exactly in their proper being and truth, than eyes can perceive which lack supernatural illumination, then surely we stand self-condemned.

The Christian mind must move in equipoise between revealed mysteries and open realities, interpreting each by the help of the other; as happens very simply and without our observing it, when we join the adoration of God's goodness with the prayerful remembrance of our friends. But of course there is no equality between our two objects of contemplation; and though the glory of the divine countenance is reflected in the looking-glass of creatures, it is not, and cannot be, all

196

reflected there. Thus the resolution to see nothing of God, but what is given back to our eyes by the creaturely mirror, is a resolution to leave out most of what there is to be seen. And, formally speaking, the superiority or excellence of revealed religion is precisely this: it tells of the special means God has taken to show us, outside the common course of nature, some part of that great overplus, which exceeds the capacity of nature's looking-glass to reflect it.

It is not even as though what natural fact does show of God were self-explanatory or self-contained. Perhaps the liveliest part of natural religion is a sensitivity to the will of God, as it comes home to us in the needs or the aspirations of our fellow-men. Yet we cannot see what their needs are, unless we know what they need to be; nor how to support their aspirations, without a vision of their goal, a goal so widely misconceived. Or again, how shall we relate the pure will of God to the perverse strivings of men, without an understanding of the atonement which forgives them, or the grace which reclaims and rectifies them?

If we are possessed by revealed truth, and not merely encumbered by credal diagrams of it, it will not deaden, it must enliven our sensitivity to present personal fact. So supernatural light strengthens the beam of natural understanding. 'I am the light of the world', says Christ in these autumn days, when night begins to crowd upon the year. And, in support of the claim, when they challenge it, 'I know whence I came, and whither I go. You, not knowing whence I come, nor yet whither I go, judge according to the flesh,' by a judgement, that is, no more than natural. For without the disclosure of our goal and our origin, how can we discern the straight from the crooked in the paths of life? It is one thing to walk from the womb in pursuit of a utopia which flees us; another thing, issuing from the hand of God, to walk towards a Mercy who comes to meet us. And what is a straight walk, on the first view, may be a very crooked walk on the second.

For a Christian, there is something absurd about the invitation to proclaim the superiority of revealed religion – to argue that we are better off with the light, the grace and the glory, the quickening water and the redeeming blood, than we should be without these things. That they are excellent, who can doubt, if only he believes them? And if there is one cause of disbelief most endemic to the natural religion we have discussed, it is probably the notorious 'scandal of particularity' – the apparent preposterousness of letting any particular set of events bear the unique importance which Christ's intervention bears for the Christian. How can Jesus have done more than heighten the perceptiveness with which we survey facts in general, and especially personal facts?

Since I cannot hope, in the last sentences of a sermon, to say anything useful in mitigation of the scandal of particularity, I will stand down once more, and give place to a more persuasive voice. In the last

197

published part of Martin Skinner's astonishing poem, *The Return of Arthur*, an unbeliever finds himself entranced in a church, gazing at a wooden plaque of the Nativity.

So Leo gazed, absorbed, a timeless glance;
And thought of all the trees that nature held
(Strange instance of a trance within a trance);
Cedars of Lebanon, green beechwoods delled
With sapphire; sombre newsprint forests felled
  At such a rate, each Sunday men were able
  To read ten acres at the breakfast table;

Dwarf fairy oaks at Lichen, harled with moss;
Trunks wide as roads, through which a cart could go;
A jungle mat a continent across
Which, piled as logs, would make the Alps look low –
And yet of all that ever grew, or grow
  (So ran his thoughts) this carving had been done
  Uniquely from a random plank of one.

Was not the contrast much the same in space,
Whose glittering forests were the galaxies?
For if the carver made a special case,
Selecting from innumerable trees
One segment, so from the vast host of these
  Could not the prime Creator, mightier far,
  Have carved his story on a single star?

And if he had, Ah, if indeed he had,
And come himself to earth, a newborn cry,
Would not the story have been just like that;
And signs accompanied, in earth and sky,
That holy abdication from on high;
  And radiant beings from about the throne
  Of Light, have made the lamplit stable known?

Now therefore to the Light of light, the threefold fountain both of being and of grace, Father, Son and Holy Ghost ...
    Hulsean Sermon, preached in Great St Mary's, Cambridge

50

The Ultimate Hope

A speaker who knows his job saves up his main point, but I'm going to spill mine out straightaway. My precious truth is this: that Christian hope is not one thing, but two. It works on two levels, and they are equally vital. There's hope for this world; and there's hope for a world beyond it. There's hope for this world so long as it lasts, and so long as it's ours to play with. For our God is a God who does nothing in vain. He has not put us here to waste our time, or to suffer mere frustration; there's something to be done here for God's glory, and for man's well-being. Certainly our faith does not promise us that the world will last for ever, or – what comes to the same thing from our point of view – that the human race will indefinitely survive to enjoy this corner of it. We are promised no such thing: we are promised that our world, while it lasts and while we last, will remain the sphere of God's creating and redeeming work; and that he will make us men his workmen. So in the short view, there's always hope; hope that frustrated in one line, we can open up another; hope that if we have to suffer, our very sufferings can help the good cause; hope that though we've wasted our chances, we may be forgiven, and allowed a fresh start. We have only to put ourselves into God's hands, for hope to spring fresh out of the present day, and reach forward and claim tomorrow.

So much for the short view. Now what about the long? As I was saying; our religion, so far from promising mankind a perpetual survival, talks to us about a fated end to human history; and scientific prediction seems to chime in with biblical prophecy: the earth will not remain for ever warm enough to support human life, or any life, indeed. And that would be that, were it not for a fantastic ray of further hope kindled in our days by space travel. Let the earth turn to ice, people say; our far-off descendants will board their spaceships and sail off into the galaxies; they will colonize some planet over there just ripe for human habitation. A fantastic hope, I call it, because the nearest habitable planet, if there is one, is likely to be a million times as far away as the moon and travel as fast as we may we shall be old and indeed dead before we reach it.

But set these reasonable doubts aside; suppose, if you like, the human race goes on for ever, by switching in due course from star to star, and hopping hither and thither over the enormous field of space. On such a supposition, would not the human race be immortal? Yes, on that supposition the human race would be immortal, if there were any such person as the human race; only there isn't. There's no such person as the human race, nor any such a thing; there's just Tom, Dick and Harry. Just Mary, Jane and Anne with all the other thousands of millions of individuals, dead, alive, or yet to be born. It is convenient to refer to the whole bunch of them as 'the human race'; but they, the individuals, alone are actual and the human race is a figure of speech, and a figure of speech is a queer sort of candidate for immortality. Tom, Dick and Harry are serious candidates for everlasting life; only in this world, and as physical animals, they just don't get it.

You may say, if you like, that human life goes on and on through history. But it's like a leaky pipe, running through sand, and fed at successive points with fresh injections of water. All along the pipe there's water in it; but all the water leaks out sooner or later to lose itself in the sand.

Such a leaky pipe is the history of mankind. As long as it lasts, these men are alive; but all the life of them leaks out and is (physically speaking) lost. Nothing and nobody runs on through the impressive panorama which historians study, or which seers venture to predict.

People say it is selfish to hope for immortal being, but it isn't because we are all in the same boat. If I'm a selfish man, I may hate the thought of my extinction. If I'm a loving man, I may hate the thought of yours. And if I'm a thoughtful man, I may hate, I must hate, the perpetual wastage of souls; of these precious products, the fine flowers of the world's growth, every one withering and fallen before it is perfect; or even if it touches some perfection, displaying its beauty for so brief an hour. And how can I be said to believe in God, if I think he has no remedy for this last frustration of his creative purpose?

But thank God (and here I return to my starting point) a Christian believer has two levels of hope. There's hope on the short view, hope within the world, that something can be made of it. But beyond that there's hope in the long view; hope that what we do in this world is not all going to leak out of the pipe of history into the sands of oblivion. So there are two levels of hope; and how stupid, how perverse it is to set them against one another: to say, 'Well, you must make up your mind; either fix your hope on this world, or fix it on a world to come. If you fix your hope on heaven, you'll not care a pin about the world's future; if you care about the world's future, you won't give a straw for heavenly bliss.' Nonsense: we are confronted with no such choice. Heaven alone gives final meaning to any earthly hopes; and to take it the other way round, we have no way to grasp at heavenly hope, than by pursuing hopeful tasks here below.

It's extraordinary, the power people have for shutting their eyes at what they don't want to see; there seems to be no limit to our capacity for putting on blinkers: and men, serious worthy men too, can go on concerning themselves with the progress of mankind, the forward march of history, while blinding themselves to the fact that there's no such being as mankind, nor any such a thing as history: but that, from the historian's point of view, the wastage of men is continuous, absolute, and final. People die off unblessed, but never mind – fix your hopes on the next generation, or the generation after that, and be careful not to notice that all those people in their turn will die off disappointed, incomplete, and old. This leap-frogging hope is fools' paradise; this is the delusive hope for ever unrealized, of which it is said:

Hope springs eternal in the human breast:
Man never *is*, but always *to be*, blest:

Achievement perpetually elusive, spilt at last over the precipice of death. The paradise of fools. But there is another paradise, and waters welling up to everlasting life: waters bright as crystal (says St John in his vision) springing out of the House of God and of the Lamb; and on this side of the river and on that, an orchard of the tree of life, every month yielding its fruit; and the leaves of the tree for the healing of the nations, so that there shall be no more curse. The throne of God and of the Lamb shall be there and his servants shall serve him; they shall see his face, and his name shall be on their foreheads.

I threw away my pearl of doctrine in my first sentence. Now let me see if I can get a second wind and a fresh start by throwing out a paradox, a sort of riddle, like this: The achievable cannot be achieved; only the unrealizable will ever be realized. 'Give me,' says commonsense, 'a manageable assignment and I'll cover it.' Well, to a don like me it looks a manageable assignment to write a satisfactory book. But the writer is never satisfied with what he has written and it's out of date before the ink is dry. It seems a manageable assignment for any citizen to get his family a position of tolerable security and a pattern of family life which will yield contentment. But the ideal balance cannot be held: care and friction invade the house; time washes away the foundations.

That which is achievable cannot be achieved; only the unrealizable will ever be realized. The unrealizable: for example, to know God and to love him. Can I catch infinite God in my little net? Plainly not. Before I even begin, the project is seen to be beyond realization. All these years I am supposed to have been learning to pray: that is, learning to join my mind with the infinite mind. And what happens when I pray? What will ever happen? Often the most a Christian can do is to put himself in God's presence: to make a mere act of blind, dry will in favour of God's purposes. If ever it seems to us that God lets a crack of light into our praying mind, can we attend to it beyond a moment? Can we walk all day in the beam of uncreated light? Or again, a Christian studies all his days to love his neighbour for God's sake. And what happens? What ever will happen? When shall you and I intercede for our friends as eagerly as we dream our selfish dreams? When serve any single person with the zeal with which we serve ourselves?

Such projects are unrealizable: and why? I have already said it: it is because I am trying to take eternity on board my narrow, perishable boat. Because it's eternity I'm trying to take on board, the project is unrealizable. But again, it's only because what I try to take on board is eternal, that there is any hope of realization. My narrow hold will not contain immortal life; but no other goods I can stow there will stand the voyage: they will leak out and perish; God alone endures.

The greatest of German philosophers said that if man's spiritual quest is not to be a mirage (and in practice we can't think it is) then we must have infinite time in a future life to achieve our unachievable task, and overtake perfection. Ah, but the perfection we seek is not the rounding-off of ourselves, each of us a little god in our little blue heaven. Our perfection lies in God himself, whom not in ten thousand years, not in ten thousand thousand ages, not in time without end, can we reach or overtake. But he, in a moment, in the twinkling of an eye, can from his side break the deadlock, by linking us to himself.

> Then long Eternity shall greet our bliss
> With an individual kiss;
> And Joy shall overtake us as a flood,
> When every thing that is sincerely good
> And perfectly divine,
> With Truth and Peace, and Love shall ever shine
> About the supreme Throne
> Of him, t' whose happy-making sight alone,
> When once our heav'nly-guided soul shall clime,
> Then all the Earthy grossness quit,
> Attir'd with Stars, we shall for ever sit,
> Triumphing over Death, and Chance, and thee O Time.

Milton put these superb lines on a clock-case. He put them there to humiliate time, to put time in proportion: time, whose cruel creeping finger shows us how the hours pass and leave our projects incomplete, our days shortened. There is the clock, ticking away our earthly existence. How many minutes by the clock do our niggardly hearts give up to the adoration of the God who is the crown and the fulfilment of our being? No doubt John Milton, like the rest of us, might reflect with shame how slowly and how dully the moments all too often passed which he spared for looking his everlasting happiness in the face. Did he find comfort at such times in the lines he had written? If he did, let's hope it was not the comfort of mere compensation – not merely that the promise of eternal bliss hereafter made up for the present poverty of his praying hours. A genuine faith knows better. The eyes of God do not look at us out of an unimaginably distant future, they look at us from the heart of the present moment. He gives himself now and with both his hands. We try to pray. We hold ourselves before him while flat minutes pass, the effort on our side is cold and ineffective. But on his side there is infinite good pleasure. The touch of our spirit on his, little as we realize it, touches the pulse of everlasting bliss. When we awake to God at last, we shall awake to the same eyes, and no other, as the eyes which look into our eyes now. There is only one God, and he is whole and entire in all his acts and ways.

Our knowledge of God now is the promise and the foretaste of heaven: apart from this present knowledge of God, we should have no clue to what heaven will be; for heaven is God. But it's just as true the other way about – without the heavenly promises God has given us, we should have no understanding of our present life with God. How could we make sense of the journey if we didn't know where the road leads? Unless the promise of heaven was shown us, how should we guess that the fitful gleams of spiritual light which visit us here flowed out from the steady and irresistable dawning of eternal day?

Compared with the sight of God in heaven our present glimpses of him seem little, or nothing, indeed; and yet they are not altogether nothing. Even today, when we pray, the hand of God does somewhat put aside that accursed looking-glass, which each of us holds before him, and which shows each of us our own face. Only the day of judgement will strike the glass for ever from our hands, and leave us nowhere reflected but in the pupils of the eyes of God. And then we shall be cured of our self love, and shall love, without even the power of turning from it, the face that is lovely in itself, the face of God; and passing from the great Begetter to what is begotten by him, we shall see his likeness in his creatures, in angels and in blessed saints; returning at long last the love that has been lavished on us, and reflecting back the light with which we have been illuminated. To that blessed consummation, therefore may he lead all those for whom we pray, he who is love himself, who came to us at Bethlehem, and took us by the hand.

preached in St Andrew's, Headington, Oxford

51

The Country Doctor

Once upon a time there was a country doctor, a pompous and unimaginative man. He was summoned to attend the wife of the squire. After the affair was successfully over, the woman, still only half alive, moaned that it was unbearable – why, she asked, does one have to suffer such pain? The doctor showed his learning. 'My dear lady,' he said, 'if you had looked as I have looked into the workings of nature, you would perceive that the nobler the animal, the more developed must be its condition when it separates from its parent; and the more developed the condition of the offspring, the greater the wrench to the parent must be. Now man is the noblest of the animals. The pain of human childbirth is the price of man's nobility.' The doctor's voice trailed in the woman's listless ear: 'That makes it no better,' she murmured, 'it hurts just the same.' At that moment her mother came into the room and showed her her son. And she began to think how it would be when she suckled him; and suddenly she remembered no more the anguish, for her joy of that little man, who was born into the world.

The Word of God brings upon human pain and strife the consolation of eternal love. It is often thought that the Christian preacher is called upon to imitate the doctor in my fable, and somehow to prove that the intolerable evils which ravage the earth are only the price of greater good. But the answer naturally provoked by such explanations is that of the suffering woman: 'That makes it no better; it hurts just the same.' Or even: 'If this is what God's love does, then for God's sake let me have a taste of his wrath.' No, God does not give us explanations; we do not comprehend the world, and we are not going to. It is, and it remains for us, a confused mystery of bright and dark. God does not give us explanations; he gives up a Son. Such is the spirit of the angel's message to the shepherds: 'Peace upon earth, good will to men ... and this shall be the sign unto you: ye shall find a babe wrapped in swaddling clothes, and lying in a manger.'

A Son is better than an explanation. The explanation of our death leaves us no less dead than we were; but a Son gives us a life, in which to live. The mother revives, as her thought attaches itself to this new life. And Mary of all mothers is most blessed, as her thought ranges forward over the happy tasks of which her life hereafter must consist, the nurture and protection of her Son. Here is a Son in whose life she can always more richly live; for he is life itself, and to live in him is to live in life everlasting. If we live in our own children we live in what must fail and disappoint us; we may even be so unhappy as to outlive them. But if we live in the Son whom God has given we have a life which will not fail, but always deepen and extend. This is the peace, this is the joy God gives: our joy is swaddled in the cradle, our peace is crucified, our glory rises from the tomb.

Mary was most blessed, because for her the natural love of parenthood could run on unbroken into the love of that Son whom God had supernaturally given. And so Christians have desired to have her prayers, not because special virtues are recorded of her, but because she has a path of incomparable simplicity into the heart of God's love. In company with her, we too have desired to find access; we have followed her through the stages of her journey. First, Jesus is in her arms, and has no life independently from her; she carries him to the temple, she presents him before God. Then, even in his childhood, he shows a mysterious life of his own. Now he walks into the temple on his own feet at his mother's side, and there detaches himself; he remains hearing the doctors, and asking them questions. She misses him and sees him sorrowing; she finds him about a business of his own, or of his heavenly Father's (it is all one) in his Father's house. Now he is something that she has not made him, his heart and mind are not under her hand; yet he returns to Nazareth, and is subject to her, for he is a child still. The day comes when he is no longer subject, but she is subjected to him: 'Whatsoever he bids,' she said to the servants at Cana, 'do it.' And so, from a mother, she came to be a worshipper; she lived in him – not in what she made him, but in what he made of her.

How blest was she, above all women; and how happy are we, if, following her progress with devout imagination, we can come to live, even for the short period of our prayer, in that Son whom God has given to us, caring for his concerns, and not for ours! For what else is it to pray, but this: that we live for a little while in the Son of God, and share in some measure the love he has for all the men with whom we have to do? That we deeply care for the fulfilment in them of his saving work, and worthily prize the work of his mercy in our own souls?

It is written, 'Unto us a Son is given.' And elsewhere it is written, 'God sent forth his own Son.' 'Unto us a Son is given,' that is, he is given to be our Son, Son of the human race; that Mary might have him for her own, and we with her might grow from a natural to a supernatural love. But he who is given to be our Son, is God's Son everlastingly: 'God sent forth his own Son.' He is our Son, and so we can come to live in his life, as Mary did. He is God's Son, and therefore, as we come to live in his life, we come to partake in the love with which the eternal Son loves the eternal Father.

The Philosopher says that the love of friendship involves some equality between the friends who love; and it is difficult to resist the truth of the saying. Between Infinite God and us there is no equality or proportion at all; and the more I dwell upon the greatness of God, the more inconceivable I find it, that there can be any friendship between him and us, or any interchange. And it seems cold comfort, and a mere fiction of words, to be told that though I can give him nothing that is of worth, he is pleased to set a worth upon it; as the whim of a stamp-collector sets a value on a slight tissue of dirty paper. That God is infinitely good, infinitely generous to my unworthiness, that he creates and sustains me not for his sake but for mine, this I can believe; but that he can so trifle as to delight in my poor and inconstant affection, this is a thought that carries no conviction with it.

But now, if he has given me his Son; if he has placed me in his Son, and his Son in me; his Son, who is the equal of himself, and in whose love his heart delights: then what matters the triviality of my response to the Eternal Father? For beneath my heart, inspiring its weak and intermittent motions, there beats the heart of the eternal Son of God. There the Father is loved; in that love he rejoices; and that love is in me, and in you; for the Son of God has put us on as a garment; he bears us in his heart, as he goes in to minister in the tabernacle of heaven. Therefore we can be content, when we pray, to let the love of the eternal Son go out in us towards his Father; we can be content to know that it is so, that it happens, and that our triviality is carried on the surface of it, like foam upon the tide.

It is not, then, that the Eternal Father has fixed an artificial worth upon us, to value us for what we are not. He has put a real and infinite worth into us, that he might value us for what we are; for he has incorporated us into his Son. There are no fictions with God, not even in his generosity. He does not turn a blind eye to our shallowness; he turns a seeing eye on the infinite depth with which he has underlaid it, the love of Jesus Christ his only Son; whom he gave to be born for us this happy morning, of the Virgin Mary, by the Holy Ghost.

Her virgin eyes saw God incarnate born
When she to Bethl'em came this happy morn.
How high her raptures then began to swell
Only her own omniscient Son can tell.
All Saints are by her Son's dear influence blest:
She kept the very fountain at her breast.
The Son adored, and nursed, by the sweet maid
A thousandfold of love for love repaid.

So now for the one eternal Son, Son of God and Son of Man, Jesus Christ, be ascribed to the Father and the Holy Ghost, all honour, glory, thanksgiving and praise, this day and ever.

preached in Christ Church Cathedral, Oxford

52

A Grasp of the Hand

It may easily happen to any of us, and especially in the wintry part of the year, to learn suddenly that an old friend has fallen ill. We go to visit him; we find him already unconscious, nothing left of his life but the breathing; and he makes an awkward job of that. Unable to talk to him, we take him by the hand. But his hand is a surprise; it is lively, fresh and warm, and he returns our grasp with all the vigour of old kindness.

No doubt it would be difficult to justify in cool reason the way a thing like this can turn our heart over. We imagine that our friend, buried deep under accumulating layers of unconsciousness, has stretched a hand to us. But a doctor would tell us that our friend has done nothing; the soul, the mind was not involved, the action was reflex or automatic. A lifetime of ready response to our greetings has got him the habit of returning our pressures; the habit is in the hand, and continues to act after the mind is gone.

That is what reason would surely say, but our heart is not convinced. The mysterious unity of personal life through sleep on into waking, through death into resurrection, fascinates us. Sleep – there now, sleep is a parallel. For he might take my hand or murmur to me in his sleep; and who can resist the impression that kind words spoken by sleeping lips come from the heart? Here again reason tells us that since the sleeper has no control over what he says, he cannot fairly be credited with meaning to say it; but instinct turns the argument upside down. He did not mean to say it, no, he just said it, and how much better that was! The expression of his kindness to us came from him because he could not hold it back, like water overflowing from a spring. What do I care for the things people mean to say? Every one in full command of his wits, the master of his hands and tongue, is up to some game; and if the game is virtue, so much the worse. Are you kind to me on principle? Is it to fill in a picture you draw of yourself as a Christian soul? Is it in execution of a plan of yours labelled 'friendship with me'? then take your kindness somewhere else, I do not care for it. Whereas, here is a sleeper who will mutter my name, here is a man unconscious yet ready to grasp my hand, yes, and here is my little child; I give him my finger and he clings to it. So Jesus clung to Mary's at Bethlehem long ago; and maybe the shepherds put their fingers into his little palms.

The moral of this strange argument is the suspicion of power; a suspicion, alas, all too well founded. God, printing on mankind the image of his own likeness, gave us some faint resemblance of that making, that self-determining power, by which he creates the world. It is this that is heavenly in us, and it is this that is satanic. Satan abused angelic power to be his own god, and we have abused our godlike power to play our own game; and our abuse of power is nowhere more seen than in our insufferable virtue, or more felt than in our synthetic kindness. Speech and thought are the beginnings of power; for even where there is no power to act, there is the power to lie, to fabricate, to invent, to deceive ourselves, to make up a story and to live in it. By this, true religion and false religion are most sharply tested. For true religion crumbles the structure of selfish invention; false religion gives to the world we make, the world God disowns, a firmness and elaboration which no irreligious thinking could ever give to it. We love the exercise of power in ourselves, it is the citadel of our being, our darling sin. We hate it in our neighbours, and in order to escape from it, we take a pathetic refuge in meaninglessness; in the seeming affection of infants, or even of brutes, uncorrupted by thought. We value slips of the tongue above sensible speech, and the muttering of sleepers above the words of wakeful men.

If the mere rudiment of power, the simple possession of conscious thought awakens suspicion, what shall we say of power full blown? The ingratitude of poor men to their rich benefactors is notorious, but it is also very natural. They feel themselves to be pawns in someone else's game of virtue, they do not feel themselves to be loved, and they are probably right. And as for political power, who credits the public smiles of public men? They are no worse men than we, indeed; no less capable of kindness in their families. But their official capacity ties them to servicing the great machine of power. Whatever faces they may make, we know we are only numbers in their arithmetic. Somewhere there may be a statesman or a prince of more than human goodness, who carries his people in his heart, and prays for them as devotedly as he governs them. But he will not easily obtain the credit of his kindness; his possession of power may not corrupt his action, but it will poison our appreciation; he will do well if he earns the favour of being accounted the least bad among necessary evils.

The universal misuse of human power has the sad effect that power, however lovingly used, is hated. To confer benefits is surely more godlike than to ask them; yet our hearts go out more easily to begging children than they do to generous masters. We have so mishandled the sceptre of God which we have usurped, we have played providence so tyrannically to one another, that we are made incapable of loving the government of God himself or feeling the caress of an almighty kindness. Are not his making hands always upon us, do we draw a single breath but by his mercy, has not he given us one another and the world to delight us, and kindled our eyes with a divine intelligence? Yet all his dear and infinite kindness is lost behind the mask of power. Overwhelmed by omnipotence, we miss the heart of love. How can I matter to him? we say. It makes no sense; he has the world, and even that he does not need. It is folly even to imagine him like myself, to credit him with eyes into which I could ever look, a heart that could ever beat for my sorrows or joys, a hand he could hold out to me. For even if the childish picture be allowed, that hand must be cupped to hold the universe, and I am a speck of dust on the star-dust of the world.

Yet Mary holds her finger out, and a divine hand closes on it. The maker of the world is born a begging child; he begs for milk, and does not know that it is milk for which he begs. We will not lift our hands to pull the love of God down to us, but he lifts his hands to pull human compassion down upon his cradle. So the weakness of God proves stronger than men, and the folly of God proves wiser than men. Love is the strongest instrument of omnipotence, for accomplishing those tasks he cares most dearly to perform; and this is how he brings his love to bear on human pride; by weakness not by strength, by need and not by bounty.

A child considered in its actual wordless state may seem no better than a kitten; but we do not view it as the animal it is, we see in it the germ of a boy, and beyond the boy, of a man. Yet not perhaps of the man that on sad calculation it will probably become; our knowledge of our fallen state betrays itself in this, that we instinctively clothe the child with an unfallen candour. We see in its simplicity, its freedom from craft or guile, its confiding physical warmth, the promise of a manhood in which power, as it grows, will remain the servant of affection. So Mary saw the infant at her breast, but with how much better reason! As he grew in stature, he grew in grace, and unfolded the exercise of a power which was love in action. He could still beg, he kept that about him to endear him; as he had pressed Mary for milk, he asked the Samaritaness for water; and there was still the day when he would be asking soldiers for vinegar. But far more, he could give; and so pure was his heart, so single in its union with the fatherly love, that he did not need to rein in his power, or measure the force of his beneficent actions. When he vindicated the humble and rebuked the proud it was without restraint; so when he drove away the demon, and so when, unsparing of his vital spirit, he healed the sick. His love was like a fire; and so he seemed, as he was, more than a man. His disciples feared him, and when in visionary trance on the mountain he blazed with light, it seemed the visible outbreak of what he invisibly was. For all his humbleness, his tradesman's hands, his common dress, his Galilean speech, he unfolded weakness into power when he spread the child into the man, and there were more in those days struck with awe and admiration than touched with any kindness. For even when power is the development of love, it may amaze us more than it warms us. But God's wisdom was not to be baffled, it took refuge once more in a folly; his power had its way by sinking back into weakness. The cross closed the scene which the manger had opened, the powerlessness of infancy was crowned by the powerlessness of defeat, and the unconscious agony of birth by a conscious agony of dying.

For God will be loved, whatever it may cost; and when he had expanded the flower of glory in his human life, he crushed it into a handful of bruised petals, for fear that power and wonder might stand between his kindness and our affections.

We must love God, it is our maker's command, and in such love our salvation lies. We must love God; yet what has love to do with 'must'? Love is free, duty cannot drive it. Yet we must love God, there is no resisting such love if we once see his face and feel the touches of his hands. The power of God perplexes us, but his weakness is still all about us; this is still the engine with which he moves our minds. By the birth in which he is born to-day, the son of God makes all mankind his own. Men's virtues indeed seldom illustrate his action more than they darken it, but all men's weakness speaks for his humiliation. Christ is every sufferer, every child; whatever hand pulls at us is the hand which clutched at Mary, and would have clutched at the friends standing round his cross, if it had not been nailed. If we would but see from how many eyes the weakness of God looks into our own, we would have no time to ask, Where is the God of Love?

According to his own express words Christ left two sorts of deputies in the world, two sorts of human substitutes for himself, beside that one divine invisible deputy, the Holy Ghost, who is the soul of all the love we have. But these are deputies of flesh and blood; the deputies of his power and the deputies of his weakness. The deputies of his power are his apostolic ministers, to whom he says. 'He that receiveth you receiveth me, and he that receiveth me receiveth him that sent me.' They speak his word, they pronounce his pardon, they give his body and his blood. The deputies of his weakness are the little and the needy; and of these equally he says, 'He that receiveth one such child in my name, receiveth me.' Neither sort of deputies represent Christ by virtue of their merits. The infirmity of the minister always hinders the word, and yet faith can hear through all their folly the voice of Jesus. And the weak, the little, are not always amiable. Are we not all both little and weak, but mostly on the side of our faults and vices? Yet faith can see the passion of Christ in all; and faith is the gift of that greater and better deputy, the Holy Ghost who will not fail us, the love of God being shed abroad in our hearts by the Spirit whom Jesus was born to bring us.

By his inspiration, then, we will receive Christ in both sorts of his human deputies; but more endearing, more revealing, more present to us at all times, are the deputies of his weakness. These are the deputies through whom his infant hands receive our Christmas gifts, and his gratitude, unlike ours, is undying. For when the nations shall stand in flocks before the everlasting Shepherd, thus shall he say to those whom he guides towards his right hand: 'Come ye blessed of my Father, inherit the kingdom prepared for you from the foundation of the world; for I was an hungered and ye gave me meat, I was thirsty and ye gave me drink, I was a stranger and ye took me in, naked and ye clothed me, sick and ye visited me, I was in prison and ye came unto me.' And when they deny that they ever did him such services, he will answer, 'Inasmuch as ye did it unto the least of these my brethren, ye did it unto me.' In these then is very God to be found, and everlasting life; and we can turn our back on idols.

As to what the eternal Judge will say to those on his left hand, this is not the time to think; for to-day is a day of gladness, a day to ring all the bells in earth and heaven, because the love of God is born into the world, so strongly armed with weakness that it must prevail. Love is nowhere more truly omnipotent than in the manger; in the speechless child we adore the Word who made the worlds, the Son of the everlasting God, the express image of uncreated glory; to whom now, therefore, with the Father and the Holy Ghost, in three Persons one love, one light, one God, be ascribed, as is most justly due, all might, dominion, majesty and power, henceforth and for ever.

preached in Christ Church Cathedral, Oxford